W9-DFJ-651

WHEN BASKETBALL WAS JEWISH

WHEN BASKETBALL WAS JEWISH

VOICES OF THOSE WHO PLAYED THE GAME

DOUGLAS STARK

University of Nebraska Press • Lincoln & London

Acknowledgments for the use of the interview transcripts
that appear in this volume may be found on pages ix–x,
which constitute an extension of the copyright page.

Set in Iowan Old Style by Rachel Gould.

For Melanie

CONTENTS

ACKNOWLEDGMENTS

Writing a book is a complex project and, much like the game of basketball, it is a team sport. This book is the collective effort of many individuals. Without them, this would not have been possible.

Once again, Bill Himmelman was a tremendous help in the completion of this book. From reviewing drafts of the narratives to fact checking and sourcing images, Bill continues to be an indispensable resource for anyone wanting to write about basketball history. Thanks once again for your assistance. Future projects continue to await us.

Additional individuals were especially helpful, including: David Smith, former librarian at the New York Public Library, who initially put me in contact with the Dorot Jewish Division. David Blittner, the grandson of Red Sarachek, for assisting in obtaining a copy of his grandfather's oral history from the New York Public Library. Matt Zeysing, historian at the Naismith Memorial Basketball Hall of Fame, who opened the Hall of Fame's archives and let me spend hours searching its oral history project from the 1980s and 1990s. Robin Deutsch spent countless hours helping to revamp my website, and was a sounding board for discussing the narratives. Sara Berkovec and Troy Gowen provided some very timely scanning. To all, my deepest thanks.

Two repositories were especially helpful in this project: the Naismith Memorial Basketball Hall of Fame and the New York Public Library. The interviews in the book can be divided into four groups:

Interviews with Norm Drucker, Sonny Hertzberg, and Nat Holman are part of the Hall of Fame's collection. These interviews were conducted in the late 1980s and early 1990s.

Interviews with Moe Goldman, Shikey Gotthoffer, Sammy Kaplan, Jammy Moskowitz, and Moe Spahn were conducted by Robert Peterson for his book *Cages to Jump Shots: Pro Basketball's Early Years* (1990) and are now part of the Hall of Fame's Robert Peterson Collection. Peterson interviewed these gentlemen in the late 1980s.

Interviews with Jerry Fleishman, Bernie Fleigel, Dutch Garfinkel, Ralph Kaplowitz, Red Klotz, Phil Rabin, and Ossie Schectman were all conducted for my first book, *The SPHAS: The Life and Times of Basketball's Greatest Jewish Team* (used by permission of Temple University Press, © 2011 by Temple University, all rights reserved). I conducted these interviews in the early to mid-2000s.

Les Harrison, Harry Litwack, Dolph Schayes, and Max Zaslofsky were interviewed by Elli Wohlgelernter, while Clifton Chanin interviewed Red Sarachek for the American Jewish Committee. These interviews are published courtesy of the American Jewish Committee William E. Weiner Oral History Library. They are housed in the Dorot Jewish Division of the New York Public Library. These former players were interviewed in the late 1970s and early 1980s.

Photographs for this book were generously provided by City College of New York, Bill Himmelman, Ed Krinsky, Long Island University, Diane Moskowitz, the Naismith Memorial Basketball Hall of Fame, New York University, the Spahn Family, and Yeshiva University.

To Rob Taylor, my editor at the University of Nebraska Press, who championed this book from our first conversation and carefully guided it to its finished product, many thanks for your support.

As always, family plays an important role—Mom, Dad, Jim, Sunday, Bennett, Nick, Rachel, and Alexis—thanks for your continued support.

During the early stages of this book, Melanie reentered my life, and she eventually became my wife. From the outset, she was enthusiastic about the project, reading multiple drafts and learning the difference between a jump shot and a hook shot. Her education continues with weekly Boston Celtics games on television, a perk of marriage. This book is for you, with love.

INTRODUCTION

Every Jewish boy was playing basketball.
Every phone pole had a peach basket on it.

—HARRY LITWACK, in Jon Entine, *Taboo: Why
Black Athletes Dominate Sports and Why We're Afraid
to Talk about It*

Within weeks after its invention in Springfield, Massachusetts, the game of basketball had spread throughout the country. Students at the International YMCA (Young Men's Christian Association) Training School quickly embraced James Naismith's new game and brought it with them when they traveled home for winter break in 1891. Almost immediately, the game was played in YMCAS, armories, and anywhere a basket, box, or crate could be nailed to a wall.

Cities in the Northeast quickly became hotbeds of the game. The introduction of basket ball (two words in those early days) coincided with the migration of millions of Eastern European Jews. Fleeing persecution and poverty, Jews immigrated to the United States seeking a better life. Mostly they landed in large cities like Boston, New York, Philadelphia, and Baltimore, moving into tenement houses and Jewish neighborhoods. The children of these immigrants sought to shed the lifestyles of their parents and embrace their new country. Becoming American was the hope, and sports provided the vehicle to achieve that goal.

Basketball quickly became a favored sport. Easy to learn and inexpensive to play, basketball attracted young Jewish children. All that was required was a ball or rolled-up rags and a goal. Thousands of Jewish children played the game morning, noon, and night. A distinct style began to emerge—more running, passing, and cutting to the basket. Soon thereafter, basketball was being referred to as a Jewish sport.

When Basketball Was Jewish chronicles the lives of twenty players from 1900 to 1960. Reading their stories reveals the game's arc from its humble origins as a club sport to its place in society at the dawn of the sixties. The game was first played in settlement houses and Young Men's Hebrew Associations (YMHAS) before transitioning to cages surrounded by chicken wire, where basketball players became known as cagers. Eventually games were held in armories, ballrooms, and arenas. In the beginning teams were organized ethnically. There were Irish, German, Jewish, and black teams before the game embraced integration, which it did before Jackie Robinson and baseball.

The early years witnessed leagues folding regularly, players jumping from one team to another, and teams affiliated with industrial companies. Some were independent, barnstorming from city to city looking for the best game. Most often, these were the New York Renaissance (Rens) or the Harlem Globetrotters, forced on the road out of necessity because they were not welcomed in any of the white leagues.

The game itself evolved from the slow, plodding, rough sport of the early 1900s to one that required more skill. The center jump after each basket was eliminated. A twenty-four-second shot clock was introduced. Scoring increased, and fans soon took notice. Eventually teams were scoring more than one hundred points a game, and players could dunk.

Basketball was not initially popular with the paying customer. It was not baseball or college football. Dances were held before or after games to drum up interest. Basketball was a weekend sport, earning the players a few extra bucks while they held regular jobs during the week. Travel was by train or car. Players carried their own bags and washed their own uniforms.

College basketball contributed to the game's growth. Double-headers in Madison Square Garden, postseason tournaments in the form of the National Invitation Tournament (NIT) and the National Collegiate Athletic Association (NCAA) tournament, and improved coaching led to better-prepared players for the professional ranks. Eventually the National Basketball Association (NBA) was founded as the twentieth century reached its halfway mark.

The country was changing from agrarian to urban. Industrialization was a big part of the development of basketball. Politics played a role too. An economic depression and the rise of antisemitism created a tense environment. Jewish players faced more discrimination on the road. The country was expanding westward. Teams were cropping up everywhere. Expansion reached the West Coast. Leagues became truly national in scope.

Basketball was growing and evolving. It was messy and beautiful all at the same time. It was part and parcel of how the country was shaped in the twentieth century. Jews were very much a part of this process. Their stories are the story of basketball. Their stories are the search for an American game. Their stories are the quest for an American identity.

WHEN BASKETBALL WAS JEWISH

. After an outstanding career as a player with the Original Celtics, Nat Holman coached at City College of New York. Courtesy of City

NAT HOLMAN

- Nat Holman enjoyed a legendary career in basketball. Holman learned the game in YMHAS and settlement houses before matriculating at City College of New York (CCNY), a school he would later make famous as a coach. By the 1920s he had become one of the game's best players, first with German-town and later with the Original Celtics, basketball's fin-est and most innovative team. Serving as the floor general, Holman established the Original Celtics as the game's first dynasty with his passing and leadership skills. Eventually he turned to coaching and helped CCNY become one of the country's top teams. Playing what was known as the "City Game," Holman led the Beavers to an unprecedented feat: winning the NIT and NCAA titles in the same year in 1950. Holman later became involved with sports in Israel.

L et me say at the very outset that basketball was not a new game on the Lower East Side. As a youngster, I would say as early as nine years of age, I played basketball at Public School 75. They had young teams. They had two divisions, 95 lbs. and 125 lbs. Now the 95-lbs. team did very well and moved on from there to Public School 62, which was down the street. Classes there went from 7A–7B, 8A–8B, and then on to high school. The basketball in that area, the games were always played in the play-ground at Stuart Park.

It was Commerce High School. There was the Henry Street Set-tlement. There was Clark House. Those settlement houses were where basketball was a big activity. On Saturday nights we competed against other institutions of a similar nature. They had a dance in between and a dance after the game. I will say this: the fellows that played basketball in that area were great ball handlers. They were tough. They moved well. They did not have the height, but they were tricky. They were sharp. I always admired them. There was a team called the Busy Izzies, and I want to tell you that in my book, they have given me more thrills than anything else that I have experienced, other than the double championship which we won at City College of New York.

The Busy Izzies had Barney Sedran, Marty Friedman, Willie Cohen, Jackie Fuller, and Alex Fuller. Sedran and Friedman were known as the Heavenly Twins. They were elected into the Basketball Hall of Fame. I played with that bunch, and I got a great deal of pleasure with them. The Busy Izzies and the University Settlement was when I was at Commerce High School.

At that time, as long as I wasn't traveling around the country playing with other teams, it was perfectly all right for me to play on any other teams on the off days. We never practiced. We had a game and we went, and I want to tell you, they were a great ball club.

There was a man by the name of Jim Gennity who was the athletic playground instructor. He was there seven days a week. Jim was a great basketball player, and he took a liking to me because I had athletic skill. I want to tell you that, I always said, I must tip my hat to Jim for inspiring me to progress in the game of basketball. There were others, but he tops the list.

You take the East Side in the summertime and you do not have the areas to play baseball. These boys had no means for automobiles to take them places, and no ballparks to play baseball. As far as I am concerned, it was the East Side that inspired me to play basketball and gave me the talent and the inspiration to move on to greater heights.

We played against college teams. We were playing sometimes, and they would not give us a college game, so we would get the freshmen to play us. Once we got in, we would make a good attraction. Know what I mean? It is difficult for me to go back that far.

Playing basketball on a floor that had dance wax on it was very difficult. My shoes had two holes up in the front and maybe two in the back, and we put Vaseline in them. This is so you wouldn't slide.

In dribbling, when you got the ball in your hand you had to tuck it under. You never threw it with one hand. I can't do it that way and then bring it back unless I hold it. We were able to change directions, pull in and draw back. Take the shot and bring it back.

It is imperative that any basketball player of any consequence has the capacity to out feint or throw a man off balance, drive in and draw back and to get the shot off. These things we gave a great deal of attention to when I was playing basketball. When I was playing baseball, I was the pitcher and I would throw that ball so fast into your lap, and I would have you worry about it too. Not only that, as I was passing it to this man here, I would hit some men right on the head, not intentionally. My intent is to get it across. I'm not concerned about you. And in doing so, I was always known as a pitcher.

I gave them many directions. With Dutch Dehnert as our pivot man, in my capacity, the other guys would get the ball to him but when they got it to me, as soon as I lifted my hand, the other guys would all break for the basket because it is in his lap. If someone else had the ball, he would be looking and looking and looking, and Dutch would be too late. You got to get the step on the man to get away.

It is nice to hear you say these things about the Original Celtics team. I concur with all that you say. On the other hand, we had to consider the personnel that was playing, the high level of personnel. It was a very important factor in my time. Today with these fellows there are eight men—five regulars and three others, one extra big man, another forward, and another guard. Today you have to have ten men. For injuries, in addition to that you have to have extra big men to take care of the center jump, to take care of the backboards, get the ball off the backboard, to tie up. You always have two men because you're the guy, you're the Angelo Luisetti. We are concerned about you. Listen, if these boys are going to go anywhere, increase their salary, you have to show that they are point getters. Do not tell me you are just a backboard man—not enough, not enough.

Dutch Dehnert was an easygoing person, a kind fellow. He never got excited. He was the kind of fellow that when he got in on a pivot play, he could wiggle and turn and move in various directions and the defensive man would whack him and everything else and Dutch never said anything to him. He got his play off, or he would bluff the pass to me. I would go in and then lift into the air; he'd spin and I would give it to him. He was a good man off the boards. I would say he was the best pivot man, the best all-around pivot man that we had at that time. He was the original pivot man. No one else got in there. When he took sick, we missed him. That is the Dutchman.

Now, Johnny Beckman. This fellow unquestionably was the fastest man on two feet. Johnny was a great shot. He would go into the air, and you could whack him and everything else. He would fall soft and would get a nice little spin with his right hand, and [with] his soft touch you would think he was not in motion. He took me out of my seat many times. I always loved to pass to him. Of course, he would feint in one direction and go off. He would get off at least three feet. That is all I needed to get the ball in there. If it were closer, than I would have to hold it up. Then he would have to buttonhook back. He was a great shooter, very fast, and took the bumps better than any man I know. He could have been a boxer. A good fighter, there was no one playing around with Johnny. He would not care if he was put out of the game. He would whack a guy, give it to him good. He was tough. If anybody hit me, he came alive. I would say if anybody was being abused somewhere and another member of the Celtics got involved, all of a sudden Johnny was getting wrapped up with him. He wanted to make sure.

Joe Lapchick played with a team up in Yonkers, and he was doing pretty well. We had Joe Haggerty before him. Haggerty was a big guy, but he didn't do much running. He did a good job off the boards. Both boards, but this guy was moving and if there was such a thing as getting into a fast break he would go down. When he [Lapchick] was married, I was his best man, and when I was married, he was my best man. We've gotten along very well. His wife today contacts me every now and then and wants to know if I'm going down to see one of the games. She would like to see me and all that. But I haven't been getting down there. I go down once in a while.

I am going to tell you something about [knee-length stockings and knee guards]. You do not know this, but inside here there are flaps. When they were hitting, they tried to slow you down for good. I am telling, you know, I got tears in my eyes many times when the guys were coming up the field and they would whack you. You are supposed to hit the ball, know what I mean? I'm going to tell you, they were very helpful. These things here, they come up to here. When you played in some of the places like the Manhattan Casino, they had wooden railings on the side. The uniforms were very, very heavy. It was to keep us warm. That was for the armories and the cold. People had their overcoats on and we had nothing on.

I played about five or six games a week. If we wanted to play seven games in a week, we played five games and two on Sunday, as it would be a doubleheader—one started at about two o'clock and then we would go to eat and then go to bed. Then we would go over there about eight o'clock in the evening for the evening game. Boy, I'm telling you, you had to learn how to conserve.

How did the body take this? I want to tell you, you had to adjust. Some guys, like Beckman, I never knew when he had time. He would go to the basket and get thrown, whacked, and then come back, come back half and he would be about ten feet ahead of his opponent. He had the quick change of direction. The guys that had it were ballplayers. I didn't have it, but I had other things. I would feint you out. I had to do all of that. That was a lunge, and then I would go the other way. Then I would come back. They would come up on me, and I would go through. All of these things are vital in our time for the little guys to do the job.

Physically? I'm going to tell you something. There are boxers 115 lbs. to 120 lbs. that go ten rounds. We guys were conditioned for that sort of thing. We did not have any time to go bumbling around or we would get pulled out the next night. Do you know what I mean? Do you know what I'm talking about? When they knew they had a tough one with doubleheaders, an afternoon game and an evening game, on Saturday night you hit the sack early. If not, Jim Furey got after you.

Jim Furey was a man who was a top salesman. What is the name of this place at Fifth Avenue and Thirty-Ninth Street, the big department store there? He was a chief buyer for the firm. In addition to that, he also ran the Celtics with his brother, Fat Tom. Between the two of them, they did the job. The Celtics broke up because there was too much money being offered. They were too good for the league [American Basketball League]. Well, they played their games and then they were ready for a coaching job or to be a part-time owner. These fellows were a great team in that era. Then the Celtics of Boston came along.

The boys [at City College of New York] went to the gym from their class work, and they would practice from four to six. I would have them on certain days maybe from four to five and then I had my assistant take over. I would hop an automobile out [of] the college gymnasium that would take me to wherever I had to go. These weekend games, I was there too. Depends on the game. I didn't miss too many. I would be at the game for one half, and after the kids were given the criticism and everything else they went upstairs. I went outside.

The boss at the college, my boss, came to me one day. Dr. Thomas A. Storey came from Stanford. He was a very bright man, hard driving, you do it my way or you're in trouble. I'm the boss. Dr. Storey called me into his office in the early years, "Mr. Holman, I want to talk to you about your schedule. I'm told you had to leave some of your classes. I'm very much concerned. I know about your basketball ability and everything else. They tell me you are playing outside a good deal, but I have to whip this out with you otherwise we may have to dismiss you." At that time, I was doing pretty well with my camp and basketball. I knew I had the students where I wanted them. We had those kids playing basketball. They moved the ball. They played at Madison Square Garden and after the game was over they would all come out with the City College flags, and they would walk to the subway, yelling and screaming. They were singing the alma mater. It was loud enough to be heard above the thunder of the street, automobiles, you name it. That gave me a thrill.

Mind you, I came from a family of seven boys and three girls and every one of those boys got an education. My brother graduated from City College, class of '03. My brother Morris was captain of the City College basketball team in 1918. Along comes his brother later as a coach. So, I say there was a great deal of enthusiasm for basketball. They loved it, and so when I got into college, I was always a stickler, a stickler, believe me, for the boys to maintain their academic standards, because I knew if they get out of here and they are dismissed and they fail, it is going to be my job. Coming from a family such as I did I appreciated what these boys were doing and I wanted them to continue. If they didn't do it I was a very unhappy coach regardless of the basketball results.

It was forty-four years ago this past summer that I connected with the camp [Camp Scatico]. Now the family is running it. I will say this, when we have these youngsters, boys and girls, we put an emphasis on good behavior. On top of that it was impossible for these children to be inspired unless the leader inspires them. I'm talking now about the counselor, so I want to say in all sincerity, I spent more time trying to locate counselors for my camp than I did going after campers. If I got the right man, and you are a camper, you are good for five years. The parents would recognize when coming up on the visits that the man [who] is handling their son is a pretty decent fellow, and their son is crazy about him.

[Barnstorming with the Original Celtics] was rough. It was very rough. When we reached our destination, we made it our business to judge the time before game time. How much time do we have to rest and when shall we eat? We would rest first and then we would get up and eat lightly. We ate heavy after the game. We had to adjust our schedules. What we were doing was part of our life, and going from one place to another, we had to make adjustments. Adjustments with playing conditions, adjustments with individuals who would play the first half and then get taken out ten minutes before the end of the first half, put them back in and start the second half. We had to adjust because we didn't have the large personnel the teams have today. As a result of that, we had to watch our conditions. The boys liked to drink their beer. They knew where their bread was buttered and they had to be right. Incidentally, to my knowledge, I don't believe any team ever beat us in a series.

We played the New York Whirlwinds in the Sixty-Eighth Street armory, and that team was composed of Barney Sedran, Marty Friedman, Willie Cohen, Jackie Fuller, and Alex Fuller. That is the team I told you about that Jim Gennity coached. We beat those fellows. The Celtics beat them, and each team won one series. We never got to play the final series. They just couldn't get together. Jim Furey could not work out the thing with the other fellows.

As a result of that, where did I go? I went to the Celtics and the different fellows all spread out. Joe Lapchick went to Cleveland. They were the Rosenblums. They were a good team, a very good team. Max Rosenblum was out there. A fellow by the name of Rose did most of the work for them. He used Max's name. He was a big operator in business. Marty Friedman played with the Rosenblums. He was a good friend of Max Rosenblum. Marty was small, about 5'7". Barney Sedran was small. Barney was about 5'6", 5'7", a little shrimp. I want to tell you, he was great. For a little guy, he had a great shot, was a good passer. He could dribble in and out and find you when he had to. Marty Friedman is a great story. He had that first international basketball tournament right after World War I. He had a beautiful trophy that he brought back from France.

The Manhattan Casino, you got off the train at 155th Street at the Polo Grounds. You walked downstairs, and there was the dance hall. Now, they had dancing before, in between, and after the games. They had a beer place. They were serving beer. They had a railing with these individual pieces all around. In order to play basketball at the Manhattan Casino, the management—I'm sure it was the Manhattan Casino people—they went out and purchased a canvas piece. They used the railings, and they had baskets on rollers and they rolled them in. Same on the other side. We played on canvas. They tied the canvas to the side of the railings. Then, at the other end, you got the baskets pushed in up to the railing. I shall never forget the hardship and the pain I developed in the legs, and others did too, because when you came down and stopped short, this canvas would give. If you had experience with that you needed some attention the following day. The court was about seventy-five by thirty. It was wide enough to get your ball handling in and many a time the thing did not bother me at all.

The cage game was played in the Eastern League and frequently I played there with tears in my eyes. The reason is that when they banged you up against the cage it was a two-by-four to keep the cage from collapsing. So when I mentioned hip pads, they were a necessity. The cage game in Philadelphia was played very, very early in its time, and the people loved it. They all wanted to get into this thing. The crowds would come, no dancing. As you got in there they had another situation that confronted them. The net was pulled down on the floor. Then they had to raise it with pulleys up to a certain point. Then they tied it behind the basket. The cage had to be taken down after the game. Once they got it, they hooked it together, the boards up on top and the boards on the bottom, they hooked them in. On the side, they had a cage that is a door that opened up. When you opened it up, some fellow had to hold it because it flew back. He held it to let the boys go in. The last guy had his troubles. The boys went in there, and that is the way the game was played. As far as the individual was concerned, it was punishment. Tom Barlow was one of the most feared guys in the game. He was tough.

Joe Lapchick and Davey Banks played for the Kate Smith Celtics at the Paramount Theatre at Forty-Fourth Street. They had a basketball court onstage. They used to play their games maybe once a week. Kate would come out and sing the opening of "God Bless America." They all enjoyed playing there. Kate was very nice to them, and they enjoyed the experience. I believe they had a game once a week, but I had nothing to do with them.

The New York Hakoahs, we had five or six Jewish kids, and we went around. I was playing with that team, just pick-up games. We got a pretty good salary as a team. I just played along with them because of the name, the Hakoahs.

Hank Luisetti will be remembered for the one-handed shot. Driving to the basket, regardless of the angle, and lifting both feet off the ground, arm extended with just a little tilt of the wrist. He was a great one. I always admired him and said in my time there were a lot of good basketball players, great players. This man came in with something different. I cannot help but tip my hat to him as one of the men that must be mentioned for the thrills that he gave me and thousands of other people.

Ned Irish was a two-fisted competitor. He did things in his own way. He was in charge of basketball at Madison Square Garden. He made up the schedule and if you had any problems you could talk with him, but the final order was in his hands. I think Ned has to be remembered for all the things that he did for basketball. He did a lot of things on his own. A lot of people did not like him. That does not make any difference to the people at Madison Square Garden. The job was being done. He packed it.

In a week, maybe a little over a week, in 1950 we [City College] defeated Bradley University twice to win the NIT and NCAA championships. For the NIT, we beat San Francisco, Kentucky, Duquesne, and Bradley. Then the following week, we beat Ohio State, North Carolina, and Bradley.

The only thing I can say about the scoring is my boys had been instructed to try and play sound basketball. I did not want any shots taken that were not legitimate shots. I did not want them to be throwing any blind passes. You do not have to score as soon as you get the ball. Let's pop it around four or five passes and then someone will get the opportunity. If he doesn't get it, fire it back in and get it going again. We're playing to win. We do not want to win the game in the first half and lose it in the second half.

In that double championship, I used Ed Warner. He was a great ballplayer. He was my original pivot man from the very start of the season. He was 6'3". He came out of Harlem and knew all the tricks. He was a pretty sharp kid. The only thing I found sometimes was that he threw the ball away. He developed into a very fine ball handler, and he moved in and out and all that. Finally, we got some of the other teams that slowed him down, and we weren't going anywhere. So I took the big fellow, Ed Roman, who was playing around the outer circle, taking outside shots or maybe following in, and took Roman and alternated the two. They were switching sides, one low and one high. The ball was moving all the time. Listen, if a guy held that ball any length of time when he was in the pivot, he was to then get rid of it. I want that ball moving. I want the body moving with or without the ball. Even if he takes a step to the right, you are standing there with your man, what the hell, you can never get away from that guy over there. Take him here. Take him there. Explore the territory.

When Joe Lapchick and I went into coaching, we were in the game about ten years and that game was moving around. It may have started picking up in Cleveland and Rochester. New York had its team. They did not have a good team, but at least they had a team. Instead of playing in Madison Square Garden, they played at the Sixty-Ninth Street Armory.

At City College, we had five games in Madison Square Garden, and maybe a fourteen-, fifteen- or sixteen-game schedule. The rest may be at home or away. The capacity at City College was maybe fourteen hundred or fifteen hundred. Recruiting was like anything else. Everybody wanted to get the ballplayers. While I was in [charge], we had friends that would help us try to bring some boys in. We talked to the high school coaches. As far as I am concerned, we all knew so-and-so was up at a certain place.

I retired [from playing] because I had reached the point that I felt it was time for me to quit. I was about thirty-two years old. Some of the boys today may be playing beyond that. It does not make any difference to me what they do today. It is what I decided to do because I had my camp, and I had the college. At that time too a fellow by the name of Harry Henschel of the Bulova Watch Company was on the board of directors of the Ninety-Second Street YMHA. He came around to see me. He said, "Nat, we are opening up this place on Ninety-Second Street. I would love to have you come over here and be in charge of the gymnasium." I said to him, "I've got the college." He said, "When you get through with the basketball season, we may make some adjustments. Now we would like you to be in charge of the Department of Health and Physical Hygiene. With your name, we feel it would be helpful." We got together on salary, and I took the job. As far as I was concerned, I met a lot of nice people there, and there were a lot of very fine students, medical students who used the top two floors when they lived there and were interning. At the same time, they had privileges in the gymnasium.

I was very interested in what was going on in Israel. I was the former president of the U.S. Committee of Sports in Israel. There is the Wingate Institute for Physical Education, and the gym is named for Nat Holman.

As far as I am concerned, I take each experience, and I take the full value out of it. I would not want to miss any part of it. What is the most exciting game? I told you before and I repeat it again, the winning of the double championship.

[Speaking of his admiration for former players at CCNY:] Mortimer Kaplan handled finances for the government. His father was a boxing manager and handled some really good boxers. His son turned out to be such a fine person and a two-fisted businessman. When he checked the books, you better look out. Then there is Marvin Davis. I had him when he was about seven years of age, and his father was in the dress business. When I had him, he was a youngster who liked to explore things under the bunks. He was looking for animals of one kind or another. He was the kind of boy that turned out to be one of our most successful men. I mention Cliff Anderson, who played basketball for me. Cliff was the head of a very successful business, and his son is now head of it. He has been very active with City College, the alumni. He played basketball for me. Cliff was an All-American. There was Bill Feinberg, who is now Judge Bill Feinberg. Today he is a judge in the Supreme Court [actually the U.S. Court of Appeals] and one of the toughest men they have there. People have done such marvelous things in the field of education, in the theater, in the arts. I can't help but admire them. What they are doing today, and they are passing everything on to their children, and the children are doing very nicely.

2. During the 1920s Jammy Moskowitz played on independent, professional, and barnstorming teams. Courtesy of Ed Krinsky.

HARRY "JAMMY" MOSKOWITZ

- Born thirteen years after the game's invention, Jammy Moskowitz learned basketball in schoolyards and settlement houses in New York City. Shooting the two-handed set shot, Moskowitz became a key player on his high school team, winning the Public School Athletic League title in 1923. Nervous before each game, Moskowitz started eating jam sandwiches to calm his nerves, thus earning his lifelong nickname. During the 1920s, Moskowitz played in the Metropolitan League and later joined the New York Hakoahs, a top Jewish team of that decade. His career playing on club, independent, barnstorming, and professional teams epitomized the early decades of the game. He later enjoyed a successful career coaching James Madison High School for thirty years, including winning two city championships.

My full name is Harry "Jammy" Moskowitz. My nickname came from the fact that I ate jam sandwiches from the lunchroom before high school games. I was born October 9, 1904, in Brooklyn, the Brownsville section. My father was a tailor, and it was sort of hand to mouth. Unions weren't recognized to get decent wages. My parents were immigrants.

I went to a public school, P.S. 84, but as a little kid—ten or eleven—we played in the street. There were ashcans, and we used them as baskets. We didn't have a basketball. The first time I saw a basketball was in the elementary school. No kids had basketballs in those days.

In those days the kids wore short pants—knickers—and black stockings. So you took the black stocking and filled it with rags or a skating hat and filled it with rags and you darned it. That was the basketball. Now, you couldn't dribble the ball. And you could not run with it. So you hit the ball up like an air dribble and you couldn't throw the ball, you had to push the ball.

In the fourth grade, they had tournaments, and that was the beginning of organized basketball. Then I played for the elementary school team on the junior team, and then I went to Commercial High School. We had good basketball players. We lost the city championship to Commerce. That was Lou Gehrig's team. Later, when Lou Gehrig made a name for himself in baseball, he had a basketball team. I played with his team for a number of games. He would play about five minutes.

I graduated from high school in 1922. I then went to Savage High School of Physical Education. It was a two-year school that trained most physical education teachers for New York City. Nat Holman graduated from there too. I played two years there. The coach was Dave Tobey.

While I was at Savage, I played semipro basketball. It was a club team, but I got paid. I played in the Metropolitan League with Greenpoint. The Metropolitan League had glass backboards about five by three, and the rim was twelve inches instead of six from the backboard. As a result, it was more difficult shooting. This was in the 1920s.

The big team that I played with in this period was the Nonpareils. They had Davey Banks, Cliff Anderson, and Joe Brennan, who played with the [Brooklyn] Visitations, and Willie Marrin. They once had Chickie Passon. We played the Original Celtics and the New York Renaissance [Rens].

I also played for the Newark Hebrew club. I earned about twenty-five dollars there in the late twenties and early 1930s. Around 1925, I was on the New York Hakoahs as well as the Nonpareils. The Hakoahs had Davey Banks and Nat Holman. The team also had Harry Riconda, a big league baseball player from 1923 [to] 1930 with the Philadelphia A's, Boston Braves, Brooklyn Dodgers, Pittsburgh, and Cincinnati. The Hakoahs were owned by a fellow by the name of Karsh. He was a City College man, and he had a partner.

Only with the Hakoahs was I on salary. The rest of the time, I was paid by the game. My salary was three hundred dollars a month. We traveled by train in the ABL [American Basketball League]. I did not have a written contract. It was a verbal contract. The Hakoahs paid expenses on the road. I was teaching at the time, but I was a substitute, so I was able to get off.

When I played against the Visitations they had Joe Lapchick at one time; Red Conaty, Rody Cooney, Joe Brennan, and Bob Grebey. They played with a lot of other teams. Joe Brennan was the greatest set shooter I've ever seen to win ball games in the last minute. He was a great shooter. He was an officer in Manhattan.

There was antisemitism when I was playing but only maybe in Prospect Hall. Prospect Hall in Brooklyn was mostly a Christian audience. It could be Catholic, it could be Protestant. I don't know the social level of the people there. The lower the social level of the people, perhaps less manners. Maybe I was hard of hearing. Nothing vicious happened to me. I didn't have firsthand experience.

The nearest I came to Baltimore, I was teaching in high school, and it was the second year I was coaching. I got a call from Hardy Coakley. He was one of those managers who would book a game and then get ballplayers to play against other teams. So he said the Baltimore team is playing Washington in Collins Casino in Baltimore, and they need another ballplayer. Can you play? I said sure I'll play. The coach of that team was Doc Sugarman. He was a great ballplayer from the East Side. We played in Collins Casino, and we played against Preston Marshall's Palace Club. I forgot whether we won or not, but I know I played well.

The first big team to travel was Elmer Ripley's New York team. They went all the way out west.

The Original Celtics in the mid-1920s were the greatest team. The only reason they lost—if they ran away with teams they wouldn't get a return engagement. So they made it close. When you make it close, a guy can put in shots, and you lose a ball game. I'll tell you the players before they started getting Joe Lapchick were Horse Haggerty, who was the center—big, husky guy, not much skill, but he could hammer. They had Johnny Beckman and Pete Barry. I played against Dutch Dehnert many times. It was a pleasure to play against him. Johnny Beckman was a great shooter and tough. Later they got Benny Borgmann, Davey Banks, and Joe Lapchick. They were the best of that era.

Before the ABL, we were playing with the two-hand dribble. From that point on, the game opened up. There were signals at the tap [jump ball]. You might put your hand on your hip and that would mean for a forward to guard the play. Or skin and cloth might be a back tap.

In those days, the best ballplayers came from the New York area and Philadelphia. In the first place, basketball was dominant in the New York City area—in the two big cities—New York and Philadelphia. As a little kid you played and before you knew it, I suppose if you were a Jewish kid, you were either a prizefighter or you played basketball. Every settlement house, every school had teams. And they developed. As a kid, everyone was playing. So before you knew it kids with talent would go up the ladder.

In 1926 I went to James Madison High School, and I stayed forty-three years. I won over five hundred games at Madison High. The players who played for me at James Madison were Rudy LaRusso, Fuzzy Levane, and Freddy Lewis, who played for the Baltimore Bullets and coached the Syracuse Nationals; the Rader brothers, Stanley Waxman, Lou Lipman, Larry Baxter, Ivy Summers, and Teddy Shriver.

I later got a degree from NYU [New York University]. I also coached at Brooklyn College of Pharmacy from 1929 to 1939 as well as high school. I started refereeing high school and college. I refereed only one pro game.

3. As a manager and coach, Les Harrison led the Rochester Royals to the 1946 N B L title and the 1951 N B A championship. Courtesy of Bill Himmelman.

LES HARRISON

- Basketball in Rochester was synonymous with Les Harrison. While a student at East High School, Harrison was consumed by the sport that was most closely associated with the Jewish immigrant sporting experience. Despite his love of playing basketball, Harrison was much more successful as a manager. He managed the Rochester Seagrams, Rochester Ebers, and Rochester Wings, all semiprofessional teams, from the 1920s to the 1940s. With his brother Jack, he purchased a franchise in the National Basketball League (NBL) in 1945. The Rochester Royals won the 1946 NBL title and the 1951 National Basketball Association championship. Most importantly, Harrison helped integrate the Rochester Royals and the Buffalo Bisons during the 1946 NBL season.

My name is Lester, but I cut it short to Les. I'm more known, I think, as Les. I was born on August 20, 1904. My Hebrew name is [pronounced] Lazer because two of my ballplayers called me Lazer. They were Bobby Wanzer and Bobby Davies. They played for me for ten years. They'd hear sometimes the Jewish name in the house. They'd be over, and all of a sudden those two picked up on Lazer. That is my Jewish name.

I was born and raised and lived my whole life in Rochester, New York. I put it on the map. In my time, the population was about twenty-five thousand people. They all moved into the suburbs. That's about it.

My mother was named Sarah Finkelstein Harrison. She was a

housewife, and my father, Abraham Harrison, sold fruit and produce, fruit and vegetables. That was his life. I did not know my grandparents. I have a brother. He's passed away. I have a sister, and she is alive. She is ninety-one. My brother's name is Jack, and my sister's is Evelyn. My sister was the oldest. I was second. My brother was third. He's passed away about twenty-one years ago. He was a lawyer.

We were brought up in the Jewish faith, and I was not exactly very religious but we conducted a respectable Jewish home and lived up to tradition, not that close and not that kosher. Especially if you would go to a restaurant, you'd get something, a steak or this or that, they are not kosher. We lived ordinary, and we lived the way most of the Jewish people lived. We celebrated the two most important holidays; Rosh Hashanah and Yom Kippur. We had a seder. I do not think we fasted. I went to cheder and I was bar mitzvahed. My brother was bar mitzvahed too.

My parents were, let's say, honest people, respectable people. My father was known as Honest Abe. My mother kept a real good house, and she did a great job raising us. I think there are a lot of things to do when you raise kids. She raised us. Jack became a lawyer. I had to go out and work when I was eighteen. I had to work. I could not go to college because my father passed away when I was eighteen. The funny part about it, he passed away on the Fourth of July. I was home and he passed away. He got sick and passed away. I became the breadwinner.

I told my mother, "I am going to give you money each week to run the house. Don't ask me questions and don't interfere and don't tell me how smart you are. Just let me. I get around. I can handle people. I was in a public market. I've learned the trade quick and fast." I could be honest or dishonest if I wanted to, but it was not in me to be dishonest. I said, "I will give you money. I can make a living. I know how to get around. Just take care of the house, that is all. I will give you money every week." And I did.

I went on my own, and I did it for twenty years, maybe a little longer. Then I got into professional basketball. That is another story. My brother helped me, and he earned his keep. He earned his way to college with me. He earned everything himself. I mean, I did not have to give him any college money or anything. In those days, you did not need too much for college. I never went to college. I just graduated high school. I had to go to work. He went to the University of Rochester, and he graduated law school at St. John's [University] of Brooklyn.

I would say we were a poor family. I had to work for every dollar we could make. We earned it honestly. At night, in the summertime, I'd play baseball, softball, fast-pitch. I played first base. I'm left-handed. In the wintertime, I played basketball. Now, how I got into the basketball business, I'm going to tell you.

In my day there were a lot of high schools. There were two high schools. One was east of the Genesee River and the other one was west of the Genesee River. I played on the East Side. We played the West Side. We beat them. In those days, twenty points was a lot of points. We beat them twenty to sixteen, and I scored sixteen of the twenty points. I said, "I like basketball." So I organized a couple of teams in the semipro ranks. Now, they were not big, but gradually I'd pick a player here or there. Gradually, we played the New York Rens. We played the Original Celtics. We were playing exhibition ball on the weekends. We did not have any salaries. Whatever we made, we divided up. We charged admissions, and I hired the hall and we played. That's it.

We made five dollars to eight dollars a man. We got a lot of money. We did not play in those days really for money. We played because you enjoyed it. I played against Davey Banks and Red Holzman. Joe Lapchick played. We beat a professional team. Remember, we got together once a week. We'd practice maybe once a week. When I could pick out ballplayers, we could win. I knew I had something on the ball that I could do with the ballplayers. For about ten years, we were the best team in town. There is no question about it.

I understood every way for the game. Not only that, I coached the team. In the beginning, we played for the Eber Brothers. They were a wholesaler of produce. Then they got into the liquor business. They did not want to go pro, and I wanted to go pro. The following year I took over, and I took my brother with me, even though he was a lawyer, and we went to Chicago and I joined the National Basketball League. The first year we won the title. The first year as an expansion team, we won the title. That's not bad. Then I got Syracuse and Buffalo into the league. Then from Buffalo, they moved quickly. After a month or two, they moved to Moline, Illinois. They moved from Moline to Milwaukee. From Milwaukee, he [Ben Kerner, owner of the Tri-Cities Blackhawks, in the region around Davenport, Iowa, and Moline and Rock Island, Illinois] moved to Saint Louis. He moved to Saint Louis and that is where he stayed and sold out [Kerner sold the Saint Louis Hawks to Milwaukee]. Syracuse was sold out to Philadelphia. That is the story of basketball.

When I would look at a player, I could tell he was good just by watching his moves, not how much he scored but what he could do and how he did it. Then I watched how he acted, too. They had to be fairly good, fairly decent. I could not take the guys that wanted to get drunk all the time or things like that, like some of the teams do. When I got into the league [the NBL], we won two championships for the league. We were the only good team at that time. There were some pro ball playing around New York City and Jersey and most of those college kids would play for the college and the next day or two they'd sneak over and play under different names and play pro ball. That was pro ball in those days. It was accepted mostly in colleges because they did not know any different and possibly did not care. This was the 1930s. I was a natural. I knew how to put people in positions and how to get the best out of them. If they had problems, there were my problems. I'd side with them and help them with this, help them with that. Anything about basketball.

You heard of George Mikan? He told me, "Les is an innovator in basketball." I came up with the thirty-second rule that they're playing with in college. They play with that in AAU [Amateur Athletic Union]. They play it in women's basketball. I've got to tell you one story. Basketball got to be lousy. You held the ball as long as you wanted. All these things we improved. We improved [by establishing] the twelve-minute quarters in pro ball. You played ten-minute quarters [previously] and [we extended them] just because we felt that they should have a longer game. If they paid admission, they should get a little more for their money.

Then there was Frannie Curran who played for Notre Dame. When he came out of college basketball, he played for Toledo and then I bought him from Toledo. Those two [Red Holzman and Frannie Curran] could stall a ball, and in Madison Square Garden with about six minutes to go, people walked out because we would exchange fouls and our guys could shoot and they could dribble. They could dribble through a dime. That is how good they were. We won two championships. We weren't bums. There were nine of us in the Hall of Fame. Not from this team but from all who played for me. Myself, Bob Davies, Bob Wanzer, Al Cervi, Red Holzman, Clyde Lovelette, Jack Twyman, Pop Gates, who coached the Globetrotters and played with the Rens, and Ed Sadowski, who coached Toronto and is from Seton Hall.

Bob Davies, Wanzer, and Sadowski are three out of the nine who played for Seton Hall College. I am on their sucker list. Every year, when they raise money for the school, you know what they do? They've got fund-raisers. I give them money. They're my favorites. In fact, we trained one year up there, and I roomed with the priest. He was a hell of a nice guy. A Jew rooming with a priest. We got along. It costs just as much to get along with a guy as not to get along with him. Why not get along with him? If he is a rotten apple, drop him. Do not bother with him. Just get along with the people you think you can get along with.

My favorite players were Bob Davies and Bob Wanzer because they were that good. The other reason is both of them, in the first twenty-five years in the NBA, they were picked as the top three backcourt combination guards. The top three were Bob Cousy and Bill Sharman, Davies and Wanzer, Dick Barnett and Jerry West. Those were the top three guards who were picked as the best guards in the league, as the best combinations.

The Rochester Royals in the National Basketball League was a better league than the BAA [Basketball Association of America]. The BAA had the arenas and the owners, and we had the talent. They could not get by, so they grabbed four of our teams from the National Basketball League. There was Rochester, Indianapolis, Fort Wayne, and Minneapolis. Our four teams joined the league [the BAA]. We let one year go by. We were the BAA. We became the BAA with their teams. Then the following year, we took the rest of the National Basketball League in. It was called a combination. The BAA with the National Basketball League merged in 1949 to form the NBA. Then in 1949–50, we became the NBA.

We [Rochester] won two titles. One we won the first year, 1945–46. In the formative years, they [the smaller cities] were all in there. Then later on some of them dropped out. It had to be big cities because if you had a smaller city, you could not get the TV people. There was no TV money in those days. Our commissioner made a deal with DuMont [Television] Network. We made a deal with the DuMont Network. The stupid ass, instead of putting on the best games, he put on the worst games. That's a commissioner. We blew that. Then it went down until we started changing the rules. When we changed the rules, it got faster, better, and then we made some deals with the networks. That is how it rose up. We did not have the NBA deal [the network deal that the NBA had; Harrison is speaking of the years prior to the BAA-NBA merger in 1949]. We might have had it earlier, but we might not have been out of basketball then if we could have got a deal and we gave them the best games. We did not. That is what the commissioner said. We did not get them. They did not get them.

We played in smaller arenas until we got into the NBA. The big change came after we left Rochester [for Cincinnati]. Fort Wayne [also] left. Fort Wayne went to Detroit. I think another one or two. Four of the teams left the small cities and went into bigger cities. Eventually we had a new commissioner. Finally it started to develop. Maurice Podoloff was the one that screwed it up. He gave them the worst games, not the best. Are you going to watch the worst game or do you want to watch the best teams that play? He gave television the worst games.

That is how basketball got started, in small cities not in big cities because the [big city] arenas had hockey. The big arenas did not have basketball. They were hockey owners, not basketball owners. Then they started to say, "Well, as long as we are doing pretty good, let's start gathering players and start to have a league," which they did. The first team they had with the BAA was Pittsburgh, which dropped out. Toronto dropped out. There were a couple more teams that dropped out. They needed teams, so they came to us because we had the players. They had the arenas, and we had the players.

The game got faster. It got better. Players started earning more money. In those days, we never had scouts. You know where the scouting was? In New York and the Sixty-Ninth Street Armory. Once a year, the East would play the West, and that is where they turned up to practice that week. That is how we'd get the players, working over there. There weren't that many big schools that were putting on basketball. They played, but they did not pay much attention to it. In the beginning, we used some of the colleges as territorial rights. If you were fifty miles from a school, you could get that player. It was in the beginning territory. Now it is not territory. Your first pick was, you get your territorial rights. So you got a team in New York, you want somebody from St. John's, you got him. You want somebody from NYU, you got him. That's all. Then the rest goes, you've got to pick from all over the United States. You get one pick.

The game today is much better. The guys are bigger. There is no comparison. Just a few of them could make it today. Bob Davies could make it. George Mikan could make it. Jim Pollard could make it. Dolph Schayes could make it. There are certain players, maybe half a dozen or eight or ten. Here and there you can spot a player. In my lifetime, the top player is Michael Jordan. Let me tell you something. I have not forgotten my smartness. I watch those games, and I watch how they play. I watched Chicago lose a game with sixteen-point-something left in the game. Scottie Pippen took a shot, a turnaround, which he should not have taken. He should have passed it around until Michael gets the ball and let Michael lose it. Let him lose the game. You don't lose your smartness, you know. I will pick four players. I will pick Michael, Larry Bird, Magic Johnson, and Dr. J. They did it all. The previous generation, I will give you four players—Bill Russell and Oscar Robertson. I would not say Wilt Chamberlain. Bob Cousy would be in Davies's class, but Davies was faster. Davies had a better shot. Cousy told me when he was playing, he said, "My model guy was Bob Davies." Cousy copied his style. Wanzer played him [Davies], and Wanzer generally outplayed him. He was a great defensive ballplayer. Michael Jordan is one of the best on defense. How can you call against him when this guy gets the ball and he suspends himself in the air? Not only does he shift to either hand, but he still makes another shift when he is up there. Doesn't he? Dr. J did a lot of running. You want to know something? If the referees call the fouls, there is no basketball. Perfectly honest. The running and the pushing and shoving, if they call it, there wouldn't be any basketball. Dr. J., they let him run. He ran with the ball and he did things that he shouldn't do. There would be fumbles. He once took off from the center of the court and he laid it right up. Everyone says it's great, but that was not basketball. I approve of good, clean basketball. They're good enough to play good basketball. If the referees started to call some of them, they eventually would still be great, but they shouldn't be allowed a lot of that stuff. It shouldn't be allowed. Our game was teamwork. Our game was teamwork. If they didn't play teamwork, they didn't play. Today, they're all one on one. You're playing me. Another guy comes up. You either pick off or let me get around them to shoot. Another thing is you stand still, try to block somebody. You say, "Go around me," and you let the guy go around them. It is all individual today, one on one.

The money today, when they got up to $100,000, I thought they were all crazy, and I stopped counting the money. One of these days, it is going to level off. The money won't be there somewhere down the line. Do you know how much they're making in Chicago, the way I understand it? On the floor, they're getting $300 a seat. Can you believe that? In Los Angeles, they're paying, these movie stars, $500 a seat. If the money isn't there, they got the TV money. Money is coming in. That's why they can afford to pay.

4. A standout player with the Philadelphia SPHAS, Harry Litwack later became a successful coach at Temple University. Courtesy of

HARRY LITWACK

- Harry Litwack and basketball in Philadelphia go hand-in-hand. Growing up in South Philadelphia, Litwack played basketball at Temple University before joining the Philadelphia SPHAS (South Philadelphia Hebrew Association), where he excelled in the late 1920s and early 1930s. Many children in Philadelphia idolized Litwack and his beautiful left-handed shot, including a young Red Klotz, later the owner of the Washington Generals. Litwack helped the SPHAS capture several Eastern Basketball League titles before retiring to pursue a coaching career. He coached Temple's freshman team for twenty years before becoming varsity coach. He led the Owls to the 1969 NIT championship and two NCAA Final Fours. He was also a referee, coach of the SPHAS, and owner of a popular summer camp.

I was born on September 10, 1907, in Galicia, Austria. My father's name was Jacob. My mother's name was Rachel. My father came here in 1910, I believe. He saved enough money to send for his family, which consisted of my mother, five sisters and a brother, and me. We landed in Baltimore when I was five years of age, and that was my start in the United States. I went to grammar school here in the States and high school and then college.

On the college level, I matriculated to Temple University in 1925 and enrolled in the Physical and Health Education Department to be a teacher and coach. I played at Temple University for four years. The last two, my junior and senior years, I was the captain of the basketball team. I received my bachelor's degree in 1930. In April 1929 I received an appointment in a junior high school on a teaching level and then started to play professional basketball.

The team was named the SPHAS, which was the South Philadelphia Hebrew Association. We were an all-Jewish team that was owned and managed by who I call, in recollection, the dean or mogul or Mr. Basketball in the Philadelphia area. His name was Eddie Gottlieb. The famous Eddie Gottlieb was my mentor on a professional level. I played and taught for quite a few years. Then, in 1931, my old coach at Temple University called me back to coach the freshmen team at the university and assist him with the varsity team. So I taught and I played professional basketball and also coached at the university for many years.

The neighborhood that I came from was an all-Jewish neighborhood, but a few blocks either way there were the Gentile and Italian neighborhoods. If you wanted to describe the neighborhood, you have to think it was like the East Side of New York. It was a very poor area of all immigrant Jews. It was called South Philadelphia. That was a really poor area. If you have to think of it, you had to think of the East Side of New York, and Brooklyn, and the Jewish section. We had streets that were lined up with peddlers selling vegetables, fruits, butcher shops, and that is where I grew up as a young kid.

My father was a shoemaker. My mother raised the family. My sisters were of an age that four of them were eligible to work [when they arrived in the States]. In other words, they were about sixteen and up. My oldest sister's name was Pauline. My next sister was Jenny. My next sister was Clara. The next one was Lenore. Then I came as the next one. Then another, younger sister that lives in Miami Beach and a younger brother who was a very good athlete but passed away at a young age. He may have been about twenty-nine or thirty. These are my family roots.

At home I spoke nothing but Yiddish because of my parents. My father still was not a citizen here. I spoke Yiddish at home to my mother and father, plus my sisters were the same way. We all spoke Yiddish at home. In Yiddish, they [my parents] could read and write. About five or six years later, my father became a citizen. In the meantime, my oldest sister got married. The next sister got married. Clara, who is still living, got married. We all spoke Yiddish at home. To this day, if a person speaks slowly, I can understand a little Yiddish and I can converse just about to be understood.

My parents were not ultraorthodox. We observed. We did not go to synagogue outside of Rosh Hashanah, Yom Kippur, and Passover. We had two sets of dishes. The house was always kosher. We all fasted on Yom Kippur. We went to synagogue. We belonged to a synagogue. I forgot the name. It was around the neighborhood. I was bar mitzvahed. I used to have a tutor come to our home maybe twice a week. I became bar mitzvahed in a synagogue, not a lavish affair or anything, just the rituals and it was over. I never pursued the biblical stuff. Today, I am not orthodox. Here and there I will go over to synagogue. Up until about five or six years ago, I observed Rosh Hashanah and Yom Kippur.

When I moved out of South Philadelphia after I was teaching school for a couple of years, my dad lost his leg. He was a diabetic and could not recover from a big cut on his toe. He died of gangrene. Before he died, he gave up the business, and we moved into a much nicer area. It was like from here to there. I lived alongside a synagogue. It was a pretty nice home. The rabbi asked me for some help starting a kindergarten, a school for children, so I gave him my basement. Every Sunday morning; I had a pretty nice, big home, and I gave it to them to use for the kids. It was in northeast Philadelphia. The synagogue is called Temple Shalom. I am still a member there after forty years, but I do not go. Once in a while they call me for a minyan. If they are short, I will go over. I did not go to synagogue every day, but I was prepared for my bar mitzvah.

My parents were born in Galicia. It is an area [straddling the border between present-day Poland and Ukraine]. They say, you are a Galician Jew. What that means, I do not know. I get all that information from my older sister who is still alive. I was always aware of being a Jew. It was pretty obvious around that area that I lived in Philadelphia. When we first came over, you were always picked on by the Italians and Catholics. So you had to stick to your own area. If you ever went to the other side, you better go along with a gang of boys. Otherwise, you would get killed. I would say I did [get into a lot of fights]. I held my own. I found out then what it was to be Jewish with antisemitism as kids. When I say antisemitism as kids, as an Italian kid of our age or a Jewish kid of our age, you had to fight your way through a lot of things. I would say through twelve, thirteen, fourteen, fifteen years of age. Later on I did not have too many people pick on me. The fact is my college coach was a Roman Catholic. He was a Catholic. He took me under his wing. I owe a lot to him because he gave me my start. He was not a Jew. He was a Gentile of the Catholic faith. Then in the profession I pursued, there were not too many Jews in the basketball profession as coaches. Here and there. Like an idol would be, I think of Nat Holman. The dean of college coaches.

Many a time when we went out to play pro ball when I was twenty-two, twenty-three, twenty-four you played certain teams that were in a Gentile area, and we had trouble after a game. Here and there a fight would start between not so much the players as the spectators. You would have a fight and they would try to get out to your car. I would not say anything serious happened, although myself, I had an experience playing a professional team. It could have been Bayonne, New Jersey. We played against a Gentile team and in between halves, we were sitting, relaxing for the second half to start, and I never even realized it, but a spectator came from the back. He did not like that I [had] pushed my opponent, because he [had] pushed me, and we both held our hands up. Nothing happened. He resented it. That was his buddy. I was hit on the head with a Coca-Cola bottle, blood streaming down. They took me to the hospital there. Some [fights] were serious. This one was a serious thing, but otherwise, you would always squelch it somehow or other. I knew the fellow. We played against each other many times. I knew the team. The team was called the Jersey City Reds. I do not think it was between him and me. It was just an incident. I pushed him, he pushed me, and the referee squelched it. A fan that was friendly with him resented it.

A guy would not say, "Watch it, you Jew bastard," or anything like that. No. Very seldom. You managed to get through it with a fight or they broke it up. The next day something else would happen. It was not until I got to college or high school that I had a couple of Gentile teammates. My high school is Southern Philadelphia High School. It was called Southern High School. Then later on it was changed to South Philadelphia High School, which took in the boys and the girls. On our basketball team, I played with three boys that were Gentile and were very nice boys. One of them became the team physician for the U.S. Naval Academy for their sports aspects. Frank Stanley was a very accomplished pianist. Abe became an engineer. I think Walt Weller, the surgeon, he may be retired from the navy, but he held one of the biggest jobs at the Naval Academy in Annapolis. Every athlete had to pass through him to say that he is physically sound to play.

[Speaking of his family:] All told there were five sisters and a brother and myself. There were seven. I did not know my grandparents. A brother of my dad's came over, his younger brother, and he was not married. The fact is he lived with us. In one little three-bedroom with one toilet, we had seven children; Mother and Dad were nine, and an uncle. Ten of us lived in that little area. One toilet. If you had to take a bath, I remember you had to go down in the basement and put a quarter in the meter for the heater to get warm, and one followed the other in bathing.

I remember that as a kid, my sisters were a little bit older than I was, outside of Rose, who was next to me. I remember as a child, I may have been nine, ten—a Saturday night of going to the Turkish bath, which was right around the corner, with my dad. So you got your bath once a week and that was the life. My youngest brother and I on a Saturday night would go to this Turkish bath with my father and that was the bath for the week. I can remember that we used to have a basement that was loaded with coal and that coal would warm the house up during the winter months. We had a meter alongside to create the heat for the sisters to take a bath in.

They [my parents] were very, very peaceful people who minded their own business. My father was a shoemaker, and my mother was a housewife. We had friends. In the evenings, I can remember as a kid coming back from the playground. By that time, they started to have lights around the playground and I would go home.

After work, [I would be with] my dad and mother, my sisters must have had dates. They were not around except my youngest sister. Next door was a tailor shop. They were the same way. They would sit and converse, day in and day out. Once in a great while, they would go to a show, a Jewish show. I know we had a shoemaker store. The next store was a plumber. The next store was a barber. On the corner was a bakery store. We knew the neighbors on the other side. A candy store. A butcher shop. It was on Eighth Street between two main streets called Snyder Avenue and Jackson. That is how they spent their days, the whole group. They were not related but each family was the same way as we grew up. South Philadelphia was divided—I do not know whether I have it somewhere—like Washington Avenue all the way down to what we used to call "the dumps," which today holds the Spectrum [arena]. The Army-Navy game is held at Kennedy Stadium. All that was not around when I was a kid. That was all built up. We used to go down because there was a lot of empty ground. We could play baseball. The rocks and sand was the place to play.

Shibe Park was maybe three, four miles away. As a young fellow, I saw many games. The greats I saw were Babe Ruth and Lou Gehrig. The Athletics had Al Simmons, Jimmie Foxx, Mickey Cochrane, Bernie Shaw, Lefty Grove, and Max Bishop. That is when they were up there. Jimmie Foxx was one of the greatest. Cochrane was a great one. He finished up in Detroit. Jimmy Dukes was a third baseman and managed in the big leagues for a while. They had a great team. I was an Athletics fan. The Phillies were always down. They reason they were sold, they broke them up because Connie Mack could not meet their salaries. He was an individual [owner]. That was his livelihood. He broke them up. In those years, I think they were in the thirties, they were great, great teams. I did not really have a favorite. I used to go out to watch them, sit up in the bleachers for a quarter. I was little bit established by then financially. As a kid, I couldn't afford it. If it was in walking distance, you would try and sneak in like a lot of the kids used to do. But it was too far away. You had to go by trolley. You could not get there any other way.

I am very, very friendly with [the comedian] Joey Bishop. He came a little later. Well, I would not say a little later. Joey Bishop did not live too far from where I lived. I would say walking distance, maybe a half mile. I came in contact with Joey Bishop through Eddie Gottlieb. Eddie Gottlieb had an interest in an adult summer camp and he needed an entertainer. I can remember sitting in the office when this incident occurred. One of our loyal fans was in the office. He says, "I could get you a comedian. He stands there on the corner and he has everybody laughing walking by. He can say things to girls and if you said them they would be insulting but he has such a manner that they laugh about it. He is very humorous." So Eddie gave him a job and Joey relates the story. We honored him one year, the former Jewish basketball players called the Jewish League Alumni; we honor an outstanding person each year. One year when Bishop was well established and had his own show, he used to kid Eddie Gottlieb, "Remember, Eddie, room and board and laundry? Changed your world, didn't it, Eddie?" He was kidding with him. He was a star, a star of shows. I see Joey here and there. He is still around. That is how he got his start. I would watch him once in a while [on the street corner], but I did not speak to him. In those days, the kids had gangs. You had a certain group, this corner, that corner, another corner, and all that. This was right around Jewish Mount Sinai Hospital, around that area, Fifth and Dickinson or Fifth and Tasker, Fifth and Morton, Fifth and Reed. That is where he came from. He lived on Moyamensing Avenue not too far from where I taught when he was a young fellow. He lived closer to the Gentile area. That is where he lived with his family. He had another brother, Mel Bishop, who is still out at the coast. He was in the theatrical business.

I played at Southern High School from 1921 to 1925. I played as a freshman. I played freshman baseball. I played freshman basketball.

I smoked cigars [as a college coach]. With maybe a minute to go and we were leading by quite a few points and knew that the game was in hand, I would stand up and go to my inside pocket, take out a cigar and take out a box of matches. When the final whistle blew, I would light up. So I preceded Red Auerbach, long before he became a famous coach. That is humorous. The fact is, up until this year, whenever I met Red at some affair, he would always come over and say, "Here you are, Harry. Here's a good cigar." He used to kid me. They [the cigars] come from an island around there [Cuba]. I get them from the Cuban distributor down in Miami. I have been getting them for about fifteen years. I get hell most of the time from my family, but it is enjoyable to me just to sit and relax and have a cigar. I could tell you a story on that [how long I have been smoking]. The last game of my college career, it was over and the following Saturday night our coach gave us a party and we went over to, I guess you would call it a taproom, a restaurant. During the course of drinking a glass of beer and having some fun, the waiter came over with a box of cigars. So between a glass of beer, he came around with a cigar, I took a cigar and put it into my mouth, and I have been smoking cigars ever since. I never smoked [cigarettes]. A pipe once in a while during the summer months at camp, but I never smoked a cigarette. I smoked cigars and a pipe occasionally years back. I gave that up. I went around with the young kids. Friends of mine started smoking cigarettes when they were twelve, thirteen, and fourteen, but I knew my parents would not like it and I had a lot of respect for them and never did it.

I would say they [my parents] sacrificed a lot for everybody in the family. Always the children. They lived a very simple life. Just like the old, old adage, you like to see your children better off than you are, and that is the way it worked.

I played three years of varsity ball and a year of freshman ball [in high school]. That is four years. I played four years of college ball. That is eight years. I played about six or seven active years of pro ball. That would be fifteen years. My mother never saw me play. My father saw me play once. The two youngest of my sisters saw me play occasionally. [My parents] were not interested in it. They did not understand it. They never knew that I was a coach or what I did. They knew that I played ball. When I was up to about age twenty-two—that was my first year playing pro ball for the Philadelphia sphas—the only guy that had an automobile was the owner, Eddie Gottlieb. We would meet at his office. It was right in the center of town. Whenever we played, we would go by his automobile, and he loaded us up. He had a specially built Ford that could hold nine players. You threw your luggage, your basket-ball bag, up on top and we rode wherever we played, twenty miles away, fifty, and seventy, whatever. After the game, he would drive us to all our different homes where we lived. He pulled down our street, on Eighth Street, and as he pulled in front of my home, I could see a light go out. My mother was sitting. Even if they [my parents] came, they would not understand the game. I would not say that it was a distance, but they were in another world and I was in another world. In those days, you had to also remember that when I got started that was at the height of the Depression.

I was making a salary teaching school. I think in my first teaching job, I got $1,500 for the nine months of the term. I was making more playing professional ball than I was getting as a salary. So you put the two together and maybe it was about $3,500. Then I got a job as a counselor at a summer camp. They started me off, I think, at $150, and with gratuities from the parents for taking care of their children all summer, maybe it was another $300 out of the summer. When you think in terms of the money at that time, I was a millionaire to what my parents had. I subsidized them. Whenever they needed six tons of coal, let us say, thirty dollars, nobody taught me, but I gave them thirty dollars and paid for the coal. By that time I could pay for my own clothing. I used to pay my mother, in those days you would call it, like paying board now. I would give her ten dollars a week. Originally, she said five. I would give her ten. So the chances are the extra five dollars here and there, she would subsidize my older sister. Here and there, when I would go to school, and I had a car by then, she would have a bag of food she made for [me to take to] my oldest sister who just got married. She married a tailor.

You never felt independent. When you look back and you saw married people out on the street with a crate of oranges to make maybe a dollar or two dollars for the day, with the Depression, you look back and I was making like $3,200, $3,300, or $3,500 [a year]. I was a millionaire. It did not faze me. It did not make my life different. I wore a little better suit but ate at home all the time except for the few times I would meet the gang at Eddie Gottlieb's office. We would get together. We were very close there. We would go to a movie pretty near three times a week. I had a little preparation for the next day's lessons. I was teaching physical and health education.

My wife is fourteen years younger than I am. I met my wife at a summer camp that I was involved with. In those days, you never made a living at coaching. You always had to have something on the side. I got lucky and got with two other fellows and we opened up a children's camp and built it up. I sold my interest and got $20,000. The other fellow sold his interest to the same individual, the third partner. We parlayed the $40,000 into another camp, built that up, and sold that for about $300,000 and built a big home.

When we owned the camp, I came in contact with a fellow that is presently the athletic director at Northwestern University in the Big Ten. He came around and conceived of an idea that basketball is growing, growing, and growing and there ought to be a chance for kids that want to develop to be able to go to a basketball camp. I knew of one. That was a camp that was run by Clair Bee, coach at Long Island University. That was in the early 1950s. He got in trouble with the scandals and did not do anything for a while. Then he finally connected with the New York Military Academy and became their director and he started a basketball camp. This young fellow [who ended up at Northwestern] was on a high school level at the time and he had asked me to come down to a clinic that he was running with Jim Pollard, who was a big name in basketball at the time, and he just got the job of coaching at LaSalle College in Philadelphia. That is how I came in contact with him, and he put the thought in my mind.

At that time, I was involved in the summer camp, Sun Mountain Camp. We used to run the camp a week prior to the opening for our regular clientele and a week after they had left before school started. We built that up and finally it became so big that in about 1959, maybe 1960, my two partners and I, we sold Sun Mountain Camp, and Bill and I, we located another spot and we opened up this basketball school. That was called the Pocono Mountain All-Star Basketball Camp. We ran that for quite a number of years, up until six years ago. I was eighty at the time we sold it. That is how I really made money, not through coaching.

[On his time with the s p h a s:] Eddie Gottlieb was a very sincere and honorable guy. If you shook hands with him on a deal he would always uphold his end of it. He said, "I can afford to pay you twenty dollars per game." He never paid on a weekly or biweekly or monthly salary like they do today. If I am not mistaken, I think I started at twelve and a half dollars per game.

The s p h a s started to play when I was a young kid of about fourteen, which was around the years, I think, World War I was going on. Around those years, 1917 and 1918, that is when the s p h a s formulated, and it was all independent. They had a league, and they called it the Eastern League, which was made up of independent teams. The s p h a s was one. The s p h a s were always an attraction because they had all Jews. St. Henry was a Catholic club. Knights of Columbus had a club. Camden, New Jersey, had a club. When that big league folded, a lot of those players moved around. That is how Eddie reorganized that team in 1929, the season of 1930. Then it went on and on until 1945. Then these big owners of the arenas came in and they wanted more revenue. That is how this league, the b a a, started.

Abe Saperstein and Eddie Gottlieb were very, very close. Eddie Gottlieb's income came from owning the s p h a s, and at the same time, he was a promoter of the games. The outstanding black team in those years, of my years, between 1930 and when the Renaissance stopped playing, the Renaissance was the best black team, the best pro team, equal to the Original Celtics. That is considered the greatest professional basketball team that ever played. The Renaissance was just as good but never got the publicity. We used to go up to play them. Once a year, we would go up to play them at the Renaissance Ballroom up in Harlem. We were the only whites. They were a great, great basketball team. The Renaissance was the great black basketball team. They came down and played in our arena. There were blacks who came to the game when they played in our arena. We would have black and white fans in our arena, but only black fans in their arena.

Abe Saperstein was in that same era, and he formed the Harlem Globetrotters out of Chicago. They would travel all over the country by bus. Of course, he put a different concept on humor.

They put on a little show all the time and you never licked the Globetrotters. Otherwise, they were not an attraction. In those days, Eddie Gottlieb would bring them in to play us, and nobody liked to be humiliated. But as an attraction, he would bring them in. Maybe they would get one hundred dollars for the game. They would go from town to town to town until eventually he started a new phase of basketball. He [Saperstein] introduced basketball internationally. He went to Israel around 1957. In 1957 at the Maccabiah Games, he had his own court. It did not have any places to play in the auditorium so he would bring his own court. He had the posts, and he built a floor on the outside. If it was not for him loaning the floor to the Maccabiah gang here in 1957, we would not have had a final game. We would have had a final game, but we would have played on dirt. They had to drive down to Haifa, get a truck, get the floor with the posts, and bring it up to Tel Aviv.

I knew Abe well. Abe was nice, ordinary. I will tell you a few facts about him. He was very, very close to Eddie Gottlieb. They both worked together. Eddie would promote the Globetrotters from town to town in the East. When this big league formed in 1946, we played one year together and he had me run the SPHAS. It had to be a year after the big league started because we played George Mikan's team. I forgot the name of that team out of Chicago. Then the following year, the SPHAS traveled with the Globetrotters. In those days it was common to have doubleheaders. Abe conceived he needed four teams. Eddie and he made a deal, and he put the SPHAS on the road because our league folded, and he gave me charge of the fellows that he did not take for the Warriors. We would play a team and the Warriors may have played the Boston Celtics and they would have a doubleheader. Now, Abe started and he got three teams. So there were four connected, including the Globetrotters, and he would go around the country.

The following year, Eddie and he made a deal that he would give him the SPHAS for one of the four teams. So they had the Globetrotters, the SPHAS, and two other teams. That was four. That team was run by Red Klotz. He ran the SPHAS. He was still very close all through that year with Abe Saperstein. The fellow that did a lot of work on those tours was a fellow by the name of

Dave Zinkoff. After the year was over, Dave was the personal secretary to Abe. After the first year of the SPHAS being with Abe, Abe Saperstein tells Red Klotz, "Tell Eddie that I will be in touch with him to get somebody else to run the SPHAS, and you get yourself a team." That was the origination of the Washington Generals. Today Red Klotz is still running the Washington Generals with the Globetrotters. They have changed. They are a big outfit today. I forget who owns them. Red Klotz, even to this day, goes with them occasionally and travels all over the world.

Red Klotz has to be about seventy, maybe more than that. About seventy-five. I met up with Red at an affair just about six weeks ago. He lives in Atlantic City. He has lived there for many years. It used to be a standing joke with the people that were around him that every time he came back from a tour, his wife was pregnant and had another child. Red must have about five or six children. He will tell you himself, he is the only millionaire that never won a ball game. As a side note, if it was not for the Globetrotters, there would not be an NBA today. They had trouble drawing people. In those days, people were accustomed to seeing a doubleheader. That was originated by a fellow by the name of Ned Irish at Madison Square Garden. People got accustomed. We had doubleheaders in Philadelphia, Boston, and Washington. That was conceived by Ned Irish. If you picked up the newspaper of a game, for example, Boston Celtics versus the Rochester Royals, and if you saw in the newspaper, "attendance 13,500 at the Boston Garden" or whatever it could hold, but if you saw that figure, you knew that if that was the capacity, you could bet all the money that you had the Globetrotters were the second part of that doubleheader. The Globetrotters went from every place, every team in the NBA, and they played a game and scheduled a game against another team. Let us say their capacity was 11,000 and the newspaper said 11,500 in attendance, you could bet all the tea in China that the Globetrotters were part of that attraction. If you picked up a newspaper and you saw attendance 2,800, you knew [the Globetrotters weren't there]. They saved the NBA. The fact is they saved them such that when Chicago went sour, they broke up the team, and Abe Saperstein thought he was slighted by not giving him the franchise to the NBA. He thought he was responsible for upholding the NBA. By that time, their [the NBA's] first president was Maurice Podoloff. He was the first commissioner. He was in ice hockey. He owned the arena in New Haven, Connecticut. The organization and all the scheduling was done by his buddy Eddie Gottlieb.

[On his early career in basketball:] I go back to the thirties. There may be Jewish ballplayers prior to that, and I am sure there were, but in the thirties, in the early thirties, every town around the New York area going down—Elizabeth, Hoboken, Paterson, Trenton, Philadelphia, Wilmington, Washington, Reading, Wilkes-Barre, and Scranton—every town had a basketball team. In the 1930s and up until I guess the late forties, City College of New York had all Jewish basketball players, NYU had quite a few Jewish players, St. Johns had quite a few Jewish players, Fordham, a few Jewish players, Long Island University had a lot of Jewish players. Around 1930 Eddie Gottlieb reorganized the SPHAS and they had a league. Let us say a team like Reading, maybe they had two or three in the town that could compete on the same level so they had to have like eight men they could import. They would import a guy from St. Johns. So you multiply that and you have got a lot of Jewish ballplayers starting to play on a professional level. Every Jewish kid would be playing, just like you have the blacks today, and emulate somebody. That is how you got a lot of Jewish players. Outside of Les Harrison and Eddie Gottlieb, most of the owners were Gentile. Barney Sedran was a former player and he took a team out of New York that was made up of a lot of Jewish players and a couple of Gentiles and they played in Wilmington, Delaware. The owner was a Gentile fellow. He owned the property, and they played there. I would not say that there were a lot of Jewish fellows that got jobs playing. To Wilkes-Barre, Scranton, and Kingston, to all those coal towns, the hall was owned or leased by the Gentiles, and they got these players to represent that town.

I never played in the Catskills, but I am familiar with a little bit about it. Wilt Chamberlain was a busboy at the Concord [Resort Hotel]. The fellow that got him the job there was a fellow by the name of Haskell Cohen. He was the one that got them all jobs. That is where the stink, the '51 [college basketball point-shaving] scandals started. That ruined Nat Holman and Clair Bee. That is where that started. Haskell was the public relations man for the NBA. He was also the public relations man for Kutchers. He got these boys summer jobs. They did not have to be from the New York area. He got them from anybody that he had a contact on. Of course, the owners of those hotels had to figure out one way to have entertainment outside of their shows. That is where the scandals started. That was in the early fifties.

When I finished college, I put one year in on the high school level at Simon Grats High School. That is when my coach called me back to assist him and become the freshmen coach at Temple University. I was there from 1941 to 1951 as the freshmen coach. In 1952 I took over [as head coach] and retired in 1973. My record was 373 wins and 193 losses. I was in the NCAA tournament in 1956 and 1958 and I won the NIT in 1969.

At Grats High School, one of the players I had on that Grats High School team was a fellow by the name of Zach Clayton. Zach Clayton became a member of the Renaissance basketball team later on. He became an outstanding referee of boxing in the country and in the world. He played with the Renaissance basketball team and later on with the Globetrotters. He was quite an athlete. He played baseball in the Negro Leagues with Jackie Robinson. He was a hell of a baseball first baseman. I had the pleasure of coaching him. The kid was so poor; he did not have a pair of sneakers to play basketball. I bought him his first pair of sneakers to play basketball. I was very, very friendly with him over the years. That kid refereed internationally, all over the world, championship heavyweight boxing matches—Joe Louis, whoever you mention, he officiated it.

We always had a pretty fair record. We were one of the few teams that hit the thousand wins early. When I took over in 1952, two years later in 1954, I got fortunate. I had a young fellow that was supposed to go to Seton Hall and his mother passed away. The coached called me up, "Would you be interested in him?" I knew the young kid through newspaper clippings in the paper. He was a very good player. I said, "Sure. Send him down to my office." From my office to his high school, it is a matter of maybe two and [a] half miles. I knew the coach. He was a teammate of mine when we played at Temple. I said, "Ike, send him down. I will pay his carfare." So he sent him down. That kid was Guy Rodgers. Wilt Chamberlain was getting all the publicity at Overbrook High School. They had two other kids, and I did not give them scholarships. I get the kid by the name of Brotski and a kid by the name of Hal Lear. There were other names on that team, which I am not going to bother you with. But Hal Lear and Guy Rodgers were the two best court combinations for many, many years. They played for me. Any time I went out to the NCAA finals after they graduated, the coaches said, "Where the hell did you get those two kids? We never saw anybody as quick and what they could do with a basketball." That is where most of my wins came from.

In 1956 and 1958 we were in the Final Four. In 1957 we won the holiday tournament at Madison Square Garden against a hell of a team, California with Pete Newell coaching them. Hell of a coach, by the way. In 1958 we repeated. We lost the first game each time; one was to Kentucky and the other year to Iowa. In those days, you played semifinals and finals. Today they only play one game.

In the 1969 NIT final, we beat Boston College. They were coached by Bob Cousy. That was his last season. He announced that he was giving up. He did not like recruiting. In the same way I had the feeling so I retired. I still had a year to go, if I wanted to. I did not like recruiting. The good recruiter is a good salesman. He can sell his college. That is the only way he can put it. I had a pretty good reputation as a player and as a coach. I told you how I got fortunate in getting a kid like Guy Rodgers. He was like a franchise. Recruiting is a tough proposition. If you and I are sitting down and I am the head coach, you are interested to be my assistant or second assistant. So I say, "Well, you know, most if it will be around recruiting. Here or there, I will need somebody on the floor, but you are the third man. He will assist me on the floor and whenever you are free, you will assist. Are you married?" "No, I am single." I say, "Well, that is good, because if you are married, how are you going to do me any good? If you have to be out on the road, you are going to have marital trouble." So you have to try to locate a guy who is what you call a jock. He would give anything in the world to become a head coach, but you have to get a start. That is how you try to get a good recruiter that will be out on the road. Then you have to have alumni friends and high school coaches that you are familiar with to recommend. You get a name and you say to your assistant, "He is playing at so and so. See what you think of him."

[On experiencing antisemitism:] No. No. On the college level? The coaching? Who knows what the other coaches thought of me. I do not know. I was always friendly. I always had a nice reputation with all the coaches. There are quite a few that I admired. John Wooden in my era was a great coach. Hank Iba in my era was a great coach. Bob Knight was a great coach, a good organizer. Bobby was the youngest head coach that the Army ever had. Dean Smith was a great coach. Great coaches are great innovators. Sometimes you see a team with great players but they do not get up there. These fellows, Dean Smith, Bobby Knight, Mike Krzyzewski, Adolph Rupp, John Wooden, were great, great coaches. Good teachers. Good innovators. You get a lot of guys that you do not even hear of that are good coaches.

I could tell you, without patting me on the back, I am sitting in the audience and they are presenting Johnny Wooden as the recipient of the coach of the year. I forget what year it was. It may have been 1956 or 1958. I am in the audience, sitting alongside my athletic director, and John Wooden was called on. He very graciously and with humility accepts the trophy. He said, "But I really do not know if I earned this recognition because in my mind there is a young man sitting in the audience who I think should have been the coach of the year and that is Harry Litwack." I did not tell him to say that. You get the reputation. People give you the reputation. I do not know. I had talks with Hank Iba and Adolph Rupp over a highball and they would say, "How do you get away playing zone? Why the hell don't you play man-to-man? You will never go too far with zone." I was a zone man, and I won a lot of games playing the zone.

I did not originate it. I started to work on the zone in 1934 when I was an assistant and freshman coach at Temple University. In 1934, the freshmen, I had Mike Bloom, Eddie Boyle, Don Shields,

Howie Black. Bloom, Shields, Don Henderson, and Black were the five starters. We had five others on the team. Those five were freshmen in 1934. So I asked my coach, "Jim." I called him by his first name. He was my coach, and I am now his assistant. I said, "Jimmy, is it all right with you if I use a different type of defense with these guys?" He said, "It is all right with me." Why did I get that thought in my head? Mike Bloom was 6'6", Don Henderson was 6'6", Shields was 6'5", Eddie Boyle was 6'4", and Howie Black was about 6'3". In those years, although the courts had to be a certain size, there were some gymnasiums where we played that were a little short. For example, at Madison Square Garden, for years they did not have an official court, 94 feet by 50 feet. Their court may have been like about 90 feet or maybe 88 feet. People never realized that. It was never brought out. So I thought, if I could get these guys to stretch their arms out, it would be tougher to get in toward the basket.

So I started what they call a three-two zone and we played it and I taught it. As the games went by and the practices went by, they got more efficient and more efficient. When they became sophomores, my coach would watch what I was doing, and he saw these kids that we were playing, and the other part of the freshmen team, they could not make a point. They could not get underneath the basket. He said, "Hey, Harry, let us work on this with these guys." So that team started to play man-to-man, but here and there we were playing the zone. Then we said, "How the hell can you get these kids to tell when to play man-to-man and when to play zone?" So we got together and I said, "Jim, how about every time we make a foul, a foul shot, or every time the opposing team makes a foul shot, if we make the foul shot, when we go back, everybody knows we are going back in the zone. If we miss the foul shot, everybody goes back and we know we are playing man-to-man. So we had a signal. That is how we started to play this thing. I innovated a few things to it but the fellow that originated it was a fellow by the name of John Lawther. He was at Penn State University in the years that I am talking about, the same era. That is how we got started and that team, when they became seniors, we used it quite often and that team won the first NIT in 1938. That was the first National Invitation Tournament held at Madison Square Garden. I was the assistant on the varsity and that is when they gave me credit for the zone starting. We won it by playing a zone. We won it against Oklahoma State that was coached by Hank Iba, who at that time was reputed to be the best coach in the United States. The type of reputation that he had, later on, you saw when he retired. He coached the Olympic team three times.

Hank was chosen three times as Coach of the Year. That is what he was thought of by the Coaches Association. But we licked him. When we would sit down to talk, he said, "Harry, I will tell you the truth. I did not know what the hell to do against the zone. We never saw it when we played." I did not have the reputation [in order to coach an Olympic team] that some other coaches had.

I never cussed at a kid. I never used foul language to a kid. I may say "damn," but I never said, "You goddamn son of a bitch." I know those words. I use them. I would never do it to a basketball kid of mine. I treated them as human beings, like they were my own kids. You had certain responsibilities. You have to get that ball off the basket. You are my point man as they call them today. This is our offense. We would go through the offense day in and day out. Dummy offense. The "live offense," we would call it. Options. Alternate offense. Dummy offense is where you pass the ball where you go, the way you go after a pass, what you do. That is five guys. Here is what I expect you to do and what you have to do and I would explain. Now we are going to practice against five guys. That is the "live offense." A kid made a pass or he did something and he did it half-backwards. "Hold it. What were you supposed to do? All right, let us do it." But yell at the kids, "You are a dumb, big horse." I would never insult a kid. Some need to be yelled at and I might say, "How many the hell times am I going to tell you?" I would not say, "How many the hell times am I going to talk to a dumb bastard like you or a dummy?" That is the difference between my style of coaching against a fellow like Bobby Knight. Bobby Knight would say, "You bastard, if I have to tell you one more time, you are sitting on the bench." That is the difference. I never used abusive language. He does that a lot of the time and a lot of the coaches follow his pattern. As an individual, Bobby Knight is a hell of a nice person, as an individual on a one-on-one basis. As a teacher, he teaches in a little bit of a style that is not mine.

When I go back in early September, that group that played for me from 1954 to 1958 will have a get-together. We do not call it an anniversary. We have met once a year like that for all these years. It created a friendship. Today, they are men in their sixties. We meet for dinner, get together, and throw crap around. The 1969 gang that won the championship at the NIT, that crowd of about twenty, will get together with a dinner. They keep in touch quite a lot and they include me in it, and I include them.

On a time-out one year in a game, I started to talk, to say what we were doing wrong and what we should do. Before we broke up, Guy Rodgers said, "Okay, Chief, gotcha." He started it. They called me the Chief. In my early days, they would call me nothing but Mr. Litwack. Never called me coach. They had that much respect for me. It was always Mr. Litwack. Some of them would call me Mr. Litwack later on, even if they knew that Guy Rodgers planted that name on me about 1957 or 1958. I can still recall a kid, he is a dentist today, Bruce Drysdale, hell of a player for me, "All right, Mr. Litwack." It is the same as the personalities in coaching. Everyone has different styles.

In forty-three years of coaching, I only had one technical called against me. The name of the referee, a good referee, was Lenny Toff. He happened to be a Jewish referee, and a good one. He refereed a lot of college games. There was one decision he made that was an obvious push on the opponent's part and he called it on my kid. I jumped up off the bench and got his attention. I said, "That is an obvious lousy call, Lenny. Kid pushed my kid." I am screaming mad. The ball was being advanced. It comes over the half-court mark and I yell at him. I said, "You missed the call." Something he did not like. He blew the whistle, and I had to sit down. That was the only technical in forty-three years. It was during the Big Five, when we had the Big Five. It may have been one of those years between 1954 and 1958. If there was a bad call, I thought, I would stand up and I would walk up and down, and the referee knew that I was mad. I never gave him the option of putting a technical on me. Sometimes a technical could cost you the game because it turned around the game and how about if you lose by a point. You have these kids running around for forty minutes sweating and toiling and here I am, their teacher, [I] defeated them. So I never refuted. I did not have that reputation. You get mad like any other coach. Like any coach, I would stand up and fold my hands, "What kind of a call was that?" I would not say it, but they would know if I got up that I was dissatisfied with the call.

If I had a loss, I would tell the kids, "Too bad. Maybe we did not play hard enough." If we lost to what I call a good team, I said, "No disgrace. We will get back at them." Personally, I would go home and I would sit and maybe smoke two cigars before I would go to bed at three, four, or five in the morning. "What should I have done? Should I have done this or this?" A victory, I took it in stride. I did not go out to celebrate or drink. I can sit down and take a drink with the coaches but not enough to get drunk or be inebriated. After a game, depending on what time the game was over, I would give them a chance to eat and give them an hour and then say, "All right boys, everybody in their rooms by 1:00 or by 1:30."

I would say I was strict with the rules. In 1957 we were going over to play at the Holiday Festival, which, by the way, we won that year. We licked Pete Newell's team, California. Pete Newell was known by his offense called the California Shuffle. He was a great coach. We were going over and we were supposed to meet and we do not see Hal Lear. Hal Lear was my big star, he and Guy Rodgers. I gave him five more minutes. So five minutes, he is not there. I tell the bus driver, "Okay, let's go." Hal Lear came over by train by himself. He paid his own train fare. He came with his uncle, and he was dressed. I did not start him. After about, I do not know, maybe five minutes. In the meantime, I am burning up. He is a great All-American, as Rodgers was. The game was nip and tuck. Now I am saying to myself, "Should I penalize these kids? If I penalize him, he is out. If I give in, he is in. Is it more important that I get the satisfaction of being a disciplinarian or should I get the satisfaction of the kids working to win a game?" So I put him in. As soon as I put him in, bang, bang, bang, bang,

bang, bang, bang we were way ahead of them. I had pity on Pete Newell, although I did not know him personally. I never tried to humiliate another coach. We were on top maybe fifty to twenty-five and Lear made the difference.

After the game was over, we won the title. We won the title. It was over, and I said, "Next time you do a thing like that, you will not play at all. I just did not want to penalize the boys, but you hurt me." So I compromised. He respected me for that. He said, "I am sorry." In fact, he was never late again. If I said, "Practice is over," he and Rodgers and a few more said, "One more goal, coach. One more. One more." They are practicing fifteen more minutes. That is what made them so damn great. Other kids on the team, if you said, "okay," they could not fly out fast enough. They put their two hours in of practice. This group from 1954 to 1958, you could not get them off the floor. That is what makes you great. It really is what makes you great.

Dedication. Want to get better. This group as a group, not only as individuals, as a group, had it. They wanted to become better. They proved it to go to the Final Four. That was a hell of an achievement. When you look at it in those days, you did not have that many teams. I think there were thirty-two teams. Now there are sixty-four. In sixty-four an ordinary team has a fairly decent reputation. The good ones, from a coaching standpoint, you will find they never look at the clock. They want to keep going, keep going, and keep going. More shooting, more shooting, and more shooting.

The difference between college and the pros. Outside of the rules, they are a little bit more lenient on the pro level, in my judgment, with palming of the ball and walking or starting on a dribble from a stationary—a little walking. They allow too much contact for the offensive man to get a position and for the defensive man to prevent him from getting [a] position. There is a little bit more pushing underneath on the pro level as compared to the college level. Outside of that, the difference is that on a pro level you have pretty near 70 percent of your talent as All-Americans, where on the college level, you may have one kid that is on an All-American basis. Mention any [pro] team and if you look at their personnel, then you would find the major part of the personnel would be All-Americans. Mention a college, maybe one kid will be an All-American.

In 1956 I was offered the job by Eddie Gottlieb, who then owned the Philadelphia Warriors, and I turned it down. In 1958, when we went to the Final Four, I was offered the job of coaching the Warriors, and both times I turned it down. I turned it down because in 1956 and 1958 I had two little children. My wife did not want me to fly all over the country. I was involved in owning a camp with two other friends of mine and I felt that my being away so much, that it would be an injustice just to let them two run the business and I get one-third of it. I thought I ought to put in my end of it. I had a good college salary. To run it with me being absent most of the time, in the summer months and during the months when you had to go out recruiting for kids, that was my feeling. Plus the major feeling was that my wife did not want me to fly all around the country.

Now, in 1958 or 1959, Eddie Gottlieb sells the Warriors to a fellow out on the coast. I forget his name, but he sells the franchise for $900,000, which was unheard-of. He originally bought the franchise for $25,000. A guy like Lester Harrison, his tongue is hanging out. Danny Biasone, an individual who owns the Syracuse Nationals, "How the hell did he do it?" They were looking for that buyer. A fellow by the name of Ben Kerner, the owner of the Saint Louis franchise that had Bob Pettit, all tongues hanging out. He sells it. Now there is no basketball in Philadelphia. They do not have a team. Eddie sells it. Now, Danny Biasone is in a little trouble and he wants to sell his franchise, Syracuse. Eddie Gottlieb at that time recommends two future owners that want to get the franchise into Philadelphia. Their names: one of them is Ike Richmond and the other is Irv Kosloff. Through the recommendation of Eddie Gottlieb telling Danny Biasone they are honest people and they will hold by, Danny Biasone sells the franchise plus the team to these two fellows, and they change the name from the Nationals to the 76ers.

When they buy, they invite me for lunch. They said, "Alex Hannum, who was the coach of Syracuse, wants to go back to the coast. So, we have got two choices. We want you to be the head coach. We know you turned Eddie down on two occasions, but we will make it interesting for you." So they did. I said, "I will talk to Estelle, that is my wife, and I will give you an answer." In the conversation, they said, "If you do not take it, then we will give the job to Dolph Schayes." Dolph knew about as much coaching as this rug knows. That is not to—great basketball player, great. I saw him right out of college come in to play for NYU against Notre Dame and as a young kid, right at Madison Square Garden, that game, he defeated Notre Dame. Great team. Yesterday he was in high school. The next day he is playing for NYU. That is not to lower his, you know—but from a coaching standpoint, [he had never coached].

I turned them down. My wife said to me, "You have had enough. You have a good college, a good college job; your camp is doing all right. How much time do you want? You cannot be a workaholic. A workaholic, it will kill you." So I turned them down. On three occasions, I had a chance to get into this. Of course, I knew a little bit about the life of a professional basketball player because I was one of them in my early days between 1930 and 1936. That is how Dolph came to the 76ers to coach. But I turned them down. Maybe I should have attempted to change gears. I did not, so I do not regret it.

Sometimes I feel bad. Why didn't I just get a taste of it? Coaching on the college level and coaching on the pro level is a little bit different. On the pro level, you know their ability. You are getting a million dollars and there is a coach that is making maybe $80,000, $90,000, or $100,000. You are going to go tell him, "Hey, you big son of a bitch, you are making a million dollars and you perform like that?" He will look at you and do something. What are you going to do? You cannot do a damn thing. The old, old adage, it is much easier to get a coach than to get an All-American that has a lousy game here and there. So you have to guide them, you have to cajole them, that is the game today.

[On money having spoiled current players:] Oh, hell yeah. No question about it. Where do you get a fellow, for example, like Charles Barkley that publically criticizes his own teammates? How would you like to be a member of that team and he is criticizing to this reporter and to this commentator or that commentator? People say, "Didn't the 76ers make a mistake in letting him go?" He has got one version. He wants to be on a team that is a contender. The other guys are working their butts off and he is saying they are inferior and they cannot play and he does not want to play with them, they stink, they do this and that. Now they have to gamble on a big guy. It had to be. They had to get rid of him. You just do not criticize your own teammates. He criticized the coach. He criticized the whole organization. A lot of them are spoiled, but he mainly is.

You install a system and they will know very quickly from their own coach's experience that they played for; you cannot teach a guy how to shoot. You cannot teach a guy how to fake a drive-in. Some have a quicker step and get noted for it. Some have a better shot. Some are just ballplayers.

Best overall fellow today is Michael Jordan. By far the best. The greatest. The best big man offensively was Wilt Chamberlain. The best backcourt years back, one of them was Bob Cousy. Elgin Baylor was a great one. An unknown who does not get as much publicity, but a hell of a shooter for the Boston Celtics was a young kid by the name of Bill Sharman. He was a great, great shooter. Go back beyond that, Joe Fulks revolutionized the jump shot. The fellow that introduced it was a kid from out at Stanford. He revolutionized the game with the one-handed shot. I really could not give you a legitimate answer for who were the best defensive players. I am sure that there are a lot around where the coach would say, "You are defending this guy." That is their star. They must have thought that this fellow was a pretty good defensive man, but by name you would not know. You are always thinking of the shooters and the dribblers and the assist men. Another great one in this era was Oscar Robertson.

Les Harrison had the Rochester Royals, which was a great team. Lester was not, by any means, the coach of that team. Bobby Davies was one of his great backcourt guys. Red Holzman played for Rochester. I tried to get him. We played the Renaissance and I needed two men and Red Holzman was one of them that I got. A fellow by the name of Red Wolfe, a New York boy, played for us. I saw him play against the Renaissance with the SPHAS when I ran them and I told Eddie, "You ought to get ahold of Red Holzman as a player." He was getting a monthly salary, and in those days you were only getting paid by the game. That is how we lost out on Red Holzman. You could see then he was a great one. There is another one, a fellow by the name of Bobby Wanzer, a great backcourt fellow.

My wife liked to watch the games, but to visualize me flying all over the country and being away for three days, being away for a week, she did not relish that. If I had it to do over, I would have taken a shot at being a pro coach. I would have gone against her will. Who the hell knows? We may have been divorced. It is just like when I sold this camp. If I held on to it the first time, I could have been maybe a millionaire by now. I sold it and bought another one. If I did not sell the second one, it was going great. I had no regrets about it. That was the way I did things. That is all.

I have never seen so much progress in a game over the years. First of all, I cannot conceive, for example, as I looked at my grandson in practice, to see a kid that is 5'11" and I looked and I see he is dunking a ball. Never would I believe that I would ever see a thing like that. Never would I believe that I would see a guy like Jordan, with two dribbles, in. Larry Bird. You can go down the list and mention twenty other guys in the league that do just as well at shooting. The physical makeup of a fellow like that could be 6'5", 6'7", 6'10" that could take the ball up court and dribble and have these outstanding moves that you only thought of years ago as a little 5'7", 5'8" guy. I never would believe that.

Today's athletes are much better. They are bigger and stronger. The same kid that is quick and is maybe a six-footer and can dribble either way, in reverse, you could get that out of a 6'8". You could get that out of a 6'9" guy. I cannot conceive of that. That is what you see in the game today, the leaping ability. Some kids will make a pass to a guy coming on the backdoor and while he is in the air. I never saw that. You saw backdoor plays, but it was always on a bounce, pass, and a layup. So the athlete today is amazing— quickness, percentage of shooting, the passing that you can see. So you could say it is a different game today. Fundamentally, it is the same damn game.

The rule makers visualize this. I remember one year the rule makers took out dunking. The fear of getting hurt, dunking and hitting, getting injured. But look at what it did from the spectator's standpoint, it is like a home run. It is like a home run. It is interesting. I know in my day, I would come back. Generally I used a zone defense. I used a zone defense mainly. If I was going to get licked, I wanted to get licked on the outside shooting. Today it is the three-point shot and the damn shot looks so easy for kids today. In my day, when I started, nobody practiced from out there. Today you go out there in your practices and every kid has a basketball on the court. In our day, when I was coaching in the early years, if we had three basketballs out for the team throughout practicing, you had a lot of basketballs.

They say, "Harry, you were born at the wrong time." Let me say, my career between teaching and coaching in summer camp, I always made a comfortable living and I was happy with it and had more than my parents ever had or more than when I was growing up. So today, I look at my grandson that I have here by my younger daughter, I go through the garage at home to get into my car, and she lined up seven or eight different pairs of sneakers. I said to my daughter, "How many the hell sneakers does David need?" She said, "Why?" I said, "I do not know. I know when I was on vacation from school when I was twelve years of age, if I got a pair of sneakers they lasted me all summer. Here I look, every time I turn around. What does a pair of sneakers cost you? Look at the damn sneakers he has, what the hell is wrong with him?" It is a different world, a different world.

[I would like to be remembered as] as a plain, ordinary, down-to-earth coach that did the best that I was able to do with the material that I got, to change offenses according to material, to be always thinking of what I could do a little bit better, and would like to win. I knew I could not win all of them. I liked to be a good winner and a good loser, although as they say, who the hell likes to lose. I tried to think of the kids' future. Basketball is not the whole world. It is part. It ought to give you an idea of what life is about, what you ought to be doing, to become a decent citizen. That is the way I felt. That is my philosophy. They all had to be eligible on my team. I would say in all the years that I coached on the college level from 1931 to 1973, that I was connected with at least 90 percent of graduations. I would say that as an individual that I tried to do the right thing from a coaching perspective and for the boys that came under my guidance. I made a lot of friends in the coaching profession and from being in the basketball camp business. I think I missed maybe two times at the Final Four. I always go every year, and I still know a lot of the coaches there.

[On basketball in Israel:] I was the coach of the Maccabiah team in 1957. That was my first trip to Israel. I lived on a desert in a tent, no showers, nothing. The whole team, the whole contingent does not have anything like this today. You have to give the Israelis a lot of credit, a lot of credit, not only for their sports and what they are doing, but for the development. That is when you see the Hilton and all of those hotels. The Ramada was just being put up, and a few others. When I see it today, and I have more time to take a tour here and there, I marvel at the development. I still say in my lifetime, and maybe in your lifetime, there will be still plenty of room for development. I never saw so many deserts and places. I cannot imagine it. The Maccabiah Games are good. I think they are run pretty fair. A lot of people will tell you that you never lick the Israelis from the standpoint of basketball for the gold medal. I can see why. You do not get the outstanding Jewish players on a college level. You do not get it. You go back and they licked us in 1957 and I had a pretty good team. They had a lot of imports. Here is a team today that played our team and that team must have played fifty, sixty basketball games. Together as a team. Here we bring over a team that has tryouts and they select the eleven or twelve boys and have a couple of workouts, and they fly them over here a few days before the first game and have a couple of workouts. Here you are playing for the finals against an experienced team that has been together and these kids are just learning. You cannot put in a system in five practice days. You have an idea. If they played more games together and the coaches had time, had more time with them. It is a combination, a combination of visiting and seeing what Israel looks like and practicing. You have more limited time than you would like to have for these boys. If they were here for two months, that is a different story. You would like to show them what Israel is like and at the same time compete. That is why you get teams that do not have that interest. Britain's closest to mind. Canada had a pretty fair team. Australia was not bad. I do not know how many teams entered. I would say maybe [at] the most three teams that could compete on a college level.

In any form that you can give help, they [Israel] could stand it. For 95 percent, it is money to do the things that they would like to do. They just do not have that. They depend on contributions. You as an individual, whatever you can do to help, you feel they need it. I could see it. They have got maybe fifty years to go to build up. The determination, yes, they have it. That is why Maccabiah is a nice thing. Give the Jewish kids a taste of it. I came across a couple of people and they are sponsoring a kid. Today it costs a kid to come over here, just plane fare, I would imagine a total of about $4,000 for each athlete. Now the Maccabiah, the United States cannot absorb all of it, so they will always need help. Wherever they have a drive or whatever they do, you try to do something for it.

I came here [to Israel] in 1957 as a coach and in 1973 as a coach. The third trip was to see my grandson. I hardly ever saw anything in 1957. I saw a glimpse. In 1973 they took us out a couple of times, and I could see changes. I think every Jew ought to be proud of what these people here have done. They ought to be proud. That is the only way you are going to have a Jew being a Jew. That is all. They know he is Jewish and he has a state. You ought to support it if you are a Jew. Some support it much, much more. Whatever you can do to support the Jewish state, you ought to do it. I support UJA [United Jewish Appeal] and support the Israel bond. That is only an investment. I am [a] member of Maccabi. Whatever they do, if they run a tournament, I support it.

[On retirement:] Up until now I have been playing golf three days a week. I played nine holes. I used to play eighteen. I just play for exercise. I would not say I like to play cards but I indulge in playing pinochle. I belong to a country club back home and when I come back from Florida I go pretty near every day. I get in a card game, yes. If I don't, I sit around and chat and talk. I do not gamble. That is how I spend my time. In the evening, I watch TV when games are on. When I am down in Florida, I call the Miami Heat. I know the general manager and he puts away a couple of tickets for me. I go down and watch them play. I watch them on TV. I watch college games on TV. I follow the game pretty much. Ron Rothstein started to coach Miami. He got them together. Then evidently they found a little thing wrong with him so they released him and they got Kevin Loughery, who I know very well. He used to come up to our camp, basketball camp. It was the Pocono Mountain All-Star Basketball Camp. We used to get a pro in once a week who lectured and demonstrated to the kids. We would give Kevin the job. It ran like three weeks. We would take him up twice. He is a nice guy. We used to have Adolph Rupp come in. Johnny Wooden came in for us.

[On recruiting Tal Brody:] Hal [actually Tal] Brody went to Trenton High School in Trenton, New Jersey. I got word that he was going to go to North Carolina State. They said he was an outstanding player and so we got in touch with his former high school coach in Trenton High School, a fellow by the name of Red Smith. Red Smith is the one that introduced us to Mike Bloom years and years back and also to a player by the name of Red Blumenthal. I went around to the home of Hal, and his father and mother were Israeli. They had a big general store. I forget the name of the neighborhood in Trenton. I located the place and introduced myself to Hal's mother. His father was busy. We were waiting for Hal. The mother was very apologetic, saying, "I do not know when he will be here." So she invited me upstairs where they lived. Finally Hal arrives. Where was Hal? He was at the YMHA practicing. Anyways, we got together and we started to talk and before we left, Hal Brody's mother said to him, "Play for this man. I like him." So I made a date with Hal to come up to the university to take the SATs. He did not have time to take the Princeton test. He wanted to make a decision. So I take him up there, the man that gave the test was in the Psychology Department and said, "Coach, I will have the results in about an hour, an hour and a half." So I said okay. So I take Hal and we walk down to what we called Broad Street. That was our campus in those days. I said, "Come on."

We go across the street and there was a restaurant. We go in and have a sandwich and sat around, came back to my office, talked with him. I said, "Come on, we will be ready." We walked to the building where he took the exam and I look at him [the proctor] and he said, "He won't pass college work." I said to him, "Come on." He was recommended by his high school, recommended by his coach. Not outstandingly, but enough grades there to show that he was going to be a good student. Well, anyways, he turned me down. Now I am boiling. This kid is recommended as a great, great player. "Well, I will tell you what. Maybe the kid was nervous. Maybe he was excited. Some kids do that when they take an important exam." He said, "If you can get him to come back here tomorrow, we will give him another type of exam."

I told that to Hal. He was very disappointed but he said, "I will be back." So I think I gave him two dollars to pay for his train fare up and back, and I gave him two more dollars to come back. He came back the next day. Once again, we go up to this building and the test. Once again, the results are that they cannot pass him. They do not think he will be able to do the college work. I said, "I cannot believe it." I am mad as hell.

In the meantime, he was being recruited by Guy Lewis of Houston. Why Guy Lewis? A player that played for me at Temple, Blumenthal, was running the YMHA and doing a little recruiting for Guy Lewis. The other coach was a fellow from Illinois. Eventually, I lost him [Brody] and he went to Illinois. Three years, all Big Ten, he got his degree and he got his master's degree. I lost track of him over the years. Sometime on the news or somewhere following four years of Maccabiah [Brody played professionally for Maccabiah Tel Aviv], the start of what they call the Olympics here, I see this kid running with the flame, the same Hal Brody. He opened up a sporting goods store. He was quite a young fellow. So I met him a couple of time. He recognized me, and said, "Oh, geez." We hugged each other. I understand he did not have a good personal relationship with his family, been divorced a couple of times. I do not know what he is doing today, but I saw him at a couple of games here.

5. Shikey Gotthoffer led the Philadelphia SPHAS to five ABL titles in ten seasons. Courtesy of the Naismith Memorial Basketball Hall of Fame.

JOEL "SHIKEY" GOTTHOFFER

- Born on New Year's Day in 1911, twenty years after basketball was invented, Shikey Gotthoffer emerged as one of the
best basketball players from New York during the 1930s. A
gym rat before the term was officially coined; Gotthoffer
always had his gym clothes on underneath his school clothes
so when the final school bell rang at three o'clock he could
go out and play. After a trade from Yonkers to Philadelphia
in 1933, Gotthoffer became a mainstay with the Philadelphia
SPHAS for ten years. In that time, he helped the SPHAS capture five American Basketball League championships while
capturing two league MVP (most valuable player) awards.
Known for his toughness, Gotthoffer was the SPHAS best all-
around player. When he retired, he was the team's highest-
paid player, at one hundred dollars a game.

I was born January 1, 1911, in New York City, on East Eighth Street,
in what is today Greenwich Village. I guess I started playing
basketball before I could read. I can't recall not playing. We had
a unique situation when I moved to the Bronx from Manhattan.
I was getting old enough to handle a basketball. We had a group
that was very much entrenched in basketball, and we consequently
built a basketball court behind the buildings that we lived in.

I was called Shikey from childhood. When my mother called
me, it must have sounded like "Shickey" or "Shikey," and kids
picked it up.

There were a group of youngsters like myself who were basketball minded. We had the Bronx Owl Seniors, Bronx Owl Juniors, and Bronx Owl Midgets. All were basketball teams. One generation moved up to the other, and all of us together built a basketball court behind the tenement houses we lived in. It was between 165th and 163rd Street on Union Ave in the East Bronx.

My parents were immigrants from Austria, but I was born in this country. My father was a designer for women's clothes. He had his own business in the garment district in Manhattan. He made women's coats and suits.

Well, I don't know what you use as a medium of poor. I guess if you say rich, then I'd say no. But I wouldn't say poor because maybe there's various differences of what poor is. We were eating every day, we had a normal life, but we didn't have the luxuries of a new car, things like that. We were clothed, we were fed. We weren't richer or poorer than the other kids on the street.

The courts that were utilized by people like myself at that time were primarily the public school courts. I can't recall when I didn't go to school dressed underneath with my basketball things so that at three o'clock I could stay in the playground and play basketball. The school had a gym, but when we played after school, it was on the outdoor court. They had an indoor gym, and they had playgrounds.

I played at James Monroe High School in the Bronx. We won the city championship three consecutive years, in 1926, 1927, and 1928. On that ballclub with me was Hank Greenberg of the Detroit Tigers. He jumped center for us. He graduated with me in 1928. The Bronx Owls made up a great portion of the James Monroe team.

College. That's a very sad story. I played basketball for [name unmentioned] and I received a dollar for playing. Somehow or other the Public School Athletic League [PSAL] of the city found out that I had received a dollar, and when I graduated junior high school and came to James Monroe, the Pubic School Athletic League wouldn't let me play my freshman year because they claimed that I had received money for playing on the outside. And since I couldn't actually defray the dollar expense at that time—after all, a trolley car was a nickel a ride, a frankfurter was a nickel—a dollar was a lot of money to get rid of. And I had difficulty getting rid of it, I remember.

Then I was vindicated, and I joined the basketball team at Monroe. Toward the latter part of my years at Monroe, before I graduated, I received offers from people who wanted me to play for their team. They were representing themselves as a team that would go out and play against another team and X amount of dollars would be paid to the individual who was organizing this, and he in turn would give a certain amount of money to the players. That happened to be five dollars in my case. I played, and the individual I played for later turned out to be a bone in my throat and was responsible for keeping me out of college.

I received scholarship offers from Brown, Providence, Temple, University of Pennsylvania, Duke, and Princeton. When the time came that I graduated high school, I received this Princeton offer. The coach's name was Whitman, and he asked me to come out to Princeton, New Jersey, because he wanted to talk to me. I went out there and spent the weekend, and I looked around and lived that life two or three days. It was much too rich for my blood— not that it was too rich for my blood, but I just couldn't handle it, put it that way. I felt that I would be a tag-on to all kinds of people I saw there. So at the end of the weekend, I told him that I didn't think Princeton was for me. He was quite annoyed with that because he felt everything was settled. I told him my story, and he rightfully told me that Princeton would not bargain my professionalism with anybody. I know that the Ivy League colleges had had players that had received money because I played with some, and I know that Columbia had a ballplayer that had played with me, and they didn't want to talk about it. They just turned it off. I just didn't feel that I belonged, frankly, that was it. I thought I wouldn't be accepted for me, I would be accepted because I was a ballplayer. So I told him, "I'm sorry," and I went home.

I decided that I was going to go to college, and I wrote to Providence College, which had offered me a scholarship. The coach told me to come up to Providence, which I did. We worked out a situation that I would get a scholarship for basketball. When the term began I started at Providence. When the time came for the basketball team to start practicing, I became part of that situation. Apparently I must have been highly touted because there was quite a crowd in the gym. I wondered why they were there, and someone told me that they were there to see me. So naturally I didn't have any trouble becoming part of that team.

When the basketball schedule came out, there was a college on that schedule whose coach was someone I had played with once; he had recruited me to play an exhibition game. He was cruel, because he recruited friends of mine who were also thrown out of college for the same reason. I had picked Providence because it was a small school, and I thought no one would know about it. But this team appeared on the schedule, and when my name was on the roster, this party wrote and said that I was a recognized professional on the Eastern Seaboard and that they would not play. I was called in when Father received that letter, and he questioned me about it, and I admitted to it, and I said that I didn't understand what makes me different than anyone else. The fact that I got five dollars doesn't make me an iron man. He said the rules are the rules, and they would have to take my scholarship; however, they would let me finish out the year. I did and then left.

I think it might have been two times for five dollars. So the big amount might have been ten dollars. One time I played in Port Chester, and the other time in New Jersey. Maybe I was aware that college players were supposed to be Simon-pure, but I felt what I was getting didn't represent anything. It was like a miniscule amount. How can you take a dollar and turn that into professional, or even five dollars? True, five dollars was a lot more than it is today, but it never dawned on me that it would cause me to be a professional. I never heard the word used. All I knew who were professionals were the Original Celtics and the Harlem Renaissance. To me, a professional was a man who takes a shot and never misses. That was my concept of professionalism. I didn't think anything like that would be attached to me. It turned out that they gave me a year's grace at Duke, and now I have two years of college. And then I went to NYU and had to pay. I didn't finish. I was nine credits short. But I realized I didn't want to teach, and that was why I was studying physical ed and health education. I realized that I didn't want to teach. It was not something I was interested in. So that closed my college career.

I didn't play at NYU. Howard Cann was then the coach of NYU, and he found out that I was going to health education so he sent word that he would like to talk to me. I knew he couldn't possibly want me to play basketball for NYU with all the commotion that had gone on with me, but I went to him, and he said, "I know you've got basketball experience. I know you're pretty good. I've heard about you. I want to ask a favor of you. I'd like you to sit with me during practice sessions and point out problems that exist and how I can alleviate them. It wouldn't be conducive to have you at the games because people would recognize you."

I said that I have no desire to sit with you at the games, but I could be helpful. So I said fine, I'll do that. So there were many days I spent at the uptown gym of NYU. What struck me as being strange—some of the ballplayers who were out there were playing for money on the side at the time. I never said anything to Howard Cann. I doubt that he knew it because he was a pretty straitlaced type of guy.

While I was at NYU, I was playing semipro ball. I was playing with pickup teams like the Knights of Columbus. That went on for some time until one day I received a call from the Yonkers Knights of Columbus. They told me they were entering the American Basketball League, and they were looking for ballplayers. I got what I considered good money, so I started playing with the Yonkers K of C [Knights of Columbus]. This was 1932 or 1933. They had some pretty good ballplayers. Joe Lapchick played for us for a while and others who were well known in basketball circles.

Then the time came when the American Basketball League was going into high gear. Cities were beginning to join in. Max Posnack of St. John's Wonder Five was playing with the SPHAS, and he wanted to go with the New York Jewels, who were made up of the old Wonder Five. They wanted Posnack to play with them. So Eddie Gottlieb, who was the owner of the SPHAS, told John J. O'Brien, who was president of the league, "Fine, you can have Posnack, if I can have Gotthoffer from Yonkers." So they ended up paying $2,500 for me. That was big, big, big bucks, and I joined the SPHAS.

I was paid fifteen dollars a game in Yonkers. Gottlieb paid thirty-five dollars a game. My salary grew as the years went on. I was voted the team's most valuable player six years consecutively. I'm only speculating, but if you tool my monies today and put them in the category of the monies they're fooling around with today with television and everything, it would be in the million-dollar class. I joined the SPHAS in 1934 and left them in 1942. By 1942 I was close to a hundred dollars a game with the SPHAS.

I was also what they called an import in the Penn State League. Gottlieb gave me permission, even though I was under contract to the SPHAS, to play twice a week when the SPHAS weren't play-ing. So I played with Nanticoke, a real mining town, and I got $150 a ballgame. The owner of the ballclub was the owner of a big gin mill, and money didn't mean anything to him.

I remember that a lot of other ballplayers were in that league. Mac Kinsbrunner from the New York Jewels, Allie Schuckman was out there. There was a scramble for the buck at the time. As time went on, as I played with the SPHAS, I guess I became more and more an outstanding ballplayer.

I played in a cage in Nanticoke. It was an enclosure with a bas-ket at each end. They played the discontinued dribble. You were allowed to take the ball and bounce around like a donkey. You could do whatever you wanted. I played maybe four times in the cage and came home with the cage's markings on me. Then they changed the whole setup and began to play on regular basketball courts.

The miners came to the game with coal dust on their faces and hands, and they'd sit on the bleachers and scream for blood. They didn't care about anything else; they wanted you to get killed in there. You were like a gladiator. And if you didn't get rid of the ball, you could get killed.

Play in the cage was continuous. The ball never stopped. When the ball came off the cage, it would take all kinds of fantastic bounces. You could bounce off until you were weak. You could play tick-tack-toe on everybody after a game because the cage marked you up. Sometimes you were bleeding and sometimes not.

Well, I'll tell you, they [the spectators] were verbal. They never became physical with you. They never wanted to kill you. While I was playing with the Philadelphia SPHAS one of the referees in the league was Doc Sugarman, who had played in the Penn State League. He was a dentist and a referee. He was a wiry guy. He was so incensed with these miners hollering for blood that one day he brought a piece of meat and put it in his jacket and went to the cage. And when they started to holler, he took the meat out and threw it into the bleachers and said, "Here, you wolves, here's meat." He told me they used to holler "Give us meat" whenever he came in after that. He was a colorful guy.

We were playing an exhibition game, the SPHAS, in Hershey, Pennsylvania, against a team from our league. Maybe it was Trenton or Wilmington. I got past my man and scored. He [Sugarman] called a foul on me. The basis for the foul was that if I could have gotten scot-free by my man, I must have done something wrong. This is what he told me. This is the kind of colorful guy he was.

If they cursed anybody, they cursed you in general. It wasn't "Jew bastard" or anything like that. The things they hollered at you were words of profanity. It wasn't a question of Jew. Although I'll tell you frankly, going back to Yonkers K of C, apparently the ballplayers I played with didn't know my religion. We were in the dressing room one day, and a fellow that played with me named Mike Platch said to me, "Well, from here on in you're never going to get the ball." I said, "What are you talking about?" He said, "Don't you know who is joining us?" He said a ballplayer from City College. His name is Milt Trupin. I said, "What does [that] mean, I don't get the ball?" I've heard about him, and he's a good ballplayer. He was outstanding at City College. And he said to me, "That Jew will never give up the ball." So I looked at him and said, "Mike, I'm Jewish." The first expression that came to him was, "You're a white Jew." I said, "What the hell does that mean?" He said, "You're different." I said, "I'm not different. You're looking for excuses."

In my era, there were many good Jewish players. This is just my own theory. Jews by the very nature of the fact that they were constantly under some kind of pressure had to do a lot of thinking and developing of the mind in order to be able to live in society and act in society. And since there was so much hatred attached to them, they had to be able to outwit a person. And I think knowing that these kinds of conditions existed that you just acquired these things as you grew up, with your family and with your friends and everything else. You learned cunning, you learned finesse, and you learned how to avoid a situation as opposed to fighting a situation. And all these things seemed to become not so much because it was Jewish on the east side of Manhattan and the Bronx and all those places the Jews settled. And they played basketball. And I guessed the intermingling of them gave them this viewpoint, and the way they did things. They thought out things instead of throwing their bodies at each other. That's a very amateurish view, I know.

Other people played all the time, too. Gentile people played all the time. It was just that you learned a little more. If you went this far, you tried to go a little farther. You acquired those skills. That's why the ballplayers that played in the old days, the ones that became generals on the court, seemed to be Jewish because they seemed to be able to analyze situations. But today you've got non-Jews out there doing the same things.

During World War II, I was a supervisor at Wright Aeronautics in New York. I built engines for B-21s. When my local board called me, they told me I was going in as 1-A [fit for general military service]. I made the request to go to officer school in the physical education area. I was sent to New Jersey, and I was questioned as to what I wanted to do. I told them I wanted to go into the health education program in Miami. They told me it was filled in Miami. They told me there was availability in the tanker destroyer unit. I told them I was not interested. I told him I would wait for an opening in Miami. My supervisor said that is not the way we do it. I went back to work, and I received a 1-A from my local board. I took it to the colonel at Wright Aeronautics. He tore it up. He told me to go back to my job and forget about it. Two weeks later, I was called down to my local board. This guy had the hots for me. He thought I was avoiding it. He said they would not let me get away with anything. I said, "I wasn't trying to get away with anything. I took it to the colonel, and he tore it up, not I." He said, "You will not get away with it. You'll go in as a private." I was there until the end of the war. I was working double shifts. I didn't play any basketball. I had to sleep sometimes.

After the war, Eddie Gottlieb asked me if I wanted to coach Philadelphia in the BAA. I gave it a lot of thought and came to the conclusion that I didn't want to do it because I felt that if I didn't make the grade there, I would have to go looking for another coaching job in another city. I had two young kids and my wife, and I didn't want to put them in a position where they would never have any friends in school because their father was moving around, and they'd have to start all over and make other friendships, and my wife would be in the same category. I decided that I didn't want to do that to my family. As a matter of fact, even in business, I chose not to become a salesman with territory, which would have yielded me a tremendous amount of dollars as opposed to being in the metropolitan area. So I stayed to be in contact with my family and be home every night.

So I told Eddie that I didn't want to do it and gave him my reasons, and he said, "Suppose you make good in Philadelphia and stay forever?" I said that's a challenge and it might, but then again it might not. I said I think basketball right now at this stage is fickle because there's no solidity in basketball. The ABL was together, yes—it had some cement—and you could say you were playing in an organized league—you had Philadelphia, Boston, Buffalo, New Jersey, and you had Pennsylvania, New York—it was a solid league. I didn't even know if the BAA would succeed. So I never went back into basketball.

Eddie Gottlieb was fair. He was honest, and he was fair. He believed in principles. If you're supposed to play forty-five minutes, give me forty-five minutes. Don't give me twenty. He also believed that a ballplayer had to start out with a certain amount of ability to play for him. Eddie learned basketball in Philadelphia. He played in the Jewish league way before my time. Eddie wasn't a good basketball player in the sense of using his body. Eddie was very burly and short, but he had a good head on him. He could analyze things and think out things. He was literally the driving force behind the NBA. Eddie created the schedules and did a lot of the organizational work. Eddie was a big wheel in the NBA. He was a teacher. He had taught for a while. Eddie had a lot of logic and brains.

Joel "Shikey" Gotthoffer · 71

One game, I was taken out because I was thoroughly exhausted, and I'm sitting next to Eddie on the bench. He is screaming for me to guard the man out there. I said, "Eddie, I'm sitting right here." He says, "What are you doing here?" He was an astute man who understood the fundamentals of the game. He was a bright man.

Eddie didn't have to coach us because he had a principle that you were professional ballplayers, you were schooled in your trade, you knew what you had to do, you had to be cohesive, and you had to be a team. The team that I played with won the league championship five or six years—seven years—was made up of a fellow by the name of Cy Kaselman, a tremendous shot; Harry Litwack for a short time; Red Wolfe; Moe Goldman; Gil Fitch; Petey Rosenberg; Inky Lautman; Red Rosan; and some others.

We had seven ballplayers. It was not like today where they have a bench of fifteen or whatever it is. You played because you were being paid. When you came out of a game, it was because you weren't conscious of the fact that you were playing in it. It had to be pretty bad.

If I could do it all over again, I would. You betcha. I didn't know there were girls around until I was seventeen years old. I didn't go to parties. We didn't have time. It sounds ridiculous. I'd go to school, come out of school and go to the schoolyard and play. At night I would go to play some more—all the time playing basketball. I played basketball, basketball, basketball. But I didn't have to roam around because the Bronx Owls had a structure. We always were there, and we played as a team and ultimately we went to college and into the professional ranks.

When I started with the SPHAS, everything was a lay-up or a set shot. Players using the two-handed set shots were coming from the West Coast. Hank Luisetti was about the first one we saw, and we looked upon him with amazement. We called it firehouse basketball because all he was doing—he didn't even know if his man had the ball—he was down the court ready to get that pass and heave. We claimed that God gave us two hands, and we used them.

He wasn't playing with the other four ballplayers. I played against him. He was very loose, and he was only interested in one thing—

shooting. I mean, like you take a kid and you tell him, "I'm going to teach you how to shoot baskets." When we played him, we played him out in the West. Bing Crosby was sponsoring the ballclub, and Hank Luisetti had a lot of good ballplayers from the colleges out there, and we were curious about what we were going to see. When you played against him, he was very loose, he wasn't difficult to guard. If he wasn't able to get away from you, he wasn't able to get his shot off, and if he got his shot off and you harassed him, it was a lousy way of shooting. Today these guys get the shot off even if they're standing on their hands, but he didn't have that facility. He would let the ball fly, and a lot of times they were air balls. And he didn't guard you a lick. If you were his man, you could walk in and score what you wanted. He lacked fundamentals, but he was a prolific scorer if you gave him the opportunity. He had developed that one-handed shot, and he could hit it.

In the ABL, I think we were on the conservative side. Shooting fouls had always been overhand, and we started to shoot them underhand. It was Eddie Gottlieb's thought that you have more control having the ball down here. And we started shooting the ball underhanded, and we were so successful. So we started to see more and more ballplayers starting to shoot underhand.

I always looked at basketball as a game of five men, they should be coordinated, that five men should contribute to the objective, and apparently there is some logic because we were quite successful.

We moved as a team, not as an individual. The man who had the ball would pass it as we moved up the court, not dribble it as they do today. Today the man with the ball is in the backcourt, and the rest of the ballplayers are down in the area where the basket is. We played on the supposition that if all the men were advancing they had to guard us that way. When we came sweeping down, we came down in full force. They didn't know where the ball was going to go or who was going to handle it. The ball always moved. The ball was off the floor. That was what we advocated. Of course we dribbled, but [for] most of the action the ball was being moved. That brought about opportunities because of the changes that were taking place.

But in the time I was with the SPHAS, the league brought about the ten-second rule, which meant that you had to bring the ball to midcourt in ten seconds, and did away with the center jump after each basket. That was what we left for the NBA.

Before we disbanded we became the darlings of Philadelphia. Connie Mack's ballclubs were no longer the darlings, the SPHAS were. We couldn't go anywhere in Philadelphia without being recognized. It was a very nice feeling. When I got off the train at Broad Street station, the redcaps would run to take my basketball bag. They knew me by name and by sight.

We were well loved. Even William Penn's statue on the top of city hall used to bow to us. Every time the SPHAS came by, he'd bow to us.

5. A player under Nat Holman at City College of New York, Moe
Spahn later played professionally in the American Basketball League.

MOE SPAHN

• In the early 1930s Moe Spahn earned a reputation as one of college's greatest players. From 1931 to 1933, Spahn was a mainstay on Nat Holman's City College of New York teams, leading the Beavers to two consecutive Eastern League titles as a junior and senior. He then joined the American Basketball League, where he was regarded as a top scoring threat. As a rookie he led the league in scoring and was often in the top five in scoring during his career. He was a member of two championship teams, the Jersey Reds and the Wilmington Blue Bombers, and also played with the New York Jewels. After his playing career, he earned a doctorate and worked in education.

I was born May 3, 1912, in the Yorkville section, Ninety-Second Street, in Manhattan. My mother had a grocery store, and my father worked in a sweatshop. I learned to play primarily in the schoolyards and played on junior high school teams [at] PS 30, on East Eighty-Eighth Street.

I went to Bryant High School in Long Island City. We had moved to Astoria. I was an All-City player at Bryant. I graduated from Bryant in 1930.

I went to the City College of New York. I had been offered a scholarship to Dartmouth, but I couldn't take it because there were too many extraneous expenses. I couldn't even pay the fare to get there. So I went to City College.

I graduated from high school in February, so I had only a half year of freshman ball. I went to summer school so I was ready to be Nat Holman's assistant as a middle freshman. I played at City College for three full years after that. We were the first team to play in Madison Square Garden. The mayor—I think it was [James John "Jimmy"] Walker at that time—wanted to open up the Garden in style so they invited City College—we were the champs that year—to play against George Washington, who were champs in that area. They had a 7'1" center. Everybody wanted to play against him. I was an All-American in my senior year. I graduated from City College in 1934.

When I got out of college, Nat Holman asked me to be his assistant, which I was for seven years. We got along very well. I'm not the pushy type. I have the greatest respect for Nat. I worked for him for seven years and never had an argument or disagreement. He was the type of coach who, when he was teaching, would worry about this little finger or that little finger. He broke everything down to slow motion; you had to walk through it. He was keeping control of the situation all the time. They had never beat St. John's in forty years, including my freshman year, and [then] we beat them four times.

After graduation from City, I played with clubs around the city for eight to ten dollars a game. In one place in Jersey, we would take the fire engines out and play in the firehouse. I never played semipro on the side while in college.

Then the Penn State League called me to play in Pittston. They had never won a championship. They could use only one professional. They paid me something like eighteen or twenty dollars plus gas. They usually had two games a week, one away and one at home. The first year there they had a cage—a net around the court—so there were no outside balls. It was netting from floor to ceiling. We dressed downstairs. The local players used to come right from the mines. They used backboards in the Penn State League. They came out a couple of feet from the net [that surrounded the court].

In 1935 I started with the Brooklyn Visitations. They played two games a week, and I had to give my first choice to their club. I picked up two games a week with Pittston. I might [also] pick up an odd game here and there.

I played for the Brooklyn Visitations only a short while. I don't know why I left them. I was offered more money by the Jersey Reds, and I went to them about 1935. They were in Union City. They played in a ballroom. Most times, the floors were very slick.

We had a couple of policemen and firemen on our team. They were very popular. Hagan Andersen came about the same time I did. Willie Scrill was on that team. Andersen was from NYU. We had pretty big centers. People don't realize that we did have big centers. They were all about 6'9" or 6'10".

The scores were a lot different than they are today. The whole emphasis was on defense. If I played against you and you scored eight or ten points, my teammates would get me in the huddle and bawl the hell out of me. "If you can't handle him, tell us, and we'll switch around." It was all defense. I would say the average game in those days ended 24–19 or 23–18. Luckily, I drew a lot of fouls. I used to average ten fouls a game, so I might be the high scorer just on fouls alone.

Speaking of Union City, the ballgame went on, and at halftime the people would go down to the bar and have a drink, and after the game they would have a dance to canned music or a band. I had the same feeling when we played against Philadelphia. A lot of young people came to the game, and when the game was over they were all out dancing.

When I started with the Jersey Reds, they were still doing the two-handed dribble. In 1938 I won [the] Most Valuable Player award in [the] American League with the Jersey Reds. There were no preseason practices for the Jersey Reds. Just signed players and started playing.

After three years with Jersey, I went up to Kingston. The Kingston Colonials had a nice court up there. Actually, we were free to play anyplace we wanted, but you couldn't play with two teams in the [same] league. They had to be freelancing. I was always paid by the game, even in the American Basketball League. I'd say if you made $2,000 for the season, you made a lot.

I was paid thirty-five or forty dollars a game in Kingston, and they paid my expenses. I would say eight hundred would be a good-size crowd. This was about the same in Union City. The court in Union City was not a ballroom. It was a large auditorium in a park.

Then the manager of the Kate Smith Celtics, Ted Collins, contacted me and told me of a plan he had to bring high-level professional ball to the Hippodrome on Sixth Avenue. We met in Kate Smith's apartment. She sat by and listened. He said he was going out to get every graduating captain from local colleges. I said, "That sounds very good. What do you have in mind for salary?" He said, "I feel very strongly that every player should get the same salary." I said, "I think that's very unfair. I've proven myself. I've committed myself to being on a winning team, and I've been very successful so far." I said, "I don't want to play if the captain of Manhattan is going to get the same salary. With my record and experience, I should be getting more money." He said, "Well, let me think about it."

The Penn State League was a difficult league to play in because there were people who had probably never even played high school ball. But I was there for about three years, and every year we won the championship. They weren't very skilled in the Penn State League because they could use only one professional. The one pro had to direct the team and organize the offense.

I drove my car to Pittston and slept in the manager's office. The Penn State League played mostly in high school gyms, but my first game in a cage was in some other building. The one thing you would tell everybody was when you go after a ball near the net, don't bend down with two hands, always grab the cage and grab the ball with one hand. That's the way you protected yourself. The spectators were about six feet from the cage.

They would yell for the home team. Everybody was drinking beer in those days. Luckily I didn't. Maybe I was a sissy. I don't know. But they used to beer up. As a matter of fact, some of our players on the Pittston team would take a beer at halftime. Let me say this, I would take a beer at the end of the game. I would lose six to seven pounds in a game, and that was the only thing that would restore me. The fans were not drinking during the game. They closed the bar during the game. I wouldn't want to give the impression that they were rowdy.

The Pittston team had a man named Granahan, who had a good shot. He could hit from thirty to thirty-five feet. Most of them were schoolyard players, or maybe a little better. None of them had played in college. It was tough. You were allowed to hold. You were allowed to grab by the throat as he was coming in. You were allowed to punch him in the chest to stop him from coming in. It was a very physical game.

There were a couple of guys in the American Basketball League who were fantastic shots. I'm talking about from half court. Billy Raven, Bobby McDermott, and Paulie Adamo, they were great shots from long distances. And then there were strong-arm guys who would push you around. And then every team had one outstanding passer. Willie Scrill, for example, I loved playing with him. There were always one or two fellows on a team who did nothing offensively but played good defense.

I also played in the Newark YMHA. I could play with our league team twice a week and play five times with anybody I wanted.

We all had somebody who had to make the substitutions. But there were some coaches that were better than others. Eddie Gottlieb was respected. He was a good coach and a good leader. But we had somebody who made the substitutions and tried to help, but I don't think he had ever played basketball in his life. In Pittston, the imported pro was the leader of the team. I made substitutions there.

At the Hippodrome in Manhattan, they took out seats to make a court. I played once in Brooklyn at the Biltmore Theater on the stage. I played about a season and a half with the Brooklyn Visitations right after college. They wore uniforms with Shamrocks all over the pants and shirts. My last pro year was 1943.

There were many good Jewish players in my era. I think it was because of the YMHAs and men's clubs. There were several beautiful gymnasiums in Brooklyn and New York. I don't know why. I guess they couldn't find baseball fields. We used to play stickball, boxball, and things of that type. But basketball itself, it was not easy to find a place to play. For example, at a very young age I was a member of the Arrows at the Ninety-Second Street Y, and they would have a league for that age level, say eleven to thirteen. We probably played twice a week in that league, but I used to live in the Y. I did my homework in the Y.

Some public schools had backboards. Some kept them [basket-ball courts] open, and some you had to scale the fence to get in.

I think you can be trained to any level of play. We were all in good shape, and we learned how to move. I would say that the black players today do things we couldn't do. We had never been exposed to them. I could touch the rim, but I couldn't go over the rim. We didn't dunk the ball. I had a pivot shot. I had three ways to go. I could fake left and go right, always stepping away from the man. Or I could fake right and go left, always stepping away from the man. Or I could go left or step out toward the center with a skyhook. But we all knew our limitations. That's why the scoring was so low. Defense, defense, defense was very import-ant. That's why the game is so much more exciting today. But I don't think any of the white boys will eventually have the ability to fly through the air.

We played against the New York Renaissance [Rens]. They were the number-one black team. They could never beat us. The Harlem Globetrotters used to play preliminary to us. They were below our ability. It was purely a white sport.

I think refereeing was much stricter in the old days than today.

Regarding antisemitism, on occasion you might hear some-thing. But if you're on a winning club you don't get much of that. In the Penn State League, they hired the one pro, and if they lost a couple of games, they got rid of him because he wasn't doing the job. But if they were winning, he could stay there forever. I was lucky, we used to win, and that was it.

I did not run into any antisemitism from players or fans in the Penn State League. Grace, the owner, would have protected me because I was producing. He was a very nice guy, and he had the team to make money.

I once played for the Original Celtics. When I got out of college, they wanted a young guy to do some running for them. There was a two-and-a-half-week Christmas vacation coming up, and they came to me. They had Dutch Dehnert, Davey Banks, Carl Husta, and Nat Hickey—the only ones that weren't there then were Joe Lapchick and Nat Holman. So they said, "Come on, give it a try, and see how you like it." So we go in their seven-passenger limousine. They had cases of beer all over the car. So I stayed with them two weeks. They were a very good team. I had to do some running because I couldn't get into the pivot play. They had Dutch Dehnert, and he invented that play, and he was that wide, you couldn't see around him. But I did very well, and they wanted me to sign with them, but I said, "No, I've got my studies. I've tasted it, and maybe a couple of years hence I'd be interested." We went up to Boston for a three- or four-day trip, and they took me on another trip toward the southern end of the New York area. But they weren't playing every day. I would say they averaged four or five games a week. I think they paid me about twenty dollars a game.

There was a certain amount of skullduggery going on. I think the Brooklyn Jewels may have fixed total scores. They were close to the Brownsville gang [an organized crime enforcement group, also known as Murder, Inc.]. I was never approached to throw a game. I think if you live in a gangster's area or if gangsters have control over it, you're in trouble.

In later years I finished my PhD in school administration. I taught at a private school in New York, and later I bought the school and its building. I also ran a summer camp and later bought it in New Hampshire. The school was the Franklin School, grades seven through twelve.

7. Sammy Kaplan (*seated front row, left*) played with the Brooklyn Dux while growing up in Brooklyn. Courtesy of the author.

SAMMY KAPLAN

- Even though he did not play high school or college basketball, Sammy Kaplan enjoyed a successful professional career.
As a youngster Kaplan played for a neighborhood team, the
Brooklyn Dux, who competed against YMHA teams. The
players booked and managed their own games, learning the
finer points of running a business. His professional career
included stops with the New York Whirlwinds, Kate Smith
Celtics, and Kingston, Troy, and Wilmington of the American
Basketball League. After World War II he became involved
briefly in politics with the American Labor Party. He later
went into the storm window business.

I was born in Brooklyn on December 22, 1912. When I was about
two years old, we moved to the Brownsville section of Brooklyn, and that's where I grew up. My parents were immigrants
from Russia. My father was a carpenter. He eventually became a
builder, and when the Depression came in the 1930s, he lost everything and got wiped out. He then retired.

I learned to play basketball in the schoolyards. Basketball was
the big sport there. We played a little baseball, but there was no
football or tennis or golf, of course. It was out of our reach. We
were too poor for that, but the schoolyard was always there, and
we could go and play. We began to learn how to play basketball
in the schoolyard playgrounds in the summer.

There were baseball fields in Canarsie, and we played once
or twice during the summer, and we also played for the park—

Nannygoat Park. It was called that because goats were in that area. That was in the Police Athletic League. When I played for the Dux club in basketball, we also played baseball once. We leveled off a field in Canarsie, and we played a few games. But that was about it.

My biggest problem coming home from school was whether I should do my homework now and have the rest of the day off or go out in the schoolyard and play immediately and then when it got dark, come home and do the homework.

I did not play basketball in high school. Most of the Brooklyn Dux club, which was formed basically on what we did in the school playground, met in the school playground and represented the playground. I think we won the championship or someone suggested that you fellows play so well at such an early age, you ought to form a team. So we formed a team, and it was called the Brooklyn Dux club. Some of the members were, I think, freshman and sophomores. I was still in public school, I think. We joined the recreation center's evening program, which was the opening of the school at night. They let us use the gymnasium to practice basketball. Also, they insisted that you hold a meeting. They wanted you to learn how to run a meeting and how to keep minutes and how to proceed in a meeting. They wouldn't let us have the gym unless we had the meeting. As young kids, we weren't interested in having meetings, but we did all right. We even had a minute book. For the meeting, we had to pay dues. Our new business might be who we were going to play the following week. We set up a booking manager who would book games by sending letters or we would meet them [the other team] on the street and talk to them and so forth. New business might be that we had found that the Ninety-Second Street YMHA was booking games, and we want the booking manager to write to them. All of the business had to do with the basketball team. All the members of the club were basketball players—maybe eight boys.

The fellow who was the treasurer complained after we found out that he didn't have the dues money we gave him. His complaint was, "What do you want from me? You gave me the 10 cents in the candy store, and I'm anxious to buy a piece of candy. I put my hand in my pocket and there's the dime. I spent it. So I haven't got the money. Don't pay me the dues in the candy store."

We also played a game called punch ball. We played it in the street. It had rules like baseball, but instead of hitting it with a stick like in stickball, you hit a rubber ball with your fist.

Sometimes we would play the team on the next corner for a dollar if we had that much in dues. We played for money. There had to be some incentive, otherwise there would be no interest in it.

In the winter we played basketball, and we joined this evening recreation program. We represented the school and eventually won the citywide championship. That was in 1927–28.

The Dux club started in 1925 and ended in 1935. I wasn't one of the original members. I came in 1926. We stayed together—most of us—until about 1935. Dux is a Latin word meaning "leader." It only had three letters, so we felt it would be the cheapest to have just three letters to sew on your shirt. That was one of the reasons. But when we went to school, Latin had to be taken in high school if you took a general course, and one of the fellows who took a general course thought "dux" would be a good name because it was just three letters and it meant "leader." But now, when you look back, everybody calls us Ducks, and we have to explain that it's pronounced "dukes" so maybe we should have done something different.

I went to Thomas Jefferson High School, but I didn't play basketball there. I didn't think I was that good. My thinking was that at some stage of the game other people may be better than you, but you eventually overcome them. I went to City College of New York at night but did not play pro ball.

When I was playing with the Dux, teams would give us expense money. Like when we played the Ninety-Second Street YMHA, everybody wanted to see us because they knew we were an outstanding team. We'd say, "We want expenses," and they'd say, "We'll give you thirty bucks." We'd say, "No, we want fifty," and there would be a big argument. We played the Newark Hebrews club, and we did pretty well against them. That was like a semi-professional team. They were paying the fellows a few dollars. So when they saw me play, they asked me to come and play with them. So I played for Newark, and they gave me like five dollars. This would be about 1935, when I was twenty-three.

Barney Sedran, who eventually became the coach and who had been an outstanding player, always wanted to promote professional basketball, but he couldn't get off the ground in those days. He was looking around to manage some team and also to rent a hall where they could play. I ended up with him. The team was called the New York Whirlwinds. That's how I began to play a little more professional basketball. This would have been 1936 and 1937.

The team consisted of college captains of City College, Fordham, Columbia, and NYU. We had Willie Rubenstein, who was captain of NYU. We had Phil Nash, who was captain of Columbia; Tony DePhilips, who was captain of Fordham; Lou Spindell, who was captain of City College; Sol Kopitko, another captain of City College; and Lou Bender, who was captain of Columbia. Then we had Chick Reiser, myself, Moe Frankel, and maybe someone else.

We were independent. We didn't belong to the league, but we played the league teams. Then we sort of barnstormed locally against local teams. I think I was getting about fifteen dollars a ballgame.

At that time Barney Sedran decided to rent the Hippodrome, a big theater in Manhattan. Billy Rose put on that musical *Jumbo* there. It sat about four to six thousand maybe. Sedran put on doubleheaders there. The Whirlwinds would play somebody, then the pro teams that existed in those days would play one another on Sunday nights. One of the teams in those days was Kate Smith's Celtics, owned by Ted Collins. They were in the league then.

In 1937–38 the Whirlwinds broke up, and Barney suggested to Ted Collins that he should take me and one or two others from the Whirlwinds. So I ended up with the Kate Smith Celtics. We didn't do too good, so Collins, who felt that he was being used by some of the other owners and promoters who were only working on a shoestring—outside of Eddie Gottlieb from Philadelphia, who had a good franchise—so he decided to give up professional basketball and that broke up the Celtics. Kate Smith was putting money into it, but Collins ran the whole thing. Once in a while she'd come to the games. The coach was Pete Berry, who had played for the Original Celtics.

Collins felt that one of the weaknesses of the professional league was that the players would play outside of the league when they had days off, and they would be exposed—people would see them—so they wouldn't come to the league games. So he decided to pay us weekly and we shouldn't play with anybody else. I didn't feel that I was getting enough money, so I went to Barney Sedran and told him I didn't think I was getting enough money. Sedran was running the Hippodrome at that time, so he said, "You play for them, Sammy, and I'll give you fifteen dollars extra." Collins was paying me fifty-four dollars a week for maybe two games a week.

When the Celtics broke up, Barney contacted the Kingston Colonials. He took the whole Celtics team—maybe he dropped one or two guys and added one or two—and we went to Kingston. I would say that would be 1938–39. We played for Kingston, and I think we won the championship of the American Basketball League, which included the Brooklyn Jewels, Philadelphia s p h a s, New Jersey Reds, and Kingston Colonials.

The following year we moved to Troy, New York, and played for Troy. We played there one year and then moved to the Wilmington Blue Bombers and played there in 1940–41 and 1941–42. They were in the American Basketball League. I was paid by the game in Wilmington. In the winter of 1942 I played for the Ebers in Rochester. Les Harrison wasn't the coach. He was the owner. I don't think we had a coach. I didn't know Harrison.

Sometime between 1935 and 1940 I played for Tunkhannock [Pennsylvania]. In those days the Penn State League allowed one or two professional players, I don't recall, and I took the place of Allie Schuckman. They said I was a team player. Everybody liked to get into the Penn State League. I think I made twenty-five dollars a game when I was only making fifteen dollars someplace else. I think they paid the [train] fare because I remember I came home on a sleeper, and I couldn't sleep because I was so happy about the twenty-five dollars. I just went up there once.

When we played, the Harlem Globetrotters played a regular game. They didn't play an exhibition game. Before the game they would put on a little exhibition, but they played a regular game.

During my basketball career I wasn't doing too much in the

off-season. I'd go up to the Catskills for two or three months and be a waiter or work on the athletic staff and play games on Friday nights. The money I made during the season was enough to carry me through the off-season because in those days fifty dollars was a pretty good salary.

There were many good Jewish players in my era. I think it was a matter of being in the poor neighborhoods, in the ghettoes. Of course we never called it the ghetto. We never felt that we missed anything. A fellow by the name of Alfred Kazin who came from Brownsville writes about the grayness and dullness of the area and all that. For us it was vibrating and so exciting and full of pep and everything.

I once read a story about Burt Lancaster. It said, "When you lived on the east side, you know, when you take a kid to Little League now, you've got to put him in the car and take him. What happened to you fellows when you were on the east side?" I said when I walked out on the street there were a thousand kids to play with. That's what Brownsville was.

I didn't feel any antisemitism. Most of the players were Jewish. Maybe some of the fans felt that way, but they never showed it.

I went into the army during the war and came out in November 1945 and played with Wilmington for 1945–46. Then I got into politics.

I was a professional basketball player so everybody in the neighborhood in Brooklyn knew me. I was brought up in the Depression so I was always socially minded and so forth. No, my father was not a socialist. The thing about immigrants, even if they were socialists, America came first with them. One of the things that was outstanding about the immigrants is that America was the greatest country. You can't say anything against it. Anyhow, I was popular because I was a professional basketball player. So since we were politically as well as socially conscious, when I came out of the army, my friend belonged to the American Labor Party, and I joined also. It was in the back of my mind that I'd like to run. So my friend and I decided to put my name forward and see if I could get the nomination from the American Labor Party for state assemblyman for the Twenty-Fourth District. There were two groups in the Labor Party—one in Brownsville and one in East New York. That was what the Twenty-Fourth District encompassed. The group in Brownsville knew me very well, and they were ready to give me the nomination, but the group in East New York, being politically, socially, and intellectually minded, they didn't go for an athlete. But eventually I got the nomination. It was only a matter of the nomination because the American Labor Party didn't have that much strength. So we decided that I would run in the Democratic primary. We won the Democratic primary. Since the American Labor Party was strong in Brownsville and East New York and weak in some other areas we made a trade. We supported them, and they supported us. So here we are with the American Labor Party designation and also the Republican designation. The American Labor Party supported the Republican [Party] up in that area where they were weak, and they supported us where we were weak.

Well, [when] I came home from the army, I noticed that for me to vote in the primaries in 1946 it was necessary for me to fill out an application and designate what party I belonged to. So my friend and I hit on the idea. You've got to fight the Democratic machine. They always had two thousand to three thousand people coming out for the primaries because the Democratic captains did some favors for everybody, and when you run against them you can't win because you haven't got the machine. We went from street corner to street corner and spoke to all the fellows who knew me because I was a professional basketball player about to sign up as [a] Democrat. When it came to the Democratic primary, we won it. So there I was with the American Labor Party and the Democratic and Republican designations. So we won the election, and I was able to bring my friend, who ran for the state senate, with me.

So when I won the election in 1946 I didn't go back to play ball. I lost the election in 1948. I went into the storm window business in New York and came to Florida in the late 1950s. I was in the building business.

8. A lifelong coach, Red Sarachek (*left*) was involved with Yeshiva University for more than thirty years. Courtesy of Yeshiva University.

BERNARD "RED" SARACHEK

• Red Sarachek cast a long and influential shadow on basketball in New York City. For more than thirty years, Sarachek had a profound influence on the development of the game as the coach at Yeshiva University. His teams were always competitive, and as he liked to say, he never cut a player. His coaching career also took him to Pearl Harbor, where he led his team to the Armed Forces title during World War II. He also coached the Scranton Miners of the American Basketball League and the Herkimer team of the New York State League. He later served as athletic director of Yeshiva University. Prior to coaching, Sarachek enjoyed a brief career as a wine bottler for Manischewitz.

I was born on October 12, 1912, on Fulton Avenue in the Bronx. I lived there until I was six, when my mother died in the influenza epidemic, and I was brought up by a grandmother. I don't think we were poor. I never knew anything about poverty. I had what I wanted according to the circumstance. When I was young, I was given what I was needed. I think I was taught not to expect too much but to have the essentials. We always had food on the table. It was a typical Jewish family. I came from the Bronx when I was six years old and was brought up by a grandmother in Williamsburg. They were kosher to an extent, but I think she was more or less from a socialistic background. At that time, there was only strictly kosher. Everything was kosher in the families then. I heard that he [my father] was a buttonhole maker and then he went into the saloon business. I have one sister. She is two years younger than me. She was born on the twentieth of October two years later. On the other side of the family [my father's side] we had an Orthodox family. The grandmother on that side was Orthodox. One of my father's brothers was Rabbi Joseph Sarachek, who was a well-known conservative rabbi. I think the only one who remained that way in the family was the rabbi.

When I was six, seven, and eight, I was already saying Kaddish every year so I had to get up very early, five o'clock in the morning at least, on the anniversary of the death of my mother and go to synagogue. I had to be taught. I went to Hebrew school. At the beginning, I was taught by the elders in the synagogue. The first time I was brought down was by my grandmother. Then it was too much for her to bring me down. I used to go to the synagogue, which was close. I went every year and then as I got a little older, I started going Friday nights and Saturdays. I still remember the days when I was in Stuyvesant and we had nine o'clock games. I had to go to what we called the first davening at seven o'clock in the morning on Saturdays. I had my uniform in the coal bin in our apartment, the tenement. I then ran to Stuyvesant High School to play Saturday games or practice and then came back about 11:30 and put the uniform away. The rabbi even knew it because he knew about the games and what I was doing there at seven o'clock in the morning. I think it didn't make a difference as long as I attended and at least I gave it a shot.

All I remember [about the influenza epidemic], there were so many dead people. I was six years old and I knew my mother was very sick. I had an uncle who was a physical education teacher in Stuyvesant who came down and took me away from the house very late at night and brought me to Brooklyn. That I remember. To my grandmother's. Then the next thing I knew, I was told that my mother died, I guess the next day or so. I didn't know about death that much. I had a good life with my grandmother, but I knew. I never had a mother, as I say, but I think my grandmother and my aunt took very good care of me. My grandmother and my aunt and another sister, aunts, and there were three rooms and they must have had about eight people living there, maybe more.

My sister came one week later. My father lived there for a while and then he moved out when I was a little older. He saw me all the time. Every Sunday while I was a kid, he took me. Saturday and Sunday he made sure I was with him.

I originally lived on Bedford Avenue and then we moved. After my grandmother died, we moved to South Second and Roebling. The house was very nice, but the neighborhood was still the same. It was a Jewish neighborhood, though we did have blacks, a couple of blacks, a couple of Italian boys and Irish boys living in the neighborhood. It was a mixture, mostly Jewish, but we had them there without any differences. I do not know if it is a Puerto Rican neighborhood or a Hasidic neighborhood today. I do not think where I lived was Hasidic. Bedford Avenue was on the other side of the road, as we used to call it, the rich people used to live on Bedford Avenue around that section. Ours was not that way. I don't remember Hasidic Jews. I knew there were Orthodox Jews and those who did not go to synagogue. These Jews were mostly immigrants. I was American born of American parents. There were others that were American born, but their mothers and fathers were not born in America. They all played punch ball the same way. It was English. Even in my house, it was English to me. I understand Yiddish. That came naturally, but I cannot speak it because my grandmother spoke English. This grandmother came over in the first immigration in about the 1870s. She came from Bohemia, which they call Austria. She spoke English because her children were born in this country so she had to speak English. There was a little Yiddish spoken in the house. There was Yiddish in the neighborhood. There were no differences. I think that was a good upbringing in itself. Even the black boy, who was the janitor's son in one of the buildings, was a good athlete and was a part of it without any differences. I do not think there were any differences at that time except if you went into another neighborhood. If you went into a Polish neighborhood, strictly Polish or Italian neighborhood, which they had, then there were differences.

When I had to go to school and I had to go to Stuyvesant, I had to go from Williamsburg before the subway was built. When I went to the subway, we had to pass like there was a borderline. Let us say Grand Street or North First Street, which was the North Side, which was Polish and Italian, you had difficulty. You crossed the neighborhood. Once you got to the Polish neighborhood, there were not many Jewish people. You were talked down to, you were shouted at, and you had to run for your life and you were abused. Like anything else, sometimes when you played ball with these fellows, it was all forgotten. It seems that athletics in itself at that time . . . but the minute you got through with athletics it was always the J.B. There were fights all the time. Of course you had to fight. You had to fight with your own. There was not a gang. At certain holidays, you would find yourself in those situations. Let us say Halloween, there used to be raids from the Polish side into the Jewish side. Then there used to be a revenge thing. The Jews left them alone. But when the Jews went, there was always . . . I do not know what it was, a fear or something that always said . . . or maybe it was the goodness that let things lie. We were pretty tough too. One-on-one, we were much tougher than them. At that time, most of the boys there always wanted to be fighters. Your only thoughts were to become a fighter. You had to fight every day. You had to have a fight when you walked out of the schoolroom, whether it was yours or the other one or you were chased by two or three. I thought I was a pretty good fighter. I thought they rated me pretty high. I think my comedown was when I had to fight in Stuyvesant with a center of a basketball team for two hours and I came back and my nose I think was a little sore. I had a fight that night with another fellow who smashed the same nose and I got two black eyes. The other guys would make appointments to fight. The older fellows would make appointments with the younger fellows to fight.

I had a pretty good life. I think my father was a very strict person. He was a very intelligent man, though he was a very tough man. He had to be in the business he was in. He made a point. Saturday night at ten or eleven o'clock he used to call, "Bernardi, come up," and then I didn't want to come up because when I was even sixteen all of the other fellows stayed down there. He said, "Well, you got a big punch ball game tomorrow at eight o'clock, you better be in shape." That was his thinking to convince me to come up early. It had to work. Otherwise, he would break my neck. It did and I understood it and some of the other fellows understood. Punch ball was the game that we played there. Stick ball we played only when we got into the schoolyard, the vacation playground at that time, but punch ball was the game. Basketball did not start until later on. When the cars started coming in, we used to jump the cars because of the punch ball, but you had two-way streets then. There were not that many cars then. Before there were cars, there were horses. We did not pay any attention to the horses. Sunday mornings was the easiest time to have a game. Sunday morning was the game to have. There were the big games because no cars were out and no horses were driven. We played in the streets on Saturday, but you never played around the synagogue, so you went to the next block.

Saturday night was the night that we all got dressed up and we snuck down to the synagogue to go to bar mitzvahs or weddings. We would sneak in and see if we could eat the food. Then at twelve o'clock, there were the crap games. I was seventeen, eighteen, and nineteen years old. I was always behind. I guess my father knew, but I thought that he thought that I was [an] angel and never played craps. Of course he did [play craps]. There is no question about it. I do not think anybody had a different life than the other one. Our fathers played cards and drank schnapps, while the kids today, their parents have their cult families, their parties and stuff like that. The kids are going to follow that thing. It is a whole different thing. I do not think we were drinkers. I think that we began to think at times. If you wanted to be in athletics, you became a health bug. You began to think. You smoked, you would smoke, but you began to think of doing things, live a little cleaner life.

I went to Stuyvesant High School, which was an excellent school. I passed the test there and went there while all the others went to Alexander Hamilton or Boys' High School. I felt I wanted to go there and the ambition was to become a doctor. After I got into the basketball setup, I played baseball and I started football, but I stopped that after an injury; I think everything went down the drain as far as studies. The physical education became a part of my thinking. I mean the health education and teaching. Not many guys went to high school. At that time, kids used to leave school at sixth grade and went to work. They went to the garment industry or any job. I used to be jealous of them, and then one time I took off from school for three months. Nobody knew I did because some of my friends were making eighteen dollars a week in the pleating industry and I got a job. I did not make the eighteen, whatever I made, but it was a heck of a lot of money, but I did not tell anybody. Then finally my father called Stuyvesant and I had a great man there, the coach, Doc Ellner, who acted like another father to me, who saved me. There was just a difference of a hair going one way or going the other way, either becoming a gangster or going to school. I do not know if there were gangs, but you knew that there were certain fellows who were in the mob, the industry, who you saw were going to develop into mobsters. They were very tough guys and they hung around. They always had some money. There were daring, and I do not think their respect for good was anywhere near the teachings that we had in our houses. I do not know if there were Jewish cops, but they used to hit you pretty good with nightsticks if you hung around the corner. If they got a complaint, they would go after you pretty much. We had candy store hangouts. We used to sit in front of a candy store. Every block had their own candy store and every block had their own group. Schmoozing, playing kick the can, jumping the sidewalk, three steps, races. We used to have these things that we organized ourselves at night. These were games, and those who did not go with us, we found those were the fellows who were drifting away into a different occupation. Whether it was crime, they were busy. You found that they started with us and then suddenly they drifted away. They became the bettors or the number takers or things like that. I think the numbers and betting were there all the time. There were fellows who were in the rackets and stuff like that who later went into the trade unions and became goons or racketeers.

I did not know of the Workmen's Circle [a Jewish mutual aid society], but there were socialistic-minded people in Williamsburg, a lot of them. I did not know about Arbeter Ring, the Workmen's

Circle group, but they were there. We had a Y. We had the Williamsburg Y. The YMHA was on the other side of the tracks over Broadway. It was not at my neighborhood. We had nothing. We used to form a club and go there. I think it was ten cents a person. First, we went to the Sabers, and that was like a young club. Then I was brought up to the bigger clubs to play for them, for the Rangers. Everybody had clubs. It was a sport club and social. That was the first thing we knew about, we used to have a meeting, Roger's Rules of Orders [*Robert's Rule of Order*, a guide for conducting meetings]. We used to have a president and everything else. We started that way. It was amazing how we did it. All by ourselves. We were going to form the Sabers with ten guys. We wore basketball shirts. You wore it over your regular shirt or you wore it under the jacket because we were proud of it. We had a fellow by the name of Vinnie and then at a funeral just the other day I met another fellow, Johnny. They were all part of my group. They were in that group there. I think that the relationship is still there. I was busy with other things, but some of these fellows who we keep in contact once in a while, they still keep in contact.

I think it was just a natural thing that the goyim is a goyim and the Jew is the Jew. I think that is what it was, but it was not with you in the one-to-one living. When you have numbers, I think that you have a problem. You and I could be of different persuasions, but we could live and talk to each other. I am not going to delve into your mind, but as a group, there could be antisemitism or antireligion or antiblack or antiwhite. You find it here now. I have a lot of friends on the one-and-one. We are brothers. You know that in itself the whole atmosphere is antisemitism. I feel it all over. I know that there is something in somebody and there is always going to be that remark. As far as we are concerned, we know how a remark could hurt us, and I make no apologies to them. If it is made, I am going to be just as abusive to them.

I had an uncle who graduated there [Stuyvesant]. Many, many years ago, he was a runner. That was one thing. I think that I always wanted to be different than a lot of them. Everybody wanted to go to Boys' High. I did not want to go to Boys' High. Everybody wanted to go to Eastern District. I did not want to go to Eastern

District. I wanted to go to something different. That is how I felt. So I wanted to go to Stuyvesant. It would have been much easier for me to go to Eastern District or Boy's High. At that time I thought of it [becoming a doctor]. But like anything else, I started playing basketball. We did not start basketball like these kids who are seven, eight years old. We started when we were twelve because there was not that opportunity to play. Today basketball in itself, it is a completely different thing. The coaching is different. It became an international setup. The coaching has become universal. We had more settlements. Down on the East Side where it actually started, we had more settlements. The East Side had settlement houses, College Settlement, University Settlement, and Rutgers's Gym, where I later played. There is where the Jewish kids played, and they played basketball. It was their game for a while. There was no CYO [Catholic Youth Organization] at that time. The CYO came up later when the churches came into the thing. The Jewish kids played it and it became a city sport. Then it went to Chicago and Philadelphia, where the Jewish people had the settlement houses. Then they called it a Jewish game like anything else. When the CYOs and churches came in, then it became a national game. Then it became an international game. To me it was a physical education activity. Then somebody found out that it could be played as a game. You would take twenty kids or ten kids in a settlement house and you would play basketball, where you would get the most out of them.

There were not many schoolyards that were open. The schoolyards and playgrounds were open on vacations, so you had baskets and you played. The balls were bad. There were no rubber basketballs. You had a basketball with a sort of binding on it that broke your fingers. There were laced balls and they were never round. The coaching was not as good as today. There was no knowledge of the game. The courts were different. They were much smaller. You played in any area you wanted. After a while, you learned movement and things like that and it progressed in that way. When the CYO came about and the churches came into this thing and they built their own gyms, then you found other boys and people coming into the situation.

Let us say you went to the Y. There was a club, the Claremont and the Sabers. We would have a challenge game with them. We would play in the schoolyard first. They had baskets and we played in the schoolyards. We played in our shirts and our long pants. We had fellows 5'2" playing who were excellent. You could not even stop them, but the game was different. It was not knowledgeable, as knowledgeable as now. The coaches themselves were not players. They were either physical education teachers or someone who had an inkling of the game and said, "Now you coach." They read books or something, old books. Little by little you yourself developed because you played it.

I think it [being a doctor] all went down the drain. Nobody ever mentioned anything about it, what you wanted to be. You made up your mind what you wanted to be. After my grandmother died, I moved with my father and my aunt, who later married my father. She was very close to me, my aunt Fannie. We were very close, and my sister, and that is when we moved out and that is how we existed. We stayed in Williamsburg. It was very good, very nice. It was a good apartment house. He [my father] was running a bar then and it was good. I wanted to [help him in the bar], but no, he wanted me to do my thing, go to school. I think he felt that that was more important. It was completely different. It was not a neighborhood of kids, very few kids. I was not small town. I was sophisticated. The others weren't. The kids from the Bronx were different, and we had kids from Manhattan and we did not have only Jewish boys there. We had some blacks, very few in Stuyvesant, but we had all different nationalities coming to Stuyvesant at that time. Mostly Jewish boys going to high school. Going to high school was a privilege that you had to go and were able to support yourself. They got jobs.

I tried out [for admission to Stuyvesant High School] in my freshman year and that was the afternoon session. I still remember that I had a pair of white shoes. It was like plain, ordinary. It was not even sneakers. It was like an old pair of white shoes, rubber soled.

I left Hebrew school when I went to Stuyvesant. I had a bar mitzvah. There was a party; about two of us were bar mitzvahed together. It was at the Williamsburg Talmud Torah, and they had a big party at the house with all the goodies. We had a fairly good-sized family. I think we were close just with the uncles for years.

I made what they called the afternoon session team. The afternoon session was the first two years, because you had two sessions in Stuyvesant. One started at 7:30 and went to 12:30 and the other started at 12:30 and went to 5:30 or 5:00. Only the first two years, the freshmen and sophomores went to the afternoon session. So the next year, he took five of us up, Doc Ellner, and brought us up to the morning session. Then you had to get some courses, and then we looked for jobs after that. I went to work for *Women's Wear*. We delivered the *Women's Wear Daily* paper. I was a paperboy for a while. Seven dollars I think we were paid for the week. I did not make enough.

Then we started playing against high schools. Doc Ellner was a very smart man. He was a chemistry teacher. He was a good thinker. He was a good fundamentalist, and he was very close, not only to me, to all the players, and that was the difference with him. I think following him or learning from him, not only basketball, but the relationship with kids. I think basically he liked children. I think that was the basic thing. He did not have any children, and I think that made the deal. There were fifteen or sixteen kids. I always started. At that time I was a guard. You had guards and forwards and center. When I started they had the center tap and there was no ten-second line. Then later on, they took the tap away, and then many years after that they put the ten-second in. You had to get over the ten-second. It was a movement game. There were no fast breaks. The games went to 14–13, 15–12. Those were the scores at that time. The high school game was thirty-two minutes; just, I think, the same as now. You just were passing around. They were all layups, always trying to make layups. There were no jump shots. You did not pass for five minutes. The game was a different game completely. It has movement, balance, and agility. I had defense. I was able to move with the ball and without the ball. Defense is concentration. The idea [is] that this guy is your enemy when he plays, even though after the game you could be friends, but he is your enemy because if he shoots two points and you shoot none, he is a better ballplayer than you. If you said you were better than me, we went out and played one-man basketball. It was one-on-one because you had to prove that you were better. You had to work and move and dribble and move. No jump shots.

The rivalries between the high schools were very big. There were not that many high schools. Number one, you did not start until January because of the football season. The guys played three sports. There were no overlaps in the season. Later on that came about. Later on in my last year, I played football for a while and I got hurt with a bad knee. I played baseball for two years and then Doc Ellner did not want me to play any longer. Now at that time, they began to overlap, so he did not want me to indulge. He felt that the best thing for me was to be in basketball. I was big in size. I was thin. I think I was about 5'9", 5'10". That was considered tall.

They had a lot of kids watching the games. Today it is all different. I do not know what it is today. They were small gyms, very small seating, but the kids used to hang around and stand around. The parents came only if we played night games. We used to play at night sometimes. My father once in a while used to sneak in. He never said anything to me because we were not living at that time together, but he used to watch the games.

I think Nat Holman wanted me to go to City College. There was recruitment, but not what you would call it now. Then somebody told me to go to New York University. Of course, they offered scholarships. Not City College. You went there for free. You had to pass a test. Certain people may not have passed. I think in the beginning first two years I was a good student and then I went down the drain. I think I did not concentrate any longer. Maybe I reached the level, you know what I mean? I did not give myself any chance after that. I think I am a history bug, more history than anything else. I think my concentration on that is more than anything else. Then a lot of health subjects, not that I am a health bug. You know, articles on health. Maybe that is a carryover. I wanted to be a doctor. I could take four years of French and I do not even know what the heck the word means. It just went out of my mind because it was rote. As a linguist, I am the worst in the business. I do not think I had that concentration anymore. Stuyvesant High School was a special high school. There was a certain amount that came in and that is it. I think it would have [been easier if I had gone to Eastern District or Boy's High]. I never regretted it. There were no girls in Stuyvesant. That is the only thing that you would miss if you went to Eastern District. Boy's High School did not have any. No matter where I went, I think that I reached some kind of a peak in studies. I think I was never able to concentrate after that. I read it, but I did not follow it. I was strictly a frankfurter and a knockwurst and a salami kid, you know what I mean? That had not changed yet.

For Hebrew school, first we went to a little store with a long table. Then from there I went to Williamsburg Talmud Torah. They were all Orthodox. I do not remember any . . . though my uncle, Rabbi Joseph Sarachek, was a conservative rabbi. There was no other place in Williamsburg but to go to an Orthodox place. It is so far back, but at times I went away and did not show up for weeks because of punch ball or some other game. I didn't really wonder what it was all about if I went, though when I did go I felt in awe and cleansed. When I went to synagogue I always felt, when I came out of synagogue, I was clean until the next thing came about and changed it. Hebrew school, after coming back from school and in the wintertime the snow and to walk there, and then in the summertime was the hardship of giving up a game. Some boys went. I do not think that in my circle many of them went. I went for a while and then after bar mitzvah, I think like anything else, you tried it a little while, you felt that urge being bar mitzvahed and being holy and feeling so elated about the thing, that you went for a while. It did not last long. Mentally, I do not think I was suited maybe because of the family attitude I had. I was brought up by a grandmother, who like other Jewish women observed the kashrut. The other side of the family was more of an Orthodox family, but I did not live with them. I was brought up by my grandmother so it did not carry over.

I do not think that I ever doubted that I was Jewish. I lived with so many there. I think every kid feels that. If you suffer some pain or some remarks about the thing, like anything else, you daydream about being something else. There were so many good things that you had such a chauvinistic attitude about being Jewish after a while. Even a gangster with a Jewish name meant something to you. If you read a paper and you find that somebody by the name of Cohen is playing for a team, you do not think that this Cohen may not be Jewish. That is something that you always had, and I was brought up with that feeling and I think it developed more and more inside me, even though I had a liberal outlook, some sort of a socialistic outlook in life. When I got to the Workmen's Circle and saw goodness, you know, I was a man. I was married then when I went there. I always had that feeling of the downtrodden, but I always felt that, to me, Judaism in itself was something to be part of. To be a part of it, and its history in itself, I indulged in history and the Bible from the point of view of history, similar to the shuls. Though I never went to a Workmen's shul, I never had a part of it, but I saw it there, at least the cultural aspects of it.

I think that it was constant, but I feel in myself that I have to be . . . I am Jewish and I will fight for it with all my being. I may give somebody an inch because of ignorance, but I cannot believe in any intolerance. I do not think any Jew could believe in intolerance, because if they do, they have not any concept of living because that is what you were brought up with. Judaism beats intolerance. I have always learned that, good or bad, a Jew is a Jew and that to me is something that you cannot get away with. In fact, I read something that was said by Groucho Marx. A Jew and hunchback passed a synagogue and the Jewish man said, "I once was Jewish," and the hunchback said, "I was once hunchback." So that is an example. I mean, it is something in your mind when you think about it, you cannot change. I do not care to change.

I think any assimilation is a loss to Judaism in itself. I think that it is so easy not to be Jewish or to get away from it. The only way a person could ever be reminded that there is intolerance or bigotry is if they get hit by it. But in itself, if there is any assimilation, we are not going to win, and little by little it dissipates in itself. Athletics was Jewish, completely Jewish then. There was nothing else but Jewish athletes. There were Jewish ballplayers, not too much, but you did not have the fields because in itself you never had access to the fields and the parks. Though there were baseball players who were Jewish that never made it because maybe there were other things. I think that as time passed the tendency of developing and increasing a person's education, going further in education, that was always prevalent in the Jewish home, so you could not do all of that. They may have been proud, you know? I think they were . . . not liberal minded in any socialistic point, but liberal in the thinking, if he wants it and if it could help him and if it can keep him as a good boy, it is more important for that reason. I think in their little way they were much more sensible than the families today. I think years ago they should have done the thinking for the whole Judaism, except in Israel, about the importance of athletics. To me, it was always important, even when I went to Yeshiva [University], which made me more Jewish conscious. I do not think I could have been Orthodox. Maybe I am lazy, you know, [too] lazy mentally and maybe [too] lazy physically to go through what an Orthodox boy in [a] yeshiva goes through. They live a very comfortable life, but I do not think that I could do that. To see what they could do made me respect [them], and I felt a great honor to be a part of them.

I had complete respect for them [while coaching at Yeshiva] that they could do all that, you understand, and still want to participate, and that was the important thing I think that Yeshiva and a lot of places should understand. If I have a youngster and I want him to continue to be in orthodoxy and to study and to be very religious, I have to get him towards me and my side, give him something that he likes or he would enjoy, and then I could do much more with him. Basketball, any sports. Not taking the place of anything. It adds to something. I have better control, I think, in my point of view, and I think it is so. I think it is so. If I want to keep a boy with me, I have to give him these things, things that he likes, that I feel he likes. If they enjoy something, it is much easier for me to give them that approach. I think so and I think that I am right and I think in time . . . Yeshiva has teams now, and they may not be the best now or in the future, but I think in time, as it goes on, more of the youngsters are participating. Whether they play with a yarmulke or not, they are playing. Though they are restricted at certain times, the Shabbos they cannot play, but they live with it and it is part of them and that is important.

There is no question that I was not the best player. I was average in itself so I had to take the next thing. I was a good defensive ballplayer and I felt that was important. I think it has been bearing out with me in all my coaching. I thought it was drilled into me by my coach in Stuyvesant. I think I was a leader. I think I was a leader, yes. I may not have been the best player, but I was the leader. I think it is more-or-less personality and your own ego. That was important. I think I just did it with my own thinking and trying to improvise in my own way too. Seeing what others did, taking the best and discounting the worst. That is what you do with your ballplayers too. You tell a kid to do the same things. Go look at the best, see what he is doing that is the best and try and emulate him. See what he is doing that you think is not right and forget about that. Think about it. Think of all you could do with it.

I think my thing was when I was in NYU and I used to go back to Stuyvesant and help him, Doc Ellner. Where I watched him and gave him a lot of my material that I began to think about, that I thought would be working. I did a great deal with him and I think he knew it and respected it. That was important. I think in the letters I received from him he always felt that way, he always said that thing, that I had this innate ability to be a coach, and I think that kept me going. I felt I wanted to coach. If I wanted to be a part of the game, I had to be there. I wanted to be an active part. I could not be a manager or a statistician. That was too low. I had to be the boss, and in order to be the boss you had to be the coach. As a player, I was assigned at that time to get the best offensive player and to work on him. Stuyvesant was a mixed school at that time. The coach was Jewish. He was a chemistry teacher. He was an intelligent man and he was compassionate and he knew how to handle the team. He was a father image more than anybody I knew. He was a great father image to me. I really do not know what a father image means, to say it, but he was somebody that you felt close to and you came to for help and he would try to help you.

One of the teachers at Stuyvesant wanted me to go to Michigan State, and I had a grandmother, Lena Goldberg, who was very sick, and I was brought up by her and she died. She was sick so I had to forego that. I do not think I had the guts to leave the old home grounds. I went to City College and I stayed there maybe a week and then I got an offer through the underground from NYU and I went to NYU. I played on the freshman team. Basketball was the game. I do not know if I could have developed any better in the other sports, but in basketball I felt . . . It was an active game. It gave me a lot of enjoyment. Howard Cann coached at NYU. Howard Cann was well known. He was a very nice man. I came from a great coach, so what I saw in college may have been a little different. I do not know if he was not as good. I do not think that there were fundamentals. I think in college, maybe now it is a little different, but fundamentally, outside of Nat Holman and maybe a couple of others were fundamentalists. Here it was a question of running and moving. You were stronger and bigger and that is what counted. The set shot was always there. That was the only shot you took, the set shot. You had to take a set shot at times from fifteen feet and then you went farther sometimes because of the defenses. Your movement was so that you could take a set shot as you can, then the layup shot.

The rules changed, but the courts were bigger in college. The courts were bigger, and the game was a little different because you played with stronger men. Your practice sessions were much more definite. They were longer. They were harder, and you played with fellows from different parts of the eastern area who came there to play basketball. The rules changed. The ten-second line came in and those things happened. That is how we played, but the game stayed that way and more development, more coaches came about, more knowledge of the game, more thinking. It was not just a plain ordinary movement. Other things came about, different phases.

I became ineligible [at NYU] and I went to work and then I came back to play some more after that. I did not want to study too much then because I thought that maybe I should have been something else than a physical education teacher. My ambition was to be a doctor at one time. Then the Depression was there. It was the height of the Depression. Like I told you, in high school I walked out of school and stayed away. I do not know, the neighborhood changed, and you wanted to do what the other ones were, there was money around and you wanted more. My thinking was rather loose at that time. I lost my grandmother and things like that happened. I was out of school for a year and then I went to night school. I went to work for Manischewitz wine as a bottler. Then I went to night school at that time and then I went from there. I was playing basketball. I used to work and play basketball. I played with a million teams then. I graduated about 1936, I think, because it was supposed to be 1935 but I went until 1936. Then there were no jobs around so I went to the WPA [Works Progress Administration] and I worked on the WPA in recreation. Then I worked in the prison ward in Bellevue and I worked in psychiatric training. A woman started the first program in recreation therapy and I went with her. I thought that was the greatest thing that I ever wanted to do and I think that was really what I wanted to be. After the Parks Department, I went into the Red Cross as a field director. I volunteered for it, though I was married. I was married in 1938. I was making twenty-three dollars a week. I was making more because I was then working with the Workmen's Circle. I was playing ball and I started to do a little refereeing. I did things like that.

I was in Franklin K. Lane High School as a physical education teacher in training and a man by the name of Hy Kaplan, who was a physical education teacher, very wonderful man, asked me if I wanted to become the athletic director, director of activities for the Workmen's Circle. I was interviewed and I took the job. It was nights. I worked from seven o'clock in the morning and then came home one, two o'clock. I sometimes worked at three jobs. The Workmen's Circle was located on East Broadway. I used to rent gyms. I used to run park games at the center. These were wonderful people. What you saw in orthodoxy, here you saw people who were so liberal minded in their thinking and looking for the best for everybody and they were Jewish minded, which is always important. The Workmen's Circle is a Jewish-minded group. You saw things there and the people you met, the May Day parades, the picnics and things like that. Those are the people I miss, Jack Zuckerman and Hy Kaplan and so many others. Workmen's Circle people came down every Saturday night. They flooded the place to see the basketball team playing. I took young kids in. Red Holzman played there, Ruby Benjamin, Nat Militzok. They all became stars. I had Red Holzman when I was coaching in Franklin K. Lane for one season. That is where he played. He was fourteen years old and from there I brought him into the Workmen's Circle. He was a great ballplayer. He was the best. He was an All-American. He was the greatest around in the city at that time.

I see everything that I did twenty-five and thirty years ago being played today, and all these coaches say so too. Some say I was ahead of my time. Then I became offensive minded. I began to think in basketball of new things to do. I started giving the ball and going the opposite way, making blocks, and going without the ball. I cannot draw Xs and Os yet. Everything came out improvised. Nothing was written down. Other people wrote what I did, and that is what happened. I think I started [innovating] right from when I was in the Workmen's Circle with the players. Of course, I had good players. We had kids from Workmen's Circle. We brought players in and they became members of the Workmen's Circle. Young kids who played for Stuyvesant, I took them. The came with me and we played. They were All-Americans in 1938 and 1939. Of course, they all were [children of immigrants]. Very few were American born. I did not even know if they were American born or not. I was with the Workmen's Circle in 1937 to . . . came back from the service and I stayed for another year after that. The athletic program faded after that. There was nothing after that.

In the time right after the Depression or during the Depression, the ILGWU [International Ladies' Garment Workers' Union] and all these organizations, the Amalgamated Union, they believed with the time that their people had, the free time, the forty-hour week, they had to give their people something. So they gave them bowling and they gave them swimming classes and calisthenics classes. They gave them a basketball team, and this was the recreation thing of socialists and the labor movement. They all had them. I worked in the clubroom meeting. After the meeting was over they used to have games, balloon handling, blowing balloons and things like that. These were the adults. This was not the teenagers. This was the English-speaking section of the Workmen's Circle. I had this program. We had boat rides and we had softball games and things like that. We had a baseball team. Softball teams we had. We played against all the other unions. We were Jewish-oriented. Some of the unions were not Jewish-oriented, but most of the people in the industry were Jewish. At that time, they were mostly Jewish. These were laborers. These were workers. In our activities, on a Friday night, I used to come down and run game nights. We had a lot of people, our picnics. A lot of people became involved to watch the basketball team. They used to come down in droves. This was a Saturday-night affair where we all went out to eat after a game.

I think it [personality as a coach] came naturally because I wanted to see things done right there. I wanted more of the discipline in the game. I wanted the player to improve. I always felt that if I stopped yelling at a person, then he may not play anymore because he knows more than me. Not only does he know more than me, but that I have no interest in him. I always tell even the worst substitute, the lowest substitute, that if I stopped yelling at you, you might as well quit. If I am not teaching you, and that was my way of teaching, then you might as well quit because you are not getting anything from me. I have already discounted you and this is important. I always made everybody feel they were part of the game. They may have had guys who felt that maybe I did not give them the right blow to play, but nobody could ever say that I did not pay attention to them.

[After leaving the Workmen's Circle], I went with the Grand Street Boys. A fellow by the name of Mike Howard, he was a wonderful man. Have you heard of the Grand Street Boys? A big social organization of politicians. They had a track team, so they wanted to have a basketball team, so I had a basketball team, and I brought some of the boys from the Workmen's Circle over, after we discontinued over there, in 1947–48. We won the AAU championship two years in a row. It was the Metropolitan AAU championship. Then they discontinued the basketball. There was nothing for them, you see. They just wanted it, maybe to fight the New York AC [New York Athletic Club]. I think that is what they did. We beat them in the AAU championship, and that was good for him [Jonah Goldstein, president of Grand Street Boys]. I think Grand Street Boys were Jewish. They had judges and everything else. Jonah came to the game and many other people came to the game. I think they forgot about it pretty soon.

I started coaching black players in the Grand Street Boys. A couple of the boys came from Stuyvesant. There was no thought of it, not in my mind, not that I saw it. I do not think there was anything doing at that time, because at that time I could have gone to the Harlem Y without any difficulty, without any trouble, and without any thinking. I do not think there was any thinking about it.

I do not know if I was well known. Sometimes you get surprised that people knew you, and I never looked. You enjoyed getting an article in the paper, a write-up. May have once in a while, but that did not mean anything. I never received the publicity that some of these other guys got, but maybe these other coaches did feel it because as we went on I always had enough players, players came to me. That was important.

In the army, I coached in Hawaii. I had some sort of a name. They picked me up and I coached in the Ninety-Eighth Division, which was what they called the Pineapple Division. It was so bad. We had mostly Jewish boys and a lot of New York people, and I started coaching in Camp Stewart and then I moved to another camp. I went into the army, I think, in 1943 in the Red Cross. I was with the American Red Cross. I joined the American Red Cross, I volunteered. I was assigned to the division. We played in tournaments. In fact, the Ninety-Eighth Division won two tournaments in Hawaii and from there I was hired to go to Scofield Barracks, which was called the Redlanders, which played other divisions, other posts, the Coast Guard and places like that.

I lost one game I think in the whole year. There was an interesting story that came about. I used to start four Jewish ballplayers. They were New York ballplayers, and we had one fellow whose name was Zeidell who everybody thought was Jewish. The other people were sitting on the bench. There were some Jewish fellows, Italian fellows, and Irish fellows. These I thought were the best. We won six games in a row, but we used to get booed by the crowd. Then one colonel came over to me one time and he said, "You know, you are a schmuck." I said, "Why?" He said, "Do you see what is going on? You could win all the games and you would be booed. Why haven't you got the sense to start three Jewish fellows instead of five?" I said, "Zeidell is not Jewish." He said, "Start three Jews, and take the others out. Then everyone will be your friend." I did it and I lost. There was no more booing. It was a different story then. They had their own in there. That was a very important thing. That is a lesson that I learned too. I do not know if it is a lesson. That is what happens today in life. In coaching, you had to think about crowds and management and things like that. That is very important. I did not bother with the crowd. It did not make any difference to me. I did not even know if they were booing my antics or if they were booing what I was doing.

I was always a very irrational man on the bench. I did not give an inch to referees or players or anybody. I think that a lot of the actions that some of them are doing now came from me. I used to argue every point with the referees. I walked the length, fought with the referees, ran at them, and did everything. I was bad. It was not good. I do not think I will ever change. It may have had a psychological effect, but I do not think that I could control myself. I was a part of the game. I was a part of the action. If I thought something was wrong, then I would yell. I talked all the time and coached. I do not think that was the attention I wanted, but it did come because it was just something that came out of me. That is all. I had no choice on it. I cannot sit down and rationalize the thing. If I am right, if I feel I am right, I am going to tell people. Of course, I was run from many games. The referee had the right to do it. I provoked him enough. I do not think a coach should act that way, not as much as I did. If any technical foul was to be called, it was to be called on me, not on them.

I could tell you, after a game sometimes I sat and had coffee and cake with the referees. I do not know if it was really forgotten in me, but I had the sociability of living with them. After a game I was completely different. Sometimes I used to work myself up before a game such that before the first call I used to be at somebody. It is all according to how I was. I never had an office. In the locker room I was just building myself up for a fight. I do not know if it did [help my team]. Maybe it hurt sometimes. I wanted to be part of the game. If I am out, I have not got a part in the game. I felt that they [my players] felt that I gave them something. I felt that they felt they were learning. I have a philosophy that if somebody feels that he getting something from you, he is learning something, if he is smart enough to feel that he has got something, and then he will take a lot more from you. I never felt that I wanted to give somebody a bad beating because I felt that I had respect for the other players and the other coach. I felt that I had to suppress these things. I always did that [told my players to hold off if the game was in hand], and all my players knew that. I never wanted to take everything away from the other coach. I felt that there would be a time that I would have to sit down there and have this thing going up my behind too. I always felt that way, and I used to threaten my players with that. If I say do not shoot, do not shoot.

We used to practice some of the things that you wanted to do, but do not do them . . . try to do something else. I do not want this other guy to get into a situation where . . . I know how it feels when you would coach Yeshiva and if you felt . . . and I used to try and teach that thing. A bunch of kids, if they keep losing by twenty-four points and twenty, thirty points every game, then when it comes about they lose all their . . . it is a Jewish word, desire to play anymore. Their pride is gone. If I could hold a game where they could lose by ten and fifteen or five points, even against the best, I feel that they have an excuse in their own mind: "If we did this. If we did something else, we could have done something else. We could have won if I had made the foul shot." I think competition. I never thought I would enjoy a game that we would win by twenty, twenty-four points. Maybe that is something in my mind. Maybe it is something that I wanted. I liked the strategy, the fight in the game. It is stupid, right? A lot of guys love this thing, but I like to be close enough so that I could do something to win a game. I wanted a part of it, so much a part of it. This was very personal. Not many people think that way. I was close with my players. Some coaches try and keep a distance. When a game started, I was not close. Close before and after. To this day, at the affair they had, they all came down and they are all part of it. Some of the fellows who I abused so much I would think would not be there. There are some that dislike me, but I do not think they would say that I was not able to teach them.

My job in the Red Cross was to take care of leaves and to help the boys with their family problems. In the division I became the coach, the recreational director. Most of the players that I had there were New York boys. Some of them were college players. Some of them were not college players that came to me and then they played against some of the pros. I had a lot of Jewish ballplayers in my division. They [captains and majors] enjoyed the idea of watching a winning team; though what they felt inwardly I do not know, but some of them did, once in a while, you heard an antisemitic expression from them. If you heard it, you went after it. I did go after it, but I either had an argument or I grabbed the guy and that was it. Of course you are in foreign territory, but I do not believe that I have to stand up. If I felt at times that it was insulting to me and to the group around me, I would become aroused. If a fellow came over to me and said, "Hey, Jew," something or other, and I knew it was between him and me just like I would say anything else. If the same person said that in front of a group of people, then it would be different for me. Then my reaction would be there. I am getting a little old now, so you got to take this thing.

I think it was three years ago, some team came down from Canada and this fellow used to be one of my students in basketball, Jack Donahue, who coached the Canadian national team, and he was playing in New York. We walked in the room and this sportswriter's a very good friend of mine, very good, he always had this Jew bit with him, but it was always on a one-to-one, it did not make much . . . there were about twenty reporters and people in the room and he walked in and he said to me, "Hey, you Jew bastard, what are you doing here?" Well, I grabbed him by the neck and I hit him in the stomach and I knocked him down and he said, "What are you doing, Red?" My friend pulled me away and he said, "What are you doing?" Even the other coach said, "Look, do not do this to Red because you will get killed," and that's what it was. The next day, he met me and he apologized to me. He said he did not mean what he said. The same remark that he would have made to me, greeting me when I am alone, when he made it there, just said it, how do I answer this? What am I, stupid enough to curse him? So I had no answer, and what I did may have been stupid in its way, but I had to do it. It just came to me, and I had to do it. That is how I feel about my personal pride in being Jewish. After that he understood it and I explained [it] to him. Now when he speaks to me, even person-to-person, I hear him saying something and he will stop. I think that is something that all the Jewish youth have forgotten about, respecting what they have. It is not a problem, but it is there.

I remember an incident. I have a friend, Ruby Benjamin, who was a policeman. He was a very close friend of mine. We were in the locker room. We just beat a team, and two kids walked into the room, the locker room, and there was a bathroom there and they had to go into this bathroom. They did not go, and I see they were going to be abusive, and we were sitting there and they passed some Jewish remarks, and I grabbed one by the neck. He was a young guy. He could have hurt me pretty bad, and I started banging his head against a locker. Ruby grabbed the other fellow, and he was smashing him up. I think my ballplayers began to see something that nobody could come in there and insult you. You should not take it. Not to abuse you or to lower you in your own esteem. Sometimes you cannot live with yourself. How can you think that night, "Why didn't I do something?" I did not feel that anybody should get away with this. I do not think they did it before, though there were fights maybe years ago between Jews and other people, but I do not think the kids . . . I think an Orthodox Jew, some of them can become more aroused than some of the other ones can. You just cannot throw it up to ignorance when you read in the paper how much abuse the Jews are getting. You cannot say that they are ignorant people. There are smart people too. There are smart people on both sides, and there should not be this abusiveness. How can we live together if I know that you are going to abuse me? That is what I feel is important.

I coached Workmen's Circle one more year after the army. We went into the AAU tournament. We lost in the final. Otherwise it would have been three championships. I left to go to Grand Street because there was nothing doing there. The activities were gone. All the ballplayers just drifted away, and I think it was a mutual thing with them. They could not go on with it anymore. They were spending a lot of money on me and the gymnasiums and everything else, and I guess the attendance in itself was not there, and I think the times changed. The Depression was over. It was after the war and the ILGWU and the rest of them were giving up all this activity because now the people were working. They did not have to give it to the workers anymore, so it changed, and that is important too.

I coached the Grand Street Boys twice to the AAU Metro championships. We beat the New York AC in the championship game. It was played in the Union Temple in Brooklyn on Eastern Parkway. We played them the year before at New York AC, and we beat them there too. When we came in there, from what I understood, Jonah Goldstein had to pay his own admission. He was president of the Grand Street Boys. He was a judge, a big judge, supreme court judge, state supreme court, and he paid his admissions in, and it was really something. I do not recall what kind of game it was, but the last time we played them, I think we won by thirteen or fourteen points the last year we played them. This was the Olympic year, and the team that won was supposed to go to Denver to play in the national championships. I think they had their tickets already because New York City and the Grand Street Boys could not get the money to take us, so they gave us a wristband instead. So we did not go. So I do not think there was a metropolitan representative. To me it was not a question of personal satisfaction, whether it was Jewish or anything else. The personal satisfaction for me is to win, and that was the important thing. To me, to win against a team with a bigger reputation and better ballplayers is more important than what the heck the personal thing is. They had the players. They had the best. I think the kids made the difference because they were playing. I think they had college ballplayers, fellows who played and finished college. At that time, my whole neighborhood would go. People came to see it, a lot of New York AC people came. We did it. Some of my ballplayers, they went to college. They were playing up in Connecticut, in New Britain and in Waterbury, and they had a coach there and they told the owner, "Look, why don't you hire our coach?" So this guy hired me, and that is when I started going into pro ball.

I think this was 1947 or 1948. We played on Sunday afternoon and on Sunday night. During the week I coached the Grand Street Boys. We used to travel, and that is how I coached these two teams. The Grand Street Boys after 1948 gave up. I worked there and then we played some of the teams in the American Basketball League, exhibition games. It was just a freelancing team. We used to play all these teams. I was getting fifty dollars, and all the ballplayers I think were getting forty dollars. That made eighty dollars on a Sunday. The fans were loaded up. I would say fifteen hundred to two thousand people. Admissions were maybe two dollars, a dollar. The Waterbury Arena, they had a place there, or we played in an armory in New Britain that did not hold too much. Then we played the next year. We played teams like Dayton with Sweetwater Clifton and we played the Harlem Globetrotters. They could not fool around with us. In fact, the morning game I beat them and then at night, and then he [Abe Saperstein] never played a mixed team after that. I had a couple of black ballplayers playing for me then, one or two of them. I brought them in from New York City. Everybody had contacts with me. They all wanted to play with the players I had. The players I had played with these fellows.

I think it was the next year that they were playing in Herkimer, New York. My team played exhibitions and then they played in Herkimer, New York. I think that was 1948. They told the owner to hire me in Herkimer, New York. That was in the oldest league in basketball, the old New York State League, and I went to Herkimer, New York. Half of the team played for Cohoes that played in the exhibition game and half the team played for Herkimer. They were called the Mohawk team. We used to be rivals. On Sunday, we used to come down and play exhibition games. This is the pro game. This was the league, the old New York State League. In Herkimer, half the team could not play in Mohawk, so some of them played for Cohoes. I coached Mohawk against Cohoes, but on Sundays we had all the players that I wanted and we played together in exhibition. That is how we played, so I had them all. Then we played the Renaissance. The Renaissance was the greatest black team around at that time. They were from New York City, and they won the pro championship. Then one of them wanted to join my teams. That is how I got another black player. Dolly King was with me, and then Eddie Younger came with me, and then the following year Pop Gates came, who was one of the greatest ballplayers around. So I had three of them. They were great.

My ballplayers were the best because they could do certain things. We beat these teams, so it did not make any difference. We played like a team. We played defense. I do not know if I was the originator of team play, but I never thought what other guys did. I did what I wanted to do. We played Wilkes-Barre, who were the champs of the American Basketball League, and we beat them in the afternoon and night game. Then they brought in Scranton, who was the last-place team, and we beat them very easily. That night when I came home at about two o'clock in the morning, I had a call from the owner of Scranton asking if I would like to talk to him on Monday about going to his team. So I said, "What is your proposition?" He gave us an excellent proposition. He wanted my players. His name was Speed Mahoney, and [there was] another guy by the name of Levy. I just forgot his name. He was the general manager. So we had a meeting with my ballplayers. We had eight. Four played for Cohoes and four played for Mohawk. He gave me a proposition, and I agreed with it. It was a lot of money for me and the ballplayers. That meant that we had to give up the exhibition games. We had a meeting that night after the games and I said, "This is the proposition we have." They voted, and it was eight to nothing to stay where they were. They did not want to go to the ABL. They were making money like it was. They had exhibition games to make it up. So I said, "Then we are going." We opened up Saturday night. I think we opened up against the

New York Jewels. I overruled the vote. I do not know if they were upset. They may have talked behind my back, but it did not make any difference. I kept some of the old ones for about a week or two and then I dropped them all out. I kept them maybe for a couple of games and then I dropped them out. That is where I made a couple of enemies. People hated my guts after that because I dropped them, but I wanted mine. What happened with this is we went there. We lost the first game I think. We won sixteen in a row. Now we are playing in two leagues. Half of them are playing for Cohoes and half of them are playing for Herkimer. I am coaching Herkimer, and I am now coaching them in Scranton.

Now we are going up there and it ends up we are in second place in the ABL. Now we are in the playoffs against the Cohoes in the New York State League. We are playing each other. So now half my team is playing on two teams in the New York State League, and they all have to play in this thing. Now we are hoping that the playoffs do not come together. Sure enough, we could have forfeited a game, but one of the teams in the American League who should have won, lost a game. That meant that we had to play in the New York State League. Against whom do you think we are playing? Cohoes. We divided the team up, and I hired some ballplayers. Some went to Scranton. Some went to Herkimer, and some went to Cohoes. Now, we played this game on the same night. Herkimer was playing Cohoes and Hartford was playing Scranton. One was played in Herkimer, New York, and the other one was played in Scranton, Pennsylvania. Herkimer beat Cohoes, and Scranton beat Hartford. So we won both games. I was the victorious coach twice on the same night, but I only coached one team. Now my problem came about. The Cohoes sued me because I did not show up with the full team. The Cohoes did not show up. I split their team. Herkimer sued me. Sure enough, the New York State League had to fold after that. They folded because they could not continue their series. Now we continue with Scranton, and we won a championship in the ABL. We beat Wilkes-Barre.

The New York State League folded because the two teams out there, Herkimer and Cohoes, were in this problem so the owners just closed up the league. They sued me, but we played. The boys were kind enough to come up there for nothing and play an exhibition game up there. We played a game in Herkimer, New York, a free exhibition game. Most of my ballplayers who played for Cohoes and Herkimer were playing for me in Scranton. I was now coaching in the ABL at Scranton. Other teams were Wilkes-Barre, Baltimore, New York Jewels, and the Philadelphia SPHAS. You went out and got them [players] and you hired them, but you could not take someone from another team, but you went out and got them. They were mostly New York ballplayers.

Now the game is international. Not only national, but it is international. It is something now internationally, Italy, Spain, Switzerland, England, every country. I did work in Israel and Italy. In Israel, a group, one of the teams, one of the organizations, sports organizations, invited me over. Then on the same trip I had a basketball clinic in Italy. They arranged them and made the arrangements. I think I was in Israel fifteen days and about eight days in Italy. I was in a place called Udine, Rome, and Vienna. They were good players, and now they are hiring state players. The coaching is getting better. The facilities are getting better from what they were seven years ago. I expect to go back this year, not as a coach. This was given to me by Yeshiva University as a gift on my retirement, a trip to Israel. With that trip, I am going to go to Italy, most likely to run a clinic there for five days and in Switzerland for three days.

They have not seen them [techniques] before, but I try to impress upon them the need for fundamentals. Everybody wants to do these things so quickly. They want to be great so quickly that they skip the most basic things. By habit, that is what the important thing is. It is a very simple thing. If I teach you how to make a layup shot or throw a pass and you do it once, you know all the terminology, all the methods of it, but that does not mean you could do it. You could only be a coach because you could only talk about it, but you are not a player. A player has to repeat things thousands of times until it becomes a habit thing, to daydream is all he has to do in a game.

They want to know how to break up zone defense and things like that. You try to impress upon them that in order to do these things you have to go through what the good coaching in the United States does. You have to teach fundamentals, and basically that is what I try to impress upon them. I do it in the States too.

I was not coaching in the N B A. I think I mentioned that I did get in a lot of trouble because I went along with the players. I think it was in the papers, in the *Times*. The owner wanted to give a cut in salary because football was coming on Sundays on television, and I went along with the players. The boys went on strike, so I went with them. I felt I had a loyalty to them because they were the ones who made me. They were players and I was a coach. You found out later, not that I had any bad thoughts about the ballplayers, but an ambitious person who wants to stay in this game would say that I could always get players, but I cannot get owners. That is a very important thing, and it was a fact. I think that that in itself gave me a pretty black eye. I do not know what it did with players, but like anybody says, players want to make a couple of cents, so after you go along with them and they want to play again, you say go and play, but you sit in the back row.

Basketball was mostly all Jews. Boxing, too, because they were the ghetto sports. It was a ghetto sport. I did not have [problems with spectators who were not Jewish] on an individual basis, but on a group basis you could always get problems. That is the basic thing on this whole thing. On a one-on-one basis, you could live with anybody. You have respect for each other and you have some dignity. When it comes to a group, then it is their upbringing and maybe our upbringing that makes it a different way of living.

I brought black players into the league. They were not the first. There were black players. I think there was an unwritten law that said that there should be one black player on a basketball team in the A B L. I had Dolly King, Pop Gates, and Eddie Younger. If I could have had more, I would have had more. I do not remember the owner's reaction. I did not live with him, but he went along with me. Speedy Mahoney, the owner, went along with me, and he is the one who said, "If you want them, you can have them." I did not look into anyone else's view on the situation. I do not know if the crowd enjoyed them. I do not think they [the crowd] would get on the players, but I think down South they would get on players. I think that the living was a little different. I remember going to a hotel in Scranton where the price was three dollars a night for a person, and they wanted maybe fourteen from Dolly King. So I walked out of the hotel and I never came back, though they wanted us to come back. I would not even have had a victory banquet at that hotel. I felt it was unfair. On an individual basis we lived together. I do not think there was this business of blacks on one side of a bench and whites on another. I think they lived together, and we still live together, those who played with us. What their civil rights thinking is and who they are for is completely up to themselves, but on the friendship and personal basis, that is completely different.

Though we spent New Year's Eves together with our families, we went out together. I think the relationship was there. I think maybe I was lucky with the type of guys I had that were able to live together. I do not think there was any falseness in it, that I had to do it. They did it because I think there was no question of color. I do not think we could have thought that way. I still think they live that way.

I started coaching Yeshiva in 1941. There was no program. I didn't know if they [the university's team] were in the college ranks. I did not know if they [the players] went to the high school. I didn't know if these fellows were rabbis or not. They had a team, and we played small teams and we had a gymnasium. We played down there [near Yeshiva], and from there I moved them up to Central Needle Trades High School and we got a little bigger. Yeshiva developed an interest in basketball in the city. Then Yeshiva became a name. I think country wide people started thinking of Yeshiva; Jewish people started putting themselves in this situation. As a Jewish person, you look for Jewish people, Jewish participants and Jewish athletics. They began to recognize something in Jews. It took time. We never had our own gymnasium. We always had to travel to a gym to practice, but we slowly developed. We had some good years, some winning years. They [the administration] let it go the way it was. I do not know if they knew it was important or not. If it was important, they would have built a gym for everybody there and they would have maybe allowed scholarships and did other things. The boys still had to go to school, twenty hours of Hebrew studies and sixteen hours of secular work, so it did not make much difference. We only practiced three days a week, and we played all the other teams.

I think there was always frustration. There had to be a benefit to it, and the benefit was that it taught you basketball, because if you work with the worst, not the worst but the poor ballplayer, at least you have to improvise and you learn to try to make them improve. That was the whole secret in coaching to me. Some of the guys start with the best, with all the scholarships, and try to get the best, and all they have to do is walk on the court and say, "Fellows, here are the basketballs. What else do you want me to do?" I think with me I had to work.

Maybe they had too much of the studies, and some of them went to different schools and others felt that when they went to Yeshiva, they did not have the opportunity to play. They were putting too much away from their education. We played everyone. We traveled to Scranton, Wilkes-Barre, Hartwick, Oneonta, Bridgeport, Hartford, Washington, and Philadelphia. Always I thought [the reception] was good because we always had the Jewish community coming out to see us. This was the biggest thing. I think they [the administration] were starting to listen to it. The papers had things in it. Strictly banging real fundamentals is how we stayed that way. I devised. I improvised. I did things like that. Some of the things that are being used today, it all came about in that time. The type of offensive plays, types of man-to-man defenses that we tried to put into effect. We did not have much time. I said if I was going to make a player I had to stay with certain things until at least he had some knowledge of what he wanted to do. They worked hard. You had always some of the men that you had to forgive for some of the things they did, but I was not the forgiving type. I think maybe if I coached now, I do not know if I could change, but I maybe would have changed and been more sympathetic to them.

I wanted something better, but I do not think I wanted another college. If you are going to get recognition, if you are going to take the worst and try and make them a little better, then you become better, and your own ego gets there. I felt that I can never knock my ballplayers. I knocked them, but on the outside, because after all, if I am a coach, if I am going to be a good coach, then they have to be good players. So we worked that way.

I started a sporting goods store as soon as I came back from the service, about 1946. I had three or four things going on at the same time. I had a family. I have four kids and six grandchildren, and I must have had some family life. They [my kids] all became bar mitzvahed and then I left it up to them. Maybe I should have been a little more forceful and tried to insist that they go further, but I think they have a Jewish feeling. They have a Jewishness about them just as I have. They were educated in Hebrew schools up until bar mitzvah, and I think one of them went a little further, but then like anything else, they drifted. You go to a high school, you want to play ball, and you have other interests and that sort of thing.

9. A star player at Long Island University, Phil Rabin played professionally for Trenton, Passaic, Kingston, Jersey City, and the Philadelphia SPHAS. Courtesy of Bill Himmelman.

PHIL RABIN

- Growing up in Paterson, New Jersey, Phil Rabin watched the Paterson Crescents play in the American Basketball League. He often found himself hanging around the team, including carrying the bags for some of the players. He made a vow that he would one day play for Paterson. He eventually enrolled at Long Island University, learning under famed coach Clair Bee. While in college, he played professionally on the side, and this caused his college career to end prematurely. He turned professional and joined his hometown team. In addition to Paterson, he played for Trenton, Passaic, Kingston, Jersey City, and the Philadelphia s p h a s. He led the American Basketball League in scoring three times.

I was born July 10, 1913, in Paterson, New Jersey. At that time it was one of the top cities for basketball. There was a professional team called the Paterson Crescents. I would carry the bags for a few of the players. Later in life, I played for them.

Growing up, we were very poor. There was no money in those days. Ninety percent of the people then were poor. We hung a peach basket in the backyard. My brothers and I would get wooden planks and put them on the ground so we could dribble the basketball. When I was ten or eleven, there was a playground nearby, and it had a basket. I went there to play basketball. I was short, but very tough.

In 1936 I was playing for Long Island University (l i u). We were rated in the top three in the country. We played at Madison

Square Garden on Saturdays, and there would be twenty thousand people who would come. Teams such as CCNY, Fordham, NYU, Manhattan [College], and LIU would play.

At the time, I was playing professional basketball for the team in Atlantic City in the Eastern League. I was way ahead of my time in playing basketball. Someone told Nat Holman, the coach at CCNY, about me. I got a call from Holman, and he said, "You are playing at Long Island University. What are you doing playing pro ball?" Clair Bee, the LIU coach, said to me, "Phil, we are playing Stanford this weekend, but I cannot let you play because you are playing professional basketball." I told the coach that I needed the money, so I did not play. I did not play, and they beat us by two points. Stanford had Hank Luisetti.

I then played with the Kingston Colonials. When I was playing for the Jersey Reds, we played the SPHAS and beat them for the championship. I wore a jacket with "Jersey Reds World Champions" on it. Eddie Gottlieb, who was the manager of the SPHAS, saw that I was instrumental in beating the SPHAS and went to the Jersey Reds owners and bought me for one hundred dollars. That is how I went to the SPHAS.

When I was with the SPHAS, we won lots of games. We would be playing, and I would be free, and I did not get the ball. So I asked Shikey Gotthoffer, Red Rosan, Red Wolfe, Inky Lautman, and Cy Kaselman why they would not pass me the ball. They said that I was making $35 a game, and they were making only $27.50. Until Gottlieb would pay them an extra $7.50 they were not going to pass the ball. When I was with the SPHAS, I made $35 a game. I was the highest-paid player in the league. Eddie was tight with money with them. In those days, there was no big money in basketball. I played the season with them, and then I signed with the Washington Brewers.

I used to travel by car or train when I went to Philadelphia. Someone would meet me at the train station and take me to the Broadwood Hotel. It was always mobbed every Saturday night. When I came in, I would stay with Dave Zinkoff. He used to announce SPHAS games. He was my friend.

The Broadwood Hotel had a big auditorium with a stage. All

the teams then had dances at halftime and after the games. Gil Fitch, who was a substitute, had a band. They played forty-five minutes between halves and for an hour after the games. It was mobbed on a Saturday night. You could not get into the game. It would seat between five and six thousand people. The crowds would go to meet girls.

The SPHAS moved the ball beautifully. In those days, we never practiced with each other. When I played for Kingston, I was from Paterson, and there were players from Troy, New York; Connecticut; Newburgh, New York; and Brooklyn. It was too expensive to practice. I played with the Jersey Reds for three years, and we never practiced. But the SPHAS were all from Philly, and Gottlieb got them to practice. In those days, you played on your own merits.

Shikey Gotthoffer was a very smart player. He was one of the better players in the American Basketball League. He played like John Havlicek. He was tough off the boards. He scored between seven and eight points a game and was great for the SPHAS. Cy Kaselman was a great shooter. He had a unique way to fake, cut to the basket, and you would give him a bounce pass to the basket. Inky Lautman was tough under the boards. He was a steady player. They got the best from around Philadelphia. There were a lot of good players in my day.

The American Basketball League was poorly run. But the best players played in that league. They experimented with a lot then. One year, we played without a backboard. One year, they allowed two-handed dribbling.

I played from 1935 to 1940, until I tore my Achilles tendon. I played another four years, but I was not as good. My best years were 1937, 1938, and 1939, when I led the American Basketball League in scoring and assists. I had torn cartilage in both knees, and I was the first person in the state of New Jersey to have both knees operated on at the same time. From 1940 to 1945, I was in defense. I was 4-F [unfit for service] for the army. I could not jump off a bench. I played until 1945.

10. A star college player for City College of New York, Moe Goldman played for the Philadelphia s p h a s in the 1930s. Courtesy of Bill Himmelman.

MOE GOLDMAN

• Basketball happened later for Moe Goldman than it did for most of his contemporaries. Growing up in Brooklyn, Goldman did not play basketball until his senior year at Franklin K. Lane High School. After a growth spurt caught the attention of the basketball coach, Goldman finally joined the team, eventually playing at City College of New York. Teaming with Moe Spahn, Goldman led the Beavers to two Eastern titles while earning All-American honors as a senior. He then turned professional and joined the Philadelphia SPHAS, where he was a mainstay for multiple championships. His lasting contribution was changing the perception of the center position from one designed for relatively slow, plodding men to one that required more athleticism.

I was born in Brownsville in Brooklyn on April 30, 1913. I learned to play basketball in high school. We played a little bit on the playgrounds, but not much. Actually, the only reason I got into basketball was because over the summer before my senior year in high school, I suddenly grew about six inches. I was the tallest one around, and when they saw me they said, "You're the center." I'd never really played any competitive basketball before. But there I was at Franklin K. Lane High School, so we played. We won the city championship that year. I made All-Scholastic in the first year I played. My senior year was the only year I ever played basketball. Then I was about 6'2", and I was the tallest guy on the team. That was 1929–30. From there I went to City College of New York. Then I was about 6'3".

City College was the only school I was interested in at that time. Somebody approached me and asked if I wanted to go to City College. I had the scholastic average to get in, and I wanted to play basketball and study. Nat Holman did not recruit me; somebody else did, but I don't remember who it was. I think it was an assistant coach who asked me to come. Some of the older ballplayers at City College, like Moe Spahn, also asked me to come. Moe Spahn played high school basketball at Bryant High School, but he got into City College a year ahead of me. I must have stayed out a year. We played two years together on the varsity at CCNY. In my three years, we lost one game each year.

I could tip the ball consistently. I was the first center man that ran. We had center men in those days—Tiny Hearn, Matty Begovich, and the rest of them. But they didn't run. But I was tall, and I was a runner.

Nat Holman was very disciplined. He was a master of fundamentals, and he insisted that you do all the things he wanted you to do. He wanted you to pass the ball and get your shot inside rather than outside. He was tough, but he was fair. He was a good coach.

Occasionally, when we had the opportunity, we had a fast break. We were all runners. It wasn't as if we brought the ball up and went slow. We were passing, running, and moving the ball all the time. But when the opportunity arose, we went in for a fast break.

When we couldn't fast break, we played a play pattern. We didn't have a real play pattern, actually; as the opportunity arose, we took it. It wasn't play number one, play number two, and play number three. We didn't do that. We moved the ball and looked for this and this and that and that, until we finally made something happen. Usually we had a pivot man, and we used give and go, pick and roll, all those things.

The physical abilities of the players today in shooting and jumping are better. Take a man that's 7' who can run like a two-footer. In our day, when you were 6'6" or taller, they never ran. You couldn't run. The Brooklyn Visitations had a tall man in Howie Bollerman, who could shoot fairly well. But as I said before, Tiny Hearn couldn't run. None of them could run.

We used the center jump after each basket. I could jump pretty well. I'd get rebounds from the big fellows. I could out jump them. I could jump and run, and I was one of the few center men who could shoot from a distance fairly accurately—two-handed set shots.

When I was at CCNY, we had plays off the center jump. If the other team had a tall center that could out jump me, we had set plays for defense off the center jump. I would usually give a signal to where I was going to tap it by nodding. We would give a signal like a face here or a nod there. We didn't use numbers or by talking to each other. You see, for every jump ball you had a moment to walk to it, and while you're walking, I'd say, "I'll try and get it to you."

I graduated from City College in 1934–35. It's very interesting how I started to play with the [Philadelphia] SPHAS. In my last year, we played Temple University in Philadelphia, and we were sitting around the hotel room after the ballgame, and somebody said, "Moe, there's somebody here to see you." He said, "It's Eddie Gottlieb."

I didn't know who Eddie Gottlieb was, and he said, "He's the owner of the Philadelphia team." So I talked to Eddie, and he said, "How would you like to play for the SPHAS?" I said, "I don't mind. I have two more games to play." And he said, "I'll offer you thirty-five dollars a game." I knew that was a little higher than New York teams were paying. They were offering me twenty-five dollars. I said, "Fine." So he said, "OK, now Saturday night you're playing against NYU. That will be your last game. Sunday night we'll be in Brooklyn playing against the New York Jewels in the American Basketball League, and this starts the second half of the season for the professionals. So you meet us at Arcadia Hall in Brooklyn." I said, "Fine."

So I found a bus that took me to Arcadia Hall, and the man at the gate wouldn't let me in. He said, "Who are you?" I said, "I'm playing for Philadelphia." He said, "I don't know you from Adam." That's how the game was then. And incidentally, I would have been the number-one choice if we had the draft system they have today.

So finally, Eddie Gottlieb comes and gets me in. I go down to meet the ballplayers, and he gives me a uniform, and I thought, "Well, I'll probably go out and watch them play and see what's happening, and meet everybody." We get upstairs and start practicing, and then we start the ballgame, and Eddie said, "Goldman, you're at center." I had never played with these fellows. I just met them that night, and I started playing the next night after I was through with CCNY. We had Shikey Gotthoffer, Red Wolfe, Cy Kaselman, Inky Lautman, and me.

Arcadia Hall was a dance hall that they converted to basketball. It could seat a couple of thousand. On an average night, the Jewels would have drawn one thousand to twelve hundred. Usually there were dances before the game, or after the game. We had dances in Philadelphia, too, but we drew much more than anybody else in the league. We would draw fifteen hundred or sixteen hundred. We played at the Broadwood Hotel. The ballroom was set up for basketball, and after the game we had dancing.

We never had salaries. We played maybe two games a week in the American Basketball League, maybe two exhibition games against teams like the New York Renaissance or teams around there, and then two days a week I'd go to the Penn State League. I played for Wilkes-Barre. Then if I had time I'd play for the Newark Hebrew Club in Newark on Sunday afternoon, and sometimes I'd go to Albany in the New York State League. I'd play seven or eight games a week. And I was also teaching school in junior high in Borough Park in Brooklyn. I ended up as a school administrator.

I was teaching school right from the beginning in 1934 when I started. If you played five, six, or seven ballgames a week, and let's say you averaged $50 a game, then you made about $350 a week. Maybe you would play for five months.

Wilkes-Barre was a different situation. In the Penn State League, teams were allowed only two imports, as we were called—professionals. The other members of the team had to be local boys. They paid me much more. They paid seventy-five dollars a game plus expenses. I played with Mac Kinsbrunner in Wilkes-Barre. In Wilkes-Barre, we played in an armory.

Most of the SPHAS were doing the same thing, playing on other teams. Each team in the Penn State League had two imports. Shikey Gotthoffer played for one team. Cy Kaselman played for one team. I would play with Kinsbrunner in Wilkes-Barre, who played for the Jewels in the American Basketball League. In the ABL, we played with each other, and in Wilkes-Barre, we played against each other.

I played in a cage in Tunkhannock in the Penn State League. It was my first ballgame in the Penn State League. They had a ball-player named Chasmadia. In the cage, you had no out-of-bounds balls. You hit the cage and bounced back. I got hit so much that day I had fifteen fouls called on me. Play never stops except for fouls and jump balls. No out-of-bounds. People were on the outside, and you were in the inside. You looked like an animal inside there. They had chicken-wire netting.

Before the season, we'd get together for several weeks for practice. We worked out against St. Joseph's and Temple and everybody else in Philadelphia. We didn't have any games with them; we just worked out with them. They were just scrimmages.

By 1942 Gottlieb was still paying by the game, but he was paying much more. They went up to $100, $150 a game. We never knew what the other fellows were making. Eddie paid us in cash right after the game.

We'd make a Christmas trip out west each year and play the teams out there for about ten days in cities like Chicago, Oshkosh, and Sheboygan [Wisconsin]. The league had no games during the holidays. We'd go out in Eddie Gottlieb's car. There would be seven of us. He had a specially built car that seated nine, with three across. We'd leave Saturday night after a ballgame. We'd stop in Harrisburg, [Pennsylvania], Fort Wayne, [Indiana], and all the other towns. We'd travel for hours and hours.

We'd play the Harlem [actually New York] Renaissance maybe twenty times a year. We'd go up to the Renaissance Casino maybe four or five times. They'd come to our place four or five times, and we'd play in other places four, five times. Maybe fifteen times a year.

At the Renaissance Casino, all the people would sit around, and they would have big crowds. They wouldn't start the game until about eleven. They had dancing first. I think we were about the only team that beat them there. At that time, they were the only black team. In the Midwest, the Harlem Globetrotters were just beginning. They took the best of the black players at that time.

I played against Willie Smith and Tarzan Cooper. They were the two center men. They used to drive me crazy.

Gottlieb was a very nice fellow. Crazy, but he only wanted to win. He was tough. He was our coach in all the years I played. He was the father of professional basketball. During the war, when the best teams could not hold up, Eddie was taking care of the expenses of some of the other teams. He had foresight. He kept it moving.

We didn't need coaching. We worked together. Everybody knew what to do. We did not need coaches. Very few teams had a coach. He [Gottlieb] made the lineups and did the substituting, and all the rest of that.

Gottlieb kept us going. We went on the trips, and we would come back and make very little money. Money was not there for a trip like that. I would say, "Eddie, why can't we take Christmas off instead of making this trip?" He said, "We are not making this trip for money. We are pioneers for the future of professional basketball."

I thought that interest in the game would grow, but not to the extent that it did. I never suspected to see salaries involved and the crowds involved, the big business involved.

There was prestige in being a professional player. In Philadelphia, we were right up there, but in the other towns where we played, they cheered you, and you left and that was about it. If I walked in the street, nobody would say, "Oh, here's Moe Goldman," like they would say today, "Oh, there's so and so." It wasn't that much prestige. But people would have been impressed if they knew you were a professional basketball player.

During my career, all we had was Jewish players. Most of the players came from South Philadelphia, which was a Jewish neighborhood. That is how it got the name. In my years, three of us came from New York and had nothing to do with Philadelphia.

Gottlieb's office was upstairs in Chick Passon's sporting goods store. He was a big man in baseball and the Negro baseball leagues. He had a secretary. He had a man who was in charge of his tickets. He had two, three, or four people working for him.

Between 1935 and 1942, the pro game speeded up some, and we had better ballplayers after a while in the way of ability. In my first year, Trenton was the team we played for the championship. They had Rusty Saunders and Tiny Hearn. They were big, and they would hit you and that's all. From hitters, we became basketball players. At the beginning, these fellows would hit you to prevent you from scoring, and they wouldn't run too fast. They would get in there and bang away. But later on, when younger players came in, the abilities were better, and the game changed, and we became better ballplayers. So hitting wasn't a factor anymore, as compared to when I started. The skills improved as time went on. Each club had some good players, like Lou Spindell, who played for Trenton. He was a good ballplayer. He graduated from City College.

Rusty Saunders was a very outstanding ballplayer, but he wasn't that much of a scorer. He could handle the ball well and pass the ball well and keep you from scoring. Tiny Hearn couldn't score two points a ballgame. He was in there to get the tip and to get rebounds, and that's about all.

The elimination of the center jump speeded the game up. The old-timers were eliminated, and you had some centers who were very good. You had John Pelkington, who played for a while in the NBL, too, and for the Jewels. Yes, there was a big change as far as centers were concerned.

It was the two-handed set for the most part. You had one or two who came along and shot one-handed, but in my time it was still two hands. Hank Luisetti changed the whole game of basketball with his one-handed shot. Nat Holman would have everybody on his teams do the same thing. For example, everybody had to shoot fouls underhanded. I was a pretty good foul shooter, but I couldn't shoot underhand. So in practice I would shoot overhand, and he would kick me in the behind and say, "Underhand." But he finally had to give in because my average overhand was very good. But I was actually the first ballplayer who changed foul shooting from underhand to overhand.

In the ABL, there was antisemitic feeling among fans in other towns. We went to Prospect Hall in Brooklyn to play the Visitations, and the first row of spectators when we went by would poke us with cigarettes. We had a lot of fights with some of the ballplayers. In Jersey City, we had fights occasionally. In between halves, we stayed upstairs. There was no place to go downstairs.

I think it was Jewish-Gentile. They'd call us "Jew bastard" or something like that. Maybe it was a little intensified for the SPHAS, but I think they did it for every team. Most of the teams in the ABL had Jewish players.

In Philadelphia, we'd get maybe 25–30 percent Jewish spectators at least. When we went to the Visitations I don't think there were any Jewish spectators. I think it was mostly Prospect Hall. Prospect Hall at that time was a non-Jewish area.

11. Bernie Fleigel (*left*) played collegiately for Nat Holman (*right*) at City College of New York. Courtesy of City College Archives Collection.

BERNIE FLEIGEL

- Bernie Fleigel was one of the greatest Jewish basketball players from the late 1930s through World War II. He replaced
  Moe Goldman as City College of New York's big man and led
  the Beavers to three successful seasons. As a senior, he was
  a first-team All-American, won the Haggerty Award as the
  best player in New York, and finished second to Stanford's
  Hank Luisetti as the country's best player. As a professional,
  he played for the Kate Smith Celtics, Kingston, Troy, Brooklyn, Wilmington, and Jersey City. He led Wilmington to an
  American Basketball League title. He decided to pursue a
  law career as opposed to joining the newly formed Basketball Association of America after World War II.

I was born on May 13, 1918, in New York, at Twentieth Street and
First Avenue. I did not play basketball in Manhattan when I was
growing up. My family moved to the Bronx when I was twelve
years old. We lived at 208th Street and Bainbridge Avenue. I was
first introduced to basketball when I was in Crescent Junior High
School and then at DeWitt Clinton High School. I was taller than
most, and it was rare for a Jewish player to be over 6' tall. We had
a schoolyard, and I always played against older guys.

I learned to play in the schoolyards. I was smart enough to use
the feint move. I would practice basketball in the schoolyards. I
was like a standing guard. I was a defensive player. I never went
past half court. I learned to defend two or three guys.

In 1933–34 we won the city championship by defeating Thomas

Jefferson in Brooklyn. I made one foul shot. It was a surprise victory. When I was growing up in the Bronx, I did not know about professional basketball. The kids in Brooklyn knew about professional basketball because the American Basketball League had two teams, the Jewels and the Visitations. Moe Goldman, who was from Brooklyn and played at CCNY, later played for the SPHAS. He graduated CCNY in June 1934, and I started in September 1934.

The American Basketball League was the only league around. It was a tough and rough league. The women would throw beer and trip us with their umbrellas. It was tough. I was the first big guy to play under the basket.

In March 1938 I was nineteen years old, and I finished college, and I went to play for the Kate Smith Celtics. She bought the Original Celtics, and Ted Collins, the manager and promoter, asked me to come to his office. He wanted me to come and play. He said, "We will be the first team to score one hundred points." I said, "Ted, how do you expect us to do that?" He said that I could score twenty-five points, Jerry Bush could score twenty-five points, and he mentioned two other players who could score twenty-five points. "Between you and them, we will score one hundred points." I replied, "Do you realize that when I played and scored twenty-five points, I was the only guy on my team shooting? With one ball, we cannot do that." I realized that Collins could not be persuaded. But Collins went for shooters, and he was ahead of his time. Eventually, teams scored one hundred points in a game.

I was with the Kate Smith Celtics, Kingston/Troy Celtics beginning in 1938–39 and went to Wilmington in 1941–42. I always played for Barney Sedran. After the service I was married, a practicing lawyer, and had one kid. I coached and played two years with the Jersey City Atoms. I played with Sammy Kaplan.

In 1940–41 we were kicked out of the armories because the U.S. Army needed them for the war effort. We had no place to play. We were playing in the Broadway Arena. Out of the blue, Barney Sedran called and said that the franchise was going to transfer to Wilmington. The team was owned by the DuPont family, and there was no problem in getting us into the armory down there. The governor and the army had granted permission.

So we went to Wilmington. Sedran was the coach and owner. I was the captain, and Sammy Kaplan came because he always played with Sedran and me. At our first game there, everyone welcomed us. It was a tremendous crowd. This was in 1941–42.

I played for three coaches. They were Nat Holman at CCNY; Barney Sedran, who is the shortest member of the Basketball Hall of Fame; and Eddie Gottlieb. Eddie liked the way I played. The SPHAS never had good rebounders, not enough strong guys. Between Christmas and New Year's, the SPHAS would travel to the Midwest and play games, and Eddie always needed an extra big man. Moe Goldman was not a good rebounder. He did not have the strength. Gottlieb liked my rebounding and my scoring and team play, and he would always want me to play when available, and when they were not playing league games. Eddie always wanted me to play, so I did. Eddie was always fair. If you played for Eddie, you knew you would be paid that night.

The SPHAS were one of the first great teams. Next to the Original Celtics, they were the best white team. They played great team basketball and were a great bunch of guys.

The Broadwood Hotel [where the games were held] was a nice hotel. There was a game and a dance. They had nice showers. It was a good, clean place. The games were incidental. The dances were the top thing. It was always crowded, with two thousand to three thousand people, mostly young and Jewish. They were knowledgeable fans who knew the other teams.

Inky Lautman was a good player. He played the pivot a lot. He was not fast but was tough. He was an important guy for the SPHAS.

Irv Torgoff was from Brooklyn, and we were friends for sixty years. He was a nice guy. He was a big guy who played with Mike Bloom and Moe Goldman. When we played the SPHAS, I had to take those three guys by myself. He was a smart player and a good left-handed shooter.

Ossie Schectman scored the first basket in the NBA as a member of the New York Knicks. Soon after that he injured himself and did not play much. He was not that big but was a smooth player. My teammate Sammy Kaplan could never guard Ossie, so I had to guard him because I was able to push him out.

Jerry Fleishman was a great player who was always in excellent shape. He played with the New York Knicks and the SPHAS. Butch Schwartz was a solid player from Long Island University. He played on the SPHAS. He wasn't sensational but a good teammate. Petey Rosenberg was a super player. He was quick, fast, and small. Cy Kaselman had one of the best shots ever. He was a great player and shooter. Red Rosan was from Philadelphia like Inky Lautman. He was a good player for the SPHAS.

Red Wolfe was from Fordham. He was a great defensive player and a nice guy. I always remember when Wolfe guarded Moe Frankel. Moe had a big ass and was known for his long shots. He couldn't dribble. He couldn't take his opponent off the dribble. But against Wolfe, Frankel would shake his ass and go around him. He did this every time. That usually wasn't his game.

Art Hillhouse was from Long Island University. He was a tall guy, about 6'11". He was not a bad center. Red Klotz was an excellent player.

Shikey Gotthoffer was sensational. He went to James Monroe High School. He was named MVP in the ABL for a number of years. He was short and stocky, but smart and fast. I will always remember the one lesson he taught me. I was guarding him, and I kept one arm on him to feel where he was, but I always kept watching everyone else. One time, he throws me into the stands. So I learned to touch my opponent, but do not let him throw you into the stands.

Bernie Opper went to Morris High School and then played at Kentucky. He was an excellent high school player. He was one of the better players for the SPHAS. Harry Litwack was a great coach and referee. He also played for the SPHAS. He knew his basketball.

Dave Zinkoff was like a ball boy for the SPHAS. He loved Eddie Gottlieb and always carried his bags. One night we were getting ready to go to Chicago, and Eddie told a few of us to go to Dave Zinkoff's father's deli and grab a bite and have some sandwiches before we traveled. So we get to the deli and go behind the counter, and we ate everything. We must have eaten $2,000 worth of food. When Eddie gets there, and it's time to leave, he says, "Will $10 cover it?" I know myself that I ate about $50 worth of food that night. But Zink was a good guy, and he always remembered us.

The SPHAS were a smart team. They had good shooters who passed the ball well, did give-and-goes, and were good underneath the boards. Gotthoffer was a bull. They were a great team and one of the best teams in the ABL for many years. After I went to Wilmington, we got Jerry Bush and Ed Sadowski and beat the SPHAS seven out of eight times one year.

The Detroit team had won the World Professional Basketball Tournament the previous spring, and we were able to sign a few of their players. We signed Jerry Bush, who was 6'3", and Ed Sadowski, who was 6'5" or 6'6". For the first time, I did not have to play center. We had a great team because of our height. The SPHAS at that time always had two or three big guys in Mike Bloom, Irv Torgoff, and Moe Goldman. In our first game against the SPHAS, Bloom outplayed Sadowski. We won, but Sadowski played poorly. Afterwards, I said, "Ed, we got you because you are a big, strong guy. You let Bloom push you around." He was steamed. The next time we played the SPHAS, he just killed Bloom. We beat everybody that year. We won both the first and second halves of the regular season, so we won the championship.

On our team, we had one standard play. Charlie Reiser would block for Chick Hoeffer, who would shoot it. Three of us would get under the boards and bat the ball back and forth. He would shoot, and we three big guys would bat the ball around if he missed, and finally one of us would tip it in. That was our sure-point play. It was a great year. Years later, the *New York Times* ran an article that said we were the best professional basketball team prior to the Los Angeles Lakers with Wilt Chamberlain and Elgin Baylor.

One year, we went to Ohio to play the Harlem [actually New York] Renaissance for four games. The first game was in Cincinnati, and before the game started, the referee called a foul on me. I told the referee, "I didn't foul him." He told me to shut up. A few minutes later, I was called for another foul. I said, "I did not do anything." He said, "I heard about you." At halftime, I went up to the referee, and I said, "I really am a nice guy. Who told you I wasn't?" He pointed to the Rens team, who were all laughing. I told the referee that they are kidding you.

The Rens had great players. We always played against each other. When they got ahead late in the game, they would get the ball, and you would never get it back. They liked to make you look like fools. They were a super team and the first really good black team.

I went into the service, but I had an enlarged heart, so I sat out a year. The next year I went in. I played on a basketball team in the service. We beat the navy [Great Lakes] team that had Bobby Davies from Seton Hall. I played on a team called the Five by Five. We had Bruce Hale, who was a great player for Santa Clara and later coached at the University of Miami. He is Rick Barry's former father-in-law. We also had Jake Ahearn and Dwight Eddleman. Our team was located in Miami Beach.

I began my time in the service at Fort Dix in New Jersey. Mike Bloom was there. Nobody wanted to leave because you were not in harm's way near the fighting. They had an extra person and announced that someone would have to go. Since I had twisted my knee and was out, I elected to go only if they would send me to a warm climate. The first stop was Miami Beach, and I stayed there for two years. Long Island University sent their freshman team down, and they needed a team to play against. That is how we started Five by Five. We played games in Tampa and then would come back. It was easy duty, and we played games.

For the first few months, I had a bad knee. I was in the aircraft specialization field. I was in Miami, then I went to Clearwater, and from there I arrived in North Carolina at Fort McCullough. I was given a broom and put on KP duty. I ran into a friend, Captain Angie Monitto, who said that I should call him. Every day I asked the sergeant if I could make a call, and he said to go back to work. After a few days, Captain Monitto came to the office and asked why I had not called. I told him to speak to the sergeant. He said, "The general wants to see you." This was during the Battle of the Bulge and a lot of the men were having horrible nightmares of what they had witnessed, so the general wanted me to put together a basketball team to help raise the morale of the troops. I said that I would if I could have a five-day furlough to visit my wife in Miami. Once I returned, I looked at a roster and found some players. One of them was Si Lobello from Long Island University. It turned out that he was shipped out two days before. He died in the first day in battle in Europe.

After that, I had a job in which I would go to the hotels and offer to buy back their furniture that was stored away when the army came in and used the hotels during the war. I did this for a year, and it was a cushy job.

I traveled with the furniture man in Miami Beach in 1944, before I went to Clearwater and Fort McClellan. I was married in St. Petersburg in November 1944, and played at Largo High School gym the day after I was married.

When I was discharged from the army, I was already married and had one child. The New York Knicks wanted me to play for them, but I could not afford to play. They offered me $6,000. I had just opened a law office. I thought I could make more money playing in the American Basketball League on the weekends. I was getting ninety a game and playing three games each weekend.

The ABL was not a minor league to the Basketball Association of America. The BAA took players from us because they did not have to pay the teams anything. I played for the Jersey City Atoms for a year and then coached them for two or three years. I quit around 1948 or 1949. I had to get serious. The competition in the ABL after the war was good. Chuck Connors, the future star of [The] Rifleman, played with Trenton.

2. One of the game's first great point guards, Dutch Garfinkel played professionally with Boston and Rochester. Courtesy of Bill Himmelman.

JACK "DUTCH" GARFINKEL

- Before the likes of Dick McGuire and Bob Cousy graced the NBA with their great court vision and slick passing skills, Dutch Garfinkel was the model for all future point guards. He introduced the "look away" pass, flashy in its day but an integral part of the modern game. His life goal was to be a professional basketball player, and to that end, he practiced all day as a child, even wearing out his sneakers once a year. He honed his reputation playing collegiately at St. John's University for Joe Lapchick before joining the American Basketball League. He joined the Rochester Royals of the National Basketball League and helped lead them to the 1946 NBL title. After playing a few more seasons with the Boston Celtics, Garfinkel became a well-respected referee in the New York City area.

I was born on the East Side, on Suffolk Street. It was rough then. In those days, we lived in an apartment. We did not have a bathroom in the apartment. We used the bathroom in the hall. My mother would take my brother and I to the public baths, which were three blocks away ,about two to three times a week. During the summer there was no air conditioner, so we slept on the fire escape. My father worked for an undertaker, and he drove the horse and wagon. There was an influenza outbreak, and many people died. My father was so busy as a helper to the undertaker that he would take five or six caskets at a time. That's how bad it was.

In East New York there were community centers. Public School

82 was located at Wonona and Dumont Streets. During the winter I played every night. In the summers I played in the schoolyards. I played ball every chance I had. I loved it, and I made up my mind I wanted to be a basketball player.

We all lived in the city. There were no fields like in the Bronx or Queens. Good baseball players were from Queens. In Brooklyn, you played basketball. There were community centers. Jewish kids were basketball minded. We played in schoolyards.

My parents did not mind me playing basketball as long as I did not get hurt. I just wore out my sneakers once a year. In the summers, they surely did not mind. In those days, my parents were busy. My father worked all the time, and [the] women were in the house cleaning and cooking. That is how life was then.

I lived in Brighton Beach in Brooklyn. As a kid, I loved basketball. I went to Public School 100. It was an eighth-grade school. I put in for high school. Thomas Jefferson had great teams, but Abraham Lincoln was only seven or eight blocks away. I elected to go to Thomas Jefferson, and I made it. In my first year, I traveled by train one hour each way from Brooklyn to East New York. I tried out for the basketball team my first year, and I did not make it. In my second year, I made it and did so for three years in a row. I am proud of that fact. In my last two years, I was a PSAL All Star as selected by the *New York World Telegram* and the *New York Journal American*.

I wanted to become a basketball player. In my first year, the team was mediocre. In my second year, we were co-champs of the PSAL with James Monroe of the Bronx. That year was the first time that the PSAL came out with new alignments for its championships. Five teams were competing. James Monroe from the Bronx, Textile from Manhattan, Newtown from Queens, and Samuel Tilden, and our team from Brooklyn. It was a round-robin tournament. We only lost once, and so did Monroe. So Jefferson and Monroe were in a playoff for the city championship. I cannot remember, but I think a Jewish holiday was coming up, so they called it off and made us both co-champs. In my third year, in 1936–37, we were the Brooklyn champions but lost in the first round to Clinton, which was a top team.

There were no big leagues then. There was one league, the American Basketball League. There were teams like the Brooklyn Jewels and the Brooklyn Visitations. There was also a team in Trenton. At Halsey Street, there was a hall called Arcadia Hall. Every Saturday night there were games, and if you brought your G.O. [General Order] card you paid twenty-five cents to see the game. I watched the games all the time. I watched attentively. They played three fifteen-minute periods, so they played forty-five-minute games. At the end of each period, the teams would go into the corner, and I would get near and listen to what they were saying. This was my learning experience. I learned by watching and picking things up myself.

In the 1920s, before my time, they played with a cage. When I watched the American Basketball League, they played on dance floors. They played in the Broadway Arena and Prospect Hall. They would put up two baskets, put out tables and serve food, and people came to watch the games.

After high school, I went to college. A man called with an offer from George Washington University. I made an appointment to meet him in a New York hotel. I got on a train, went to New York, and waited. He never showed. Meanwhile, the athletic director at St. John's called and asked me if I would like to play for them. This was the second year for Joe Lapchick as coach. I said yes immediately. I wanted to play there because there was a team, the Wonder Five, and they had a guard named Max Posnack. He was a great passer. That team was great and lost only two or three games in three years.

In those days, there was a freshman rule, and you could not play on the varsity. So I watched Max. I idolized him. He became a friend of mine. He was a lovely man. He settled in Washington DC. I am glad it happened that way. I played at Madison Square Garden. I got publicity. It made my name, and I played for Lapchick.

When I was at St. Johns, I used to see the SPHAS play the Jewels. Eddie Gottlieb was the coach then. I would watch all the teams. They were a great team and won many championships. They had great shooters. Cy Kaselman was a great set shooter. Shikey Gotthoffer was a strong defensive player. They had terrific ballplayers.

The Visitations had a lot of fans who were antisemitic. They did not like Jewish kids. Prospect Hall, where they played, had two or three balconies. They threw stuff down on the players. They would put lit cigarettes into the players. There was no worry with the Jewels. Most the fans of the Jewels were Jewish.

After college, I played pro ball for a year in the ABL, and then the war came. I played for the Baltimore Clippers. I was paid twenty-five dollars a game, and I had to pay all my own expenses. There were lots of New York players, and we traveled by the Pennsylvania Railroad. I did not care. I was playing ball. The team disbanded and became the Trenton Tigers. Lapchick made me the freshman coach at St. John's. I got away on the weekends for ball games. I would play three games and then go back to camp.

The next year I somehow connected with Gottlieb. I signed with the SPHAS and played with them for two years. I made about forty or fifty dollars a game. Those teams had Inky Lautman, Petey Rosenberg, Red Wolfe, Red Klotz, and Red Rosan. We won the championship one year I was there. We made peanuts for the playoffs. We got one hundred dollars a man. The halls had only one thousand people in attendance. The payoff was tiny, nothing to speak of.

In the army, Gottlieb contacted me. I spent two years at West Point as an enlisted man. I played for the SPHAS. I was there with Bernie Opper, and he played for Adolph Rupp. He was the only Jewish captain at Kentucky. I asked Gottlieb if we could sign Opper so he could also play for the SPHAS.

After inspection, four of us would leave to go to New York City. Bernie and I would go to the SPHAS, and the other fellows would travel to their teams. We ended up playing each other on the weekends. Afterwards we would drive back to West Point for inspection on Monday morning. I never slept in those days.

I took the Long Island Railroad to Philadelphia. There was a hotel, the Broadwood Hotel, and they had a ballroom with dances. The guys would meet the girls, and the girls would meet the guys. I would check in, get a few hours of sleep, and get up and put my uniform on. I would take the elevator to the ballroom, and there was a court. After the game, I would go back to my room, shower, and go back down to the dance. I would dance with the women. I would pick up a date. That was the life of the hotel.

Dave Zinkoff was a good friend of Gottlieb. They were nice to Bernie and me. They always took us to the Jewish community. They would sit with us at the deli and have franks, corn beef, and knishes. They took care of us and treated us to late dinners. Eddie always wanted to win.

The SPHAS were a great team. They won many championships. They were the greatest ballplayers for that era. They were great shooters. They played all the great teams, the Rens [New York Renaissance], and the [Harlem] Globetrotters. They were noted for winning championships. They played defense and took good shots. If you had to dribble, then you did. If you did not, then you didn't. You looked to pass to the other guy who was in position to shoot. They always wanted to win and had great teamwork.

We were smart players from the East. Gottlieb was called the Mogul. During the war years, he wanted the league to continue, so he called his players and other players and had them play for other teams. He did that so the league could go on. He was quite a promoter. He, Ned Irish, and Walter Brown formed the Basketball Association of America. Later, in 1950, it became the NBA. He kept that league alive. He was all basketball. When he went to the NBA, he did all the scheduling. He did it alone by hand.

After I finished with the SPHAS, I joined the Rochester Royals of the National Basketball League. It was one of the greatest teams I played for. They had Red Holzman, Al Cervi, Bob Davies, Fuzzy Levane, John Mahnken, and Bobby Fitzgerald. We won one championship.

After I left the SPHAS, I played for the Royals and then for the Boston Celtics of the NBA. Honey Russell was the coach then, and he coached at Seton Hall. He developed great players. Then Doggie Julian from Holy Cross came in. He let me go. Honey called me, and he was in upstate New York near Schenectady, Glens Falls, and Saratoga. I got fifty dollars a game and ended my career there.

I met my wife, Lillian, and I was looking toward the future. I became a physical education teacher for twenty-seven years. I retired and have a pension. I was also a salesman until two or three years ago. I sold advertising specialty items. Anything with an imprint on it, I sold it. I also get a pension from the NBA, which helps me.

I was also a referee for twenty-seven years. I got two dollars or four dollars a game. I took the IAABO [International Association of Approved Basketball Officials] test and passed, so I was eligible to referee New York high school games. I also passed the CBOA [Collegiate Basketball Officials Association] so I could referee college ball. One year Maurice Podoloff, the commissioner of the NBA, called me and asked if I would like to referee a few professional games. It was a tryout for a weekend in Maine. I just made it back for Monday morning to teach. It would interfere with my teaching job so I did not do it.

13. Ossie Schectman scored the first two points in N B A history on November 1, 1946. Courtesy of L I U Athletics.

OSSIE SCHECTMAN

- On November 1, 1946, Ossie Schectman made history by becoming the first person to score a basket in the new Basketball Association of America (later the N B A). As a member of the New York Knicks, he scored the first two points against the Toronto Huskies in a game played in Canada. His basketball skills as a solid guard were honed playing for Clair Bee's Long Island University squads that won two N I T championships, in 1939 and 1941. After graduating he joined the Philadelphia S P H A S and was a member of teams that won two American Basketball League titles in five seasons. He played only one year with the Knicks, when they lost in the playoffs to the eventual champions, the Philadelphia Warriors. He then rejoined the A B L, this time starring with Paterson, New Jersey.

I started playing basketball in Brooklyn at an early age, and I was involved with settlement house teams. That was my early competition. I had an older brother who was a good athlete. I watched various teams in the neighborhood, amateur clubs, teams in Brownsville, and I picked up different moves from the players. I grew into my game. I improved a great deal. I was a dedicated athlete, and I played hard. I was a pretty good point guard who would run the offense and play strong defense.

Playing basketball in those days was confined to smaller areas. The physical setup was not too much. The ceilings were low, and there were ten men on the court. You played in a figure eight, and there was lots of movement. It was devoid of long set shots.

When I was in junior high and high school, I went to Arcadia Hall in Brooklyn to see the Brooklyn Jewels play in the American Basketball League. The Jewels were represented by the St. John's Wonder Five. I got to see the SPHAS play. With them, it was more of a team concept. I tried to emulate certain players. That was the way I learned to play. A couple of the SPHAS were from Brooklyn, like Moe Goldman, who played at CCNY, and Irv Torgoff, who played at Tilden High School. Shikey Gotthoffer was from the Bronx. I used to follow them.

In high school, I lived in Flatbush and played for Tilden High School. My senior year in Brooklyn we won the championship. I was a fairly good student. In 1935, during the Depression years, Clair Bee, coach at Long Island University, managed a beach club in Manhattan near Brighton Beach. It was a private club, and he recruited local players to get them jobs. They earned decent salaries and worked at the private beach and played exhibition games. It was one of the factors why I attended Long Island University and played for Clair Bee. I could have gone to other schools, like St. Johns and City College of New York. LIU became a powerhouse. My sophomore year, we played the best teams in the country and went undefeated. That 1938–39 team was the best group of players that New York saw in those days.

When I got out of college in 1941, there was some type of draft in the American Basketball League. A New York team chose me. I got a call from Eddie Gottlieb, and he wanted to know if I would like to play for the SPHAS. I told him I would if he could work it out. He arranged it, and I went to the SPHAS.

I enjoyed playing with the SPHAS. It was a haphazard league, and players were paid on a per game basis. With the SPHAS, it was a stable situation. If you got hurt, you would get paid. Eddie was very understanding.

One incident I remember as a player occurred in Wilmington, Delaware. It was quite a rivalry between the SPHAS and Wilmington, although I didn't know what created it. It was a Sunday afternoon in the armory, and there was a skirmish on the court. The closest guys were wrestling with each other, and I stepped in to separate them. Some fan came out of the stands and punched me in the jaw. I had an impacted wisdom tooth and was taken to the hospital.

We sometimes played exhibition games with the Harlem [actually New York] Renaissance, an all-black team. We would have a game in Troy, New York, then the next night in Albany, New York, and then we would go to Cleveland, Ohio. They were very good. Some of them could have played in the American Basketball League. Eddie was also involved with Negro League baseball. Eddie and Bob Douglas, owner of the Rens, worked out the exhibitions. When we played in Harlem, we were the only white people in the building.

The Rens loved to make us look bad. They would put on a display of ball movement, and we would be chasing after them. Douglas would call a time-out with a minute left just to prolong the showtime.

The SPHAS played at the Broadwood Hotel. There were four or five of us from New York who were on the team, and on Saturday night we would leave New York Penn Station on a 6:00 p.m. train and it would take two hours. We arrived at Market Street in Philadelphia and would walk over to the Broadwood Hotel. It was a four- or five-block walk. The ballroom was on the second or third floor. The ballroom was where we played the game, which could seat about two thousand or three thousand people. We dressed downstairs in the health club and would take a small elevator in the back to the game. Eddie would come down and see if all the guys had come in. He had a habit of walking up to us and straightening out our jerseys. Today I can still see Eddie Gottlieb, between periods, yelling at us, "Give me a period."

We would play the ball game, and at halftime the stage would be set up for music and dancing. Behind the stage there was a dressing room, and he [Gottlieb] would talk to us there during the half. Dave Zinkoff was the announcer. We would stay over at the Broadwood Hotel, and the following day we would drive to Wilmington for the next game. His parents [Zinkoff's] owned a deli, and we would stop and pick up food for the trip.

I heard about some of the antisemitism the team faced when they traveled to the Midwest. In the early years they had *Hebrew* printed on their jerseys. They were an easy mark in places like Ohio and Indiana.

I played for Grumman Aircraft after graduation from LIU in 1941–42 and then went into the service in 1943 and came out in 1946, after the war.

The BAA, forerunner to the NBA, was formed for the 1946 season. I was signed by the New York Knicks and captained the team that year. I scored the first two points in NBA history. It was November 1, 1946, with the New York Knicks against the Toronto Huskies in Toronto, Canada.

14. Ralph Kaplowitz starred at New York University before serving five years as a fighter pilot during World War II. Courtesy of New York University Archives, Photographic Collection.

RALPH KAPLOWITZ

- Ralph Kaplowitz grew up playing basketball on the streets of New York. After leading DeWitt Clinton High School to a city championship as a senior, he enrolled at New York University, where he played under Howard Cann. Prior to his senior year, he was drafted into the army and served five years as a fighter pilot. He flew thirteen missions in the Pacific Theater. After his discharge he joined the Philadelphia SPHAS and helped lead the team to its last American Basketball League championship. The following year he became an original member of the New York Knicks. Midway through the season he was traded to the Philadelphia Warriors and was a part of the first BAA championship.

I was born on the East Side of New York on May 18, 1919. My brother, Danny, who was two years older than I, played basketball. He wanted someone to keep him company. He forced me to go with him to the schoolyard. I did not want to play. I did not want to do anything. He stuck his finger in my ear and dragged me to the schoolyard and forced me to play with him. He taught me. Once I got interested, he did not have to worry about me anymore.

My first memories of playing basketball are in the schoolyard. I played one-on-one with my brother. He was a very good shooter, so he taught me what he knew. Ultimately, he played for DeWitt Clinton High School, and I played for the Creston Junior High School. I was only thirteen years old and was a substitute, but my team won the PSAL championship.

My parents were not concerned about me playing basketball. They were not interested, and as long as I was out of the house, it was okay.

The game of basketball was about friendships in the schoolyards. We played three-on-three. If you won with your threesome then you stayed on the court. Then another threesome came on, and you played until you lost. Then you stood on the side until it was your turn to play again. It was more social than anything. It was a bunch of kids playing a game.

I learned to play by playing. Just by being there and doing what we saw. I played at YMHAs. As I got older, there was a YMHA on Fordham Road. I played pickup games there five-on-five. That is all I remember until I got older and played in high school for DeWitt Clinton High School. I did not play in a cage. We used the two-handed set shot all the time. That is all we knew.

Basketball seemed to be a Jewish sport then. We played in the schoolyard, and I would say 90 percent of the kids were Jewish. A few were not. Lou Rossini, who was ultimately the coach of New York University, was one of the kids, and we played together.

My brother was on the DeWitt Clinton High School team, and I was able to get up to the main school after one year at the annex downtown. Because of my brother, the coach of the team was willing to look at me. I made the team at DeWitt Clinton, and we had a pretty nice team.

My senior year, we were undefeated and won the PSAL championship, and that is when I got a scholarship to New York University. Howard Cann came to our championship game, and we played against Seward Park High School. Butch Schwartz, who ultimately played for the SPHAS, was the other center on this high school team that we beat. We were friends all these years.

I played on the freshman basketball team at NYU, but I got hurt and tore the cartilage in my knee, and I missed most of the season. The NYU team was pretty good, but they had a mediocre season. So, when I was a sophomore, I was the only member of the freshman team that Howard Cann moved up to the varsity. So I was on the first team, and we had a very good season. We won eighteen games in a row mainly because of me. It was a mediocre team that I joined, so I was what they called a sophomore sensation. We lost the last game to the City College of New York; otherwise we would have had a perfect season.

The following year Bobby Lewis, who was an excellent ballplayer the previous season, graduated and so did some of the other players. So I was left as the fulcrum of the new NYU team. We had a mediocre season. From there, unfortunately, my senior year we went to war in Europe. There was a draft in my senior year. I was drafted into the U.S. Army on August 13, 1941. I spent five years in the army. I became a fighter pilot flying P-47 planes with single engines. I flew thirteen missions in Japan.

I went to Camp Upton, New York, as a draftee. I immediately applied for the flying school. At the time, a draftee was in the service for one year, because there was no war at that stage. I wanted to get into flying, so they sent me to Jefferson Barracks, Missouri, where I would take an examination to get into the cadets. I took the examination, and I passed, so they sent me to Chanute Field, Illinois, where I went to air mechanics' school. I was waiting for them to accept me into flying school.

Meanwhile, I played on the basketball team in December 1941. I was in Chicago on a weekend when the announcement on the radio said that we were attacked at Pearl Harbor. Therefore all the soldiers—I was a private at the time—had to report back to the barracks. I went back to the barracks, and I found out more about Pearl Harbor. Meanwhile, we went about our normal duties.

I played basketball at Chanute Field with a bunch of All-American ballplayers, like Bill Hapac from the University of Illinois. We were undefeated in the six games that I played with them before I got called to go to cadet school to take up flying.

I went to cadet school, but on the way there we had a game with Chanute Field against Scott Field, another team in the air corps. The fellows said to me, "Before you go and are on your way, we are making you the captain of the team." I scored thirty-seven points, and I did not miss a shot. That was my going-away present. Then I got on the train and went to Kelly Field, Texas, where I had six weeks of preliminary training.

We went to school to learn code, navigation, nothing to do

with actually flying. Consequently, I went to Fort Worth, Texas, for primary flying school. This was three months primary, three month[s] basic, and three months advanced. In flying school primary, you had light airplanes where you learned to fly. So we flew in the morning. In the afternoon we went to classes. In the second half, we flew in the afternoon and went to classes in the morning.

I used to get airsick in the airplane, so the instructor would bank the airplane to one side for me to heave. Fortunately, he was in the front, and I was in the back, so when I threw up in the back it went elsewhere and not to him. After we finished, I would be all right for a while. We would do some maneuvers. My instructor realized I was a good learner and I was a good pilot, so he did not report me. He said that if you threw up, they washed you out. But he did not say anything. Ultimately, I got used to it, and I did not throw up anymore.

One day when I was soloing, I used to fool around in the airplane, like flying too low when I was not supposed to. By the way, I was the first in my class to solo after eight hours of instruction. If I were caught, then they would throw me out. I was caught. When I came back to the field the instructor who caught me came up to me and told me to go back to the barracks because you are finished. I went back to the barracks. I got a phone call from my instructor, who said to me, "Kaplowitz, you stupid fool, get your ass down here." I talked him out of it, but he said that I would need to take a flight test with the lieutenant. It was a civilian flight school, so they had a lieutenant in charge.

The next day I went up with the lieutenant, and I was in the backseat, and he had me do all the maneuvers. I thought I did well. When we landed, I went up to the front of the wing, and he was still in the cockpit. I could see that he had a big F on the charts. I had failed. He said to me, "Maybe it is not your fault. Maybe your instructor was not so good." I said, "Lieutenant, I cannot blame my instructor. If I am not good enough, then wash me out, and I will thank you for saving my life, because I think I am pretty good. If you do not think so, then I do not want to be any part of flying." He said, "We will see what we can do." My instructor came to me and said, "We decided to give you another chance." I said, "If I am not a good pilot I do not want to be here." He said, "We will see. We will manage." Anyways, I behaved myself for the rest of the term.

I graduated. We had a party. The guy who gave out the assignments, gave you an airplane to fly, the dispatcher, came over to me and said, "Kaplowitz, you are a good pilot. You could fly anything the air corps could give you. We pulled a shitty on you and made you worry. But do not worry anymore. You can fly, and if you pay attention, you will not have any problems." So I thanked him, and I graduated.

I went to the next phase, which was flying BT-13s. I finished and did well and graduated. Then I went to advanced flying school. At advanced, you had fast airplanes. So I did well there, and I graduated and got my wings on August 5, 1942.

I then was sent to Savannah, Georgia, where I was for the next few months. I had thirty days before Savannah. I went home and asked Norma to come to Savannah to see if she liked army life, and if so we would get married. As soon as she came I made up my mind that we would get married. A judge married us on August 29, 1942.

Meanwhile, off the base there was a Jewish family named Rosensweig. They would invite Jewish soldiers to come to their house every Friday night to have services. When she [Mrs. Rosensweig] heard that we got married by a judge, she said, "Ralph, if you have children they won't be considered Jewish unless you are married by a rabbi. I will take care of it." So she arranged a chuppah with the Jewish people. The other Jewish soldiers were witnesses. Norma and I were married a second time in October by this couple, the Rosensweigs, in Savannah, Georgia.

At Savannah, I was flying a British dive-bomber. From there we were sent to Waycross, Georgia, where I flew A36s, the forerunner of the P51. I then went to Tampa, Florida, and there I flew B39s, B61s, and the A36s. From there we went to Lakeland, Florida, and we still had A36s. I piled up flying time and was promoted to first lieutenant. After Lakeland we went to Dalhart, Texas, where we got P47s. After P47s, we went to Galveston, Texas. My wife went home with our baby daughter, and I was on my way overseas. I got my promotion to captain because I was a flight leader.

We sailed on a carrier to Hawaii. We were going to be there for three days. Every one of the pilots was rushing to get a reservation to a hotel. I made a telephone call to the hotel. I told them, "I am Captain Kaplowitz, and I just came off a carrier," so they should think I was a captain in the navy. A captain in the navy is a full colonel. A captain in the air force is only a captain. I had a reservation, and when I arrived at the hotel I came up to the desk and said I was Captain Kaplowitz. They honored my reservation, and I got a room. I took about eight or ten guys with me.

We left a few days later by carrier to go to Eniwetok [Atoll]. We tested the airplanes and then we went to Saipan. We flew to Saipan with our airplanes. From there we saw the B29[s] that ultimately flew to Tokyo, Japan, and back. We saw them taking off at night and coming back the next morning. Most of them were pretty well shot up. Some of them did not come back. That is what I saw on Saipan.

From Saipan, we flew to Tinian, a small island. From Tinian, we were told we would fly to an island off Okinawa, the front lines. The time came that we were to fly the 750 miles over Iwo Jima, and a P25 would lead us because we were over water. We got into formation. I do not know how many planes, but it was a whole wing. I had my planes. I was a flight leader. I flew on somebody else until we got to Iwo Jima, which were the front lines. The planes were set down, and we were ready to go to war, which we did.

I flew my first mission, which was a fighter sweep. We had fuel tanks added to the airplane, and it was a two-hour flight to the southernmost island [of Japan], Kyushu. On the way over somebody yelled out, "Bogeys" [unidentified aircraft, presumably hostile]. The other planes immediately dropped their wing tanks. I did not because I was not sure they were bogeys. When they came closer, they were our airplanes. I still had my wing tanks, but the others did not. I had plenty of gas to get over to Japan looking for the enemy, but they never came up. Before we left the island on the way home I dropped my wing tanks on the island. Maybe I could have killed somebody. That was my first mission. I had twelve more missions.

I had a couple of close calls flying. On one flight, I was leading a flight of eight to go to Shanghai. On the way there, I tested my guns, and they would not fire. They were jammed for some reason. I did not want to report it because you had to wait several days to go on another flight. After a few hours of flying, I did not want to have to abort and go back. So I stayed without the guns. We got to Shanghai, and I saw three Japanese destroyers tied up at the docks. I called out that I am going after them, so I started dive-bombing. I got to where I felt it was the right moment, and I dropped my two five-hundred-pound bombs. I shot the middle destroyer, and it blew up in flames. I got out of there. Nobody fired at me. I reported it. Ultimately, the other flights concurred that a ship was sunk, so I received credit for sinking the Japanese destroyer. They gave me a medal. I already had two air medals. Now they gave me a third.

The other close call happened when we were passing a couple of islands that were held by the Japanese. This island was well fortified with coastal guns, which we did not know about. On the way back from every mission, my commanding officer would come by and strafe the island. I had just come by from a mission to try and locate a missing pilot. I received word to go back and try to dive-bomb the coastal guns on the corner of this island. My commanding officer was shot down between this island and the next island. He was stranded on a buoy that was in the middle of the water.

Meanwhile, those guns were shooting down seventeen American pilots who were trying to rescue this major. Unbeknownst to me, I am now going to the area that I was told from twelve thousand feet to drop the bombs at forty-five hundred feet. I go into my dive at twelve thousand feet, and my guys are going to follow me. All of a sudden, the bullets are flying by my cockpit. I look up, and I do not see anybody there. I realize that fire is coming from down below. There is a wall of fire, and I cannot get out. I cannot pull out. I am thinking that I will go the other way. By this time, I am now at eighty-five hundred feet, and I can see my altimeter going round and round. My airspeed is 550 miles an hour. There is nothing I can do. I press the button to drop the bombs and all of the sudden the firing stopped. I pull out and go out to sea and watch from there. I do not know where my other planes are. When I returned to the base, I heard that the Japanese picked up the major.

When we rescued the major he told us a story. He was picked up and taken as a prisoner of war, with his hands tied behind his back and a rope tied around his neck. He was stabbed at with sticks, and people were throwing rocks. When they finished with him, they put him on the other island in a cave where he lived with another navy pilot that was captured in the Battle of Okinawa. When we rescued him, he mentioned that he had seen so much firepower. He did not know how some of our planes lived through it. I think I was one of the planes he saw, because if they did not stop firing I would have had it. That was the worst situation that I was in while I was overseas.

The *Enola Gay* made a drop on Hiroshima on August 6. On August 9 I was leading a flight of four escorting a b24 on the island Kyushu, which is the southernmost island of Japan. I was flying back and forth over the island taking pictures of the island for the eventual invasion of Japan. Meanwhile, at the briefing that morning, they told us to stay away from the west side. I was flying escort with the b24s when they dropped the bombs on Nagasaki, but I did not know this. I looked over to the west and saw terrific clouds, which turned out to be the clouds of the atomic bomb dropped on Nagasaki. I said to myself that was the reason they kept us away, because of thunderstorms in the area. When I got back from the mission, they said over the loudspeaker that a bomb was just dropped on a Japanese island that was twenty thousand times more powerful than anything we had. At that point, I realized what it was, and I said to myself that the war is over, and I am still alive. Thank God.

The next day or two, we got into our aircrafts and heard that the Japanese were making a last-ditch stand. We got into our airplanes with the engines running, waiting to take off. When word came after a half hour, there was nobody coming, so we knew the war was over. We got out of our airplanes. The next we heard, the Japanese were coming to our island in a white airplane, a bomber painted green, and they were going to land at our field. The generals from our army were there to meet the generals from their army. They signed a treaty in Tokyo, and the war was over.

I got orders to come home in early November. We flew to Guam, and we got into a B29, and we flew to Hawaii. On the way to Hawaii, which is an overnight flight, I said to the lieutenant, "Why don't you go back and sleep, and I will fly the plane with the navigator. I will wake you up when we get to Hawaii." He said fine. He went back, and I took over, and we flew to Hawaii. The time came to land, and I woke up the lieutenant, and he came and landed the airplane. We stayed in Hawaii for a day until we got washed and showered. It was a terrific shower. I loved it.

Then we got ready to go back to the states. I did the same thing as before, and I flew, and I woke the lieutenant up, and he landed the plane. We got to the states on November 27, 1945. They made a party for us and gave us gifts, and we then left on a train for Mitchell Field [Long Island, New York]. I got checked out of the army and came home with flowers for my wife and my child, and I was home to stay.

When I came out of the service, it was the end of 1945. I got a phone call from Eddie Gottlieb, the owner and coach of the SPHAS. He invited me to a game in New York between the SPHAS and the New York Gothams at the Saint Nicholas Arena in New York. My friend Irv Davis, who I played with at NYU, was now playing on the SPHAS. My other friend Sonny Hertzberg was playing on the New York Gothams.

I came down to the game, and Eddie pulled me aside and said, "I am ready to play you tonight." I said, "No, I want to hear what you have to say." He said, "I would like you to play for me. I will pay you $150 a week whether you play two games or three games." I said, "That is okay with me." And we shook hands on the deal. He had a very good reputation as an owner and manager, and I felt we did not need a contract. His word was good from what I heard from other people, so I was content. In that game, they lost, and my friend Sonny Hertzberg scored forty points to beat them. That was terrific shooting. That was my beginning with SPHAS.

I had heard about them before I played with them. They were great players like Shikey Gotthoffer, Moe Goldman, and Red Wolfe, all terrific names. All the old-time basketball players knew about them.

I played a half season with the SPHAS. I joined them in December 1945, and the season ended in March 1946. I played half a year.

I did rather well. We won the American Basketball League championship. In the finals, we beat Baltimore. I was the most valuable player to his team, and that was the end of my playing for the Philadelphia SPHAS.

All the home games for the SPHAS were in the Broadwood Hotel. It was on the third floor where they had these games. It was a game and a dance. We used to play three, fifteen-minute periods. In between periods, the people would come on the floor and have their dance. After the game, they danced as well. We played all our home games every Saturday night. The New York players, like me, Jerry Fleishman, Ossie Schectman, and Butch Schwartz, would take a train from Penn Station and go down to Philadelphia to make the game. I remember going up to the third floor, getting dressed, and playing the game and going home. The place held about three thousand people, and I believe they were sold out every night.

Eddie knew a lot about basketball. He knew a lot about ballplayers. He knew good players from bad players, and he was very much a manager and a promoter. That is how he got his team. The people all loved him. I thought he was a very compassionate, honest, and sincere person. You could believe everything he told you. There was no bull. I loved him for it.

Inky Lautman was a terrific player for the SPHAS. When we played, Eddie Gottlieb used to pick on Inky Lautman a lot. We were playing a game at the Broadwood Hotel, and Eddie says to Inky during a timeout, "Inky, you are playing terribly. You are not getting the ball off the backboard. You are not clearing the ball. You are not passing the ball. You are not doing anything right. What is wrong is with you?" Inky said, "Eddie, you insulted me." Eddie said, "I would never insult you." Inky said, "You called me a horse's ass." Eddie said, "You are wrong. I never called you a horse's ass. I said you are playing like a horse's ass."

Irv Torgoff was a terrific basketball player for Long Island University. He was a terrific professional player. He played with the SPHAS before I ever got there.

Jerry Fleishman and I are buddies. We played together with the SPHAS and Philadelphia Warriors. He was a terrific scrapper, a fighter. He was always an asset to the team he played for.

Dutch Garfinkel was a passer. He could shoot as well but was known for passing the ball to the open man on the team.

Butch Schwartz and I first met when DeWitt Clinton played Seward Park High School. He was the other center against me. We played one another. He was a fighter and a scrapper and tough off the backboard.

Art Hillhouse was a 6'7" center, and he was always good at getting the ball off the backboard and helping his teammates get the ball.

Petey Rosenberg was short and a dribbler. We played together on the Philadelphia Warriors. He always came into the game to freeze the ball in the last few minutes by dribbling around so nobody could touch him, and we kept possession of the ball.

Chink Morganstine joined us in the second year with the Philadelphia Warriors. I did not know too much about him.

Cy Kaselman was Eddie's assistant coach of the SPHAS and Warriors. I never saw him play, but I heard he was a fantastic shooter, and he played with the SPHAS in the early years under Eddie Gottlieb.

Moe Goldman played for City College of New York and also for the SPHAS. I understand that he was an excellent player for the SPHAS.

Red Klotz was a little fellow that played with the SPHAS. Ultimately, he was the one who played with the Washington Generals against the Harlem Globetrotters. He played with them as a foil for the Harlem Globetrotters.

Shikey Gotthoffer was one of the great players for the SPHAS. The reputation he had was of being one of the greatest. I never saw him play. I heard a great deal about him.

Bernie Opper also played with the SPHAS. I believe he played with me with the SPHAS when I played with the team in 1945–46. I do not know too much about him. Howie and Lennie Radar played for Long Island University.

Ossie Schectman was a terrific player, a terrific shooter, and an all-around player. He played for his team. He was a terrific player to have on your team. He played team basketball.

Dave Zinkoff was the announcer for the SPHAS and also with the Warriors. I think he was a publicity man, and he announced the players for the SPHAS and Warriors.

Harry Litwack was a coach of Temple University and a great friend of Eddie Gottlieb. He used to come to all our games with the SPHAS and Warriors. He sat on the bench and maybe gave Eddie some information about the players and teams.

I believe that when you say SPHAS you have to mention Eddie Gottlieb. He was not only a promoter, but he was the sweetest person you ever wanted to meet. So when you mention the SPHAS, you mention Eddie Gottlieb in the same voice. He was the SPHAS. I believe that he once was a ballplayer himself. He eventually formed the SPHAS.

The style was teamwork, moving, passing, running, and shooting the ball. It was about making sure you were getting free of your opponents by helping your teammates, by blocking out for them, by blocking out the defense and allowing your teammates to get free as well as yourself to get free of your opponent.

The American Basketball League was the only league in existence at that time. It was comprised of other local teams—Wilkes Barre, Scranton, Baltimore, Trenton, New York, Paterson, Hartford, and Bridgeport. We used to travel by car. In addition, Eddie arranged other games as well. We played up in Troy, New York, against the New York Renaissance, which was an all-black team. I think they won 98 percent of their games.

There was one game in Troy, New York, with the SPHAS against the Rens, and it was a feature game. There were twenty seconds to go, and we were ahead by eight points. They scored a basket, and one of the players took the ball out from underneath their basket. As he threw the ball in, the Rens intercepted it, and they scored in two seconds. Now we only had a six-point lead. The same player threw the ball in, was intercepted, threw it in again, and the same thing happened. The ball was intercepted, and they scored a basket. Now we only had a two-point lead. The same player threw the ball in the third time, and they intercepted the ball and scored. Now the score was tied with ten seconds left. They scored the winning basket and won the game.

The reason I tell this story is because ultimately the basketball players of New York had a dinner honoring the owner of the Renaissance, Bob Douglas, and at the end of the dinner they asked each player to stand up and tell a story about the Rens. I stood up and told this story, and I did not want to mention whom that player was. Suddenly, Eddie Gottlieb stood up and yelled out, "That player was Irv Davis." I said, "I know, but I did not want to mention his name." Eddie remembered everything about every game that was played.

During the summer of 1946, it was rumored that a big league was being formed. By August, it came true. Ned Irish from Madison Square Garden sent me a telegram stating that a professional league is being started, and he would like me to play for his team. So I called the number, and I spoke with Fred Podesta. He offered me $4,000 for the season to play. I told him I was not interested. I figured that I could make $4,000 playing for a local team instead of the big leagues. He insisted that I speak with him. I said that "I am not ready to talk for $4,000." He said he would get back to me. The next six weeks, he called me practically twice a week to speak with me. Each time, he raised the amount. Norma was walking up and down the living room saying, "Take it. Take it." I kept saying, "Not yet. Not until I am satisfied that we settled." I told him I wanted $8,000. Before long, we settled on $6,500, but I insisted on $1,500 up front, and they agreed. I got a check for $1,500 and a contract for $5,000. Norma sat down with a sigh of relief.

When I played for the Knicks, I played in the very first game against Toronto. I scored six points. We won that game, 68–66. I felt that the coach did not know the players and did not know the game. He did not know basketball. I did not like him and neither did the other players.

During the first year of the Basketball Association of America, Toronto was not used to basketball, only hockey. They would call the jump ball a face-off, like in hockey. They probably never saw a Jew, and the Knicks were mainly a Jewish basketball team. We had Schectman, Gottlieb, Kaplowitz, and Rosenstein. Fans were yelling, not against one ballplayer, but all ballplayers, "Abe, throw the ball to Abe. Abe, throw the ball to Abe." This kept going on, which we ignored. We heard this about Saint Louis as well, but we ignored them.

I played with the Knicks for half a year. By January 1947 I got a letter from the coach that my contract was sold to the Philadelphia Warriors. Eddie was the coach, and I had to report by January 17, which I did. I started playing with Philadelphia, and I was the sixth man on the team because they had a pretty good team, with players like Joe Fulks, Howie Dallmar, George Senesky, Angelo Musi, and Art Hillhouse. The rest of the team was Petey Rosenberg, Jerry Fleishman, Matt Goukas, and Jerry Rullo. Jerry Fleishman and I were like the sixth and seventh men on the team. I used to go in for Angelo Musi to pump up the team and give them some life. Jerry and I had that role on the Warriors.

We beat the Knickerbockers in the first round and then Saint Louis. We won the championship by beating Chicago by winning four out of five games. I played in most of the games. Some games I played well, and other games I did not play so well. When it came time for the playoffs I saw lots of action, and I felt that I was really helping the team. So I did pretty well. For winning, we received $2,140 each. That was 50 percent of our salary for the year.

The next season I got a contract from Eddie for $5,000. I said, "We won the championship. I should get more. Last year I got $6,500." He said, "That is all I can afford to pay." I did not like it. I felt that $5,000 was not enough. I played that year, and my heart was not in it. I did not do too well. It was the worst season for me. As a result, when the season was up, I did not get a contract renewal, and I was out.

I spoke to Jerry Fleishman, and he said he got the same contract. He said to Eddie, "We won the championship. Why can't I get more money?" Eddie said, "Because now I own you, and I can do with you what I want." That was the contract, and that was it.

During our trips to Philadelphia, I would have a chance to talk to other players. Hank Benders was on the team. He said to me, "Ralph, you would make a good insurance man. Why don't you get in contact with Herbert Angstreich from the Equitable Life Insurance Company? All you have to do is sell one $5,000 policy, and you make enough money for a week, then you can take off and go to the beach." I said, "That sounds pretty good to me." When the season ended, I got in contact with Herbert, and he told me about the insurance business. I liked what I heard, and I signed up, and that is how I got into the insurance business, which I did for fifty-five years and did rather well.

While I was with the insurance company the first four years, I joined up with the American Basketball League. I played for the Paterson Crescents, and Ossie Schectman was on that team. I found out that my contract was sold to Hartford. So I went to Hartford and stayed with them for the next four years. I was a star. Every time I met the coach Leo Merseon of Paterson, he admitted the worst move he ever made as a coach was getting rid of me to Hartford. At Hartford, I averaged 13.9 points a game.

I also played with Bridgeport for one year, and I do not remember too much about that. At the time, I lived in Astoria, and we used to travel up to Hartford and Bridgeport every weekend. I do not remember too much about the players or the team.

As a player, I was a shooter. When I played with a team I felt you had to play as a team. You could not do it by yourself. There was passing and cutting to the basket, moving, and moving without the ball. Getting in position to get a shot off and making long shots. Doing anything that could get you free of your opponents.

15. As coach and owner of the Washington Generals, Red Klotz helped spread the game to more countries than anybody. Courtesy of the Naismith Memorial Basketball Hall of Fame.

LOUIS "RED" KLOTZ

• For more than seven decades, Red Klotz did more than anyone to promote the game globally. As the founder, owner, and coach as well as a player for the Washington Generals, Klotz traveled with the Harlem Globetrotters, serving as their foil and bringing basketball and joy to fans around the world. Once, in 1971, the Generals finally beat the Globetrotters on a last-second two-handed set shot from Klotz. He learned the game in South Philadelphia, playing in the warm-up games for the Philadelphia SPHAS before finally joining them during World War II. He later played for the 1948 Baltimore Bullets title team of the Basketball Association of America.

I grew up in South Philadelphia, and that neighborhood was all about basketball. I lived in a Jewish area. Basketball was a sport that excited us. We were poor families, and all we needed was a pair of sneakers and ball and pair of shorts. You could play soccer or basketball. I got interested when I was ten years old, and I never stopped.

The game was for poor people. So we played basketball, from morning to night. We played it right. We played fundamental smart basketball.

Everything was outdoors then. You did not have indoor courts then. We played outdoors from morning to night as long as the weather was right. I watched the better players, and you learned from observation. Then you would practice what you saw, and that is how I learned. It paid off.

My parents did not even know I was playing basketball. I had to sneak out of the house. I would drop my bag out the back window and get on the trolley and get off at Fifth and Bainbridge. [At] Fifth and Bainbridge [we] played in a cage, the ceiling was low, and you had to shoot the ball right between the ceilings to get it in. While we were playing if you got pushed into the cage you bounced off and kept playing. That was the beginning of playing in the cage. We played at Fifth and Bainbridge, and we learned a lot by playing in the cage. I could shoot that ball.

In high school, I was the best player in the city. I was a little Archibald of Philadelphia. I was probably one of the first point guards. They did not have point guards, but if you had put a finger on me and say point guard, I had fifteen assists and fifteen points. I was happy to set everybody up, and we beat everybody. We won city championship after championship.

I was supposed to go to Temple University for college, but they had a racial quota. I had to wait for Mendy Snyder to graduate. They wanted me to go to Brown Prep, that was like a pre-college, and in my case it was a stall. My best friend, Chuck Drissen, who was a great star, went to Villanova. He was a great player for Germantown, and he said, "Come over here. Coach Al Severance would love to have you." So I went over there, and we were heroes at Villanova. We were the only two Jewish players in the whole university, I think.

Eddie Gottlieb started the SPHAS with Hughie Black and Harry Passon. There was a Passon Sporting Goods in Philadelphia. These three men started the SPHAS, and gradually Gottlieb took over. Eddie played on the SPHAS in 1918.

I played preliminary games with the SPHAS Reserves before the SPHAS would play. While I was in high school at South Philadelphia High School, I was playing for this team on the side that played preliminary games to the SPHAS. Before that I played with a midget team called the Outlaws, who played exhibitions in the ballroom where the SPHAS played. We were a smart little team, and nobody could beat us for our age and height.

The SPHAS were the Los Angeles Lakers of the day in Philadelphia. Philadelphia played in the American Basketball League, which was the equivalent of the NBA today. We had Cy Kaselman and a lot of Philadelphia players. We had Ralph Kaplowitz from New York, Irv Torgoff, and Butch Schwartz. These two cities, New York and Philadelphia, mixed to form the SPHAS. The SPHAS won championship after championship in the American Basketball League.

We played at the Broadwood Hotel at Broad Street on a ballroom floor with a balcony. On the weekend, it was a social night. It was a nice hotel with a good health club and nice ballroom, where we used to play our games. People came dressed on the weekends to see the games. One of our players had his own band, Gil Fitch's band. Kitty Kallen started her career with that band. Before the game ended, Fitch would get off and get ready for the social evening. About fifteen hundred people attended the games. It was a social evening, and a lot of guys met their wives there. It was enjoyable, and people came dressed properly. We were princes out there.

We won the championship before I went into the military. It was a great team. Scoring in those days was half of what it is today, maybe even less. It was a different game then. We did not have a shot clock. So you can run the clock off and win the game without even shooting if you had the lead. It was a smaller game than played today. It was a team game. We did not stress one star, even though we had them.

The team was very popular with the Jewish people, but we also had other people and gradually had non-Jews on the team. There was another Klotz on the team in 1918, Babe Klotz, and he happened to be Polish. I am not, but we have the same name.

For a while, we were all Jewish. It was not that Eddie Gottlieb wanted all Jewish players, but it just so happened that they were the best players of the time.

He was a tough coach. You would not want to be in halftime listening to what he had to say. He was a fundamental, smart coach, but he was strict, and if you made a mistake you were in trouble. In those days, the ball moved around. It would not hit the ground unless you were going to drive. The movements were smart; there were picks and blocks.

Eddie liked New York players. They were smart too. He had

some great players. Dutch Garfinkel was a great player. He was good all around—defense, offense, and team player. He is one of the all-time greats to me. That is the type of player that belongs in the Hall of Fame.

Cy Kaselman and Petey Rosenberg were great players. I played with them. I was the youngest player on the team. We had a fellow on the team, Red Wolfe from New York, who later coached in a New York college. He was the oldest redhead on the team, and I was the youngest. Eddie kept that group together for years, and to get on that team you had to prove it. I did. I proved I belonged on that team, and gradually I became part of that team.

Rosenberg had a great hook shot and was a smart player. I played with him in the military, and he was a dear friend of mine. Kaselman had one of the greatest three-point shots that ever was. He would shoot it a mile in the sky, and it was beautiful to watch. He could shoot that thing. Red Rosan was a great driving type of player, and he played for Temple. Si Boardman was another great set shooter–type of player from New York. Ralph Kaplowitz was a great player. Butch Schwartz and Irv Davis were from New York.

Harry Litwack was my idol as a player. As a kid, he was the player I watched on the SPHAS all the time. He was my man, and he became a great teacher and coach at Temple. His style of play is not lost today.

The uniforms were red and blue and patriotic. They were very colorful uniforms. Eddie was ahead of his time. To play for the SPHAS in Philadelphia before the NBA was the tops. You could not get any better than that. There was no money to be made, by the way. Eddie did not pay much. Nobody paid much in those days.

We were paid by the game in those days. You did not need a contract with Eddie. He had a reputation, and he did not owe anybody anything. He did not pay much, but he did not owe anybody anything.

We traveled in a car with a floor in the back. Dave Zinkoff was lying on the floor. He graduated from Temple University and became a great announcer. Dave did a lot of good work for basketball and charities. Dave Zinkoff was the publicity man. He used to put out a paper, and when I first turned pro I was in his paper. He was a great guy.

The SPHAS played against New York teams, and most of the players were Jewish. The Jersey Reds were a great team. The team in Paterson [New Jersey] was good. We used to play in lots of armories. Madison Square Garden was the place to play, and if you played there you hit the top. There were no teams out in the West. That came about later.

When the team was on the road, it faced some antisemitism, but you still have it today. It hasn't left yet. We had fights in the armories at different places occasionally. The audience was on top of you in places, and they would throw things at you. They would call you names. We got even with them by beating them good on the court. You had to keep a deaf ear, otherwise you would be in fights all the time.

Basketball was not the biggest thing then with the press, but we did have a column and box scores. We were news. There was the *Philadelphia Ledger*, *Philadelphia Inquirer*, *Philadelphia Record*, and *Philadelphia Daily News*. They covered the team. The *Jewish Exponent* always had nice stories. We were their heroes. The *Philadelphia Bulletin* had Bill Dallas as a writer.

I was in the military for a few years, and my commissioned officer was Cy Kaselman. He played for the SPHAS and was a great star. We had Petey Rosenberg, who played for the SPHAS and for the BAA champion Philadelphia Warriors. I was stationed in Las Vegas, New Mexico. It was Camp Luna, air transport command. We had a very good team and played all around New Mexico and Arizona and Texas until they shipped us overseas. After the war I returned to the SPHAS and became player/coach, and I took them everywhere until I formed my own team, the Washington Generals.

The BAA formed in 1946. Eddie had the first franchise in the BAA with Philadelphia. They were the Warriors. I took the SPHAS on exhibitions against the Globetrotters. I first went to try out for the Boston Celtics, and they had a full group. So I went over to the Baltimore Bullets, and we beat the Warriors for the title in 1948.

There were a lot of American Basketball League players who played in the BAA that first year. Ossie Schectman, who I played with, became one of the first players with the New York Knickerbockers. Ralph Kaplowitz, who was a great star playing with us, played with the Philadelphia Warriors and won a championship. Petey Rosenberg was on that Warriors team that won the championship. Cy Kaselman was a coach on that Warrior team with Eddie Gottlieb.

In 1952–53 I formed the Washington Generals. Abe Saperstein asked me to form a team because when I took the SPHAS out on exhibition, I was beating the heck out of the Globetrotters. He knew that was the type of opposition he needed to tour all over the world. The teams they were playing were local, and they were not good enough competition. After I formed my own team, I turned the SPHAS over to one of my players, Pete Monska, who continued to coach the team for another year or two until it disbanded. There is no truth to the rumor that Eddie Gottlieb sold me the SPHAS. Whoever had that story and how it got out I have never known. Eddie Gottlieb took the team with him when he left this earth.

The new generation does not know about the SPHAS. The older generation knows about the SPHAS. Once in a while when there is a story about Eddie Gottlieb, the SPHAS is revived a bit, and it makes people think that there is more to basketball than the NBA.

A group of players from Kansas City contacted me and wanted to use the SPHAS name in honor of the Philadelphia SPHAS. It is an all-Jewish team in Kansas City. I helped them out, and they have a team called the SPHAS. They knew about the SPHAS, and I sent them information about the SPHAS. They were attracted to the Jewish history of the SPHAS.

Eddie Gottlieb was not only one of the top people in the country for basketball, he was also one of the originators of the NBA. He should have been the first president [of the NBA], but it was a hockey man, Maurice Podoloff, who did not know anything, and Eddie was coaching him. Eddie made the schedule for the NBA for almost twenty years with no computer. That is how brilliant he was. You could not win an argument with Eddie Gottlieb.

People don't know, but the NBA was a failure for a lot of years. We kept them alive for years as we toured with the Harlem Globetrotters. They were begging us for doubleheaders. We played for Eddie and Philadelphia and then for Ben Kerner in Saint Louis. They needed that money to stay alive. They lost franchise after franchise after franchise for years before they made it to the age of television. That goes for baseball as well.

By the way, Eddie had a black baseball team in Philadelphia, and Saperstein had a black baseball team in Chicago. They were very successful. They were a big help with blacks and sports. Abe continued on with the Globetrotters.

We were playing the game and playing it right. The fundamentals you see played today are the same fundamentals that we played with, only we played it right. Today it is superstars, and the European teams are getting better than our teams because they are running it by the book.

We played so many years overseas that we introduced basketball to a lot of the world. We carried our own baskets and plywood floors. They did not even have them in those countries. We played in bullrings and soccer fields, wherever we could put the court down. The people loved it, and gradually each year the kids started playing. When we first started there was nothing but kicking the soccer ball around. They are still kicking it around, and soccer is still the top sport in the world, but now if you go there are baskets hanging everywhere. They love basketball. They have had American coaches, and the right ones. They learned the fundamentals, and we gave clinics for years. We played all around the world, including China right to Japan and Korea. We played everywhere. What you see coming into the N B A today, a hundred players from overseas playing solid, fundamental basketball.

It all started with players like the s p h a s. Then it went to the West Coast with Hank Luisetti from Stanford, who introduced the new style of basketball, the one-handed shot. He introduced back dribbling. He sensationalized the East, and he came and played against Temple University, who were the national champions that year. Temple had beaten them in Philadelphia in a tight game. He played against Long Island University in Madison Square Garden, and he scored fifty points. He dribbled behind his back and was taking one-handed shots. The whole country from that point on came on. Later you had Jerry West taking jump shots. That was unstoppable. Basketball was born with people like Eddie Gottlieb and Clair Bee. Ned Irish and Walter Brown made it go, but the hard way.

16. A referee, Norm Drucker eventually was the supervisor of officials for the NBA. Courtesy of the Naismith Memorial Basketball Hall of Fame.

NORM DRUCKER

- A Brooklyn product who starred at Erasmus High School, Norm Drucker enrolled at City College of New York, where he played for Nat Holman. Drucker teamed with Red Holzman and Sonny Hertzberg to form several strong Beaver squads, including the 1942 team that made it to the National Invitation Tournament. After serving in the U.S. Army, Drucker joined the American Basketball League before embarking on a notable career as a referee. He refereed on the college and professional levels and later became the N B A's supervisor of officials. He also worked in the New York City school system.

I got involved in the local community centers playing ball, lots of ball. I played for Erasmus High School for a coach by the name of Al Badain, who is still around. I still see him. After high school, I went to City College of New York through a man named Bobby Sands, who became the assistant coach at City College. At that time, I wasn't even thinking of going to college. Mostly, kids in my neighborhood did not go to college. But I did go, and I played for Nat Holman. I went to City College in 1940, played for Nat Holman on the 1941–42 team when we were in the National Invitation Tournament. That was Red Holzman's last year, and it was a good team. Then Holzman left, and the following year I played on a team that was not that good. We did not have any power or big men. Then I went into the service in February 1943 before the end of the season. I spent about thirty-six to forty months in the army and overseas in Europe. Then I came back to school, assuming that I was going to go back, which I did. I was playing ball for Nat Holman, but by that time I had been married and nearly four years in the army, and I could not take Nat Holman. I am not saying anything bad about the man, but the way he exacted discipline and his way of doing things, after being four years in the army, I realized I was no more a student. I was a man. So I went and played in the American Basketball League. I played with Trenton, Troy, and Elizabeth.

At that time I was playing guard. I'm 5'11", and in those days I was considered big. I was not a great ballplayer, but 5'11" was a good size. I graduated and went into the city school system. I played basketball until about 1950, and then I started refereeing. I went into the school system about 1949. I started refereeing in my last year of playing, just boys' club games and things of that nature. I just had an affinity for it. I felt I liked it, and I was good at it. I refereed in 1950. I got into colleges, did not do big games, but some games in 1950–51. Then I went into the old American Basketball League, and Matty Begovich, who was on the St. John's Wonder Five, an all-timer, who was the supervisor of officials, he said, "Why don't you come in and see if you can handle the pro games?" Well, it was rather difficult because I knew some of the ballplayers.

When you referee, you really should not know them. It worked out, and in 1953 I got to know a man by the name of Haskell Cohen, who was the publicity director of the old NBA. I call it "old" because it had a name change. It was the Basketball Association of America, and then it became the National Basketball Association. It was a change in name because they took in some of the old National Basketball League teams, teams like Rochester and Syracuse and so forth. He called me. I worked one game; it was a rather rough game. I came into the league in 1953, and I stayed there until 1968, I think. Then I went to the American Basketball Association [ABA] for seven years and came back to the NBA, refereed another year, 1975–76, and then became a supervisor in 1977 until 1981. So all in all, I was in pro basketball from 1953 to 1981.

My first game in the NBA, I was teaching at a school in Brooklyn. Haskell Cohen needed an official in Baltimore, and this was like at 2:30, and I get a call from Maurice Podoloff. I thought it was a gag, but in those days, the commissioner did a lot of things. Today a commissioner has a big office and does only the important things. I answered the phone with some smart remark, like "This is Pat Kennedy," who was then the big-name referee of the time, and when he spoke, I realized it was Mr. Podoloff. He said, "We have a problem. Could you get to Baltimore for an 8:00 game?" I never refereed in the pros. I had heard stories, how tough it was, you do not blow the whistle. I said, "Yes, I could." I made a train, got to the game, got dressed, and was waiting in the locker room. The other official never showed up. At five minutes to 8:00 p.m., they forced me to go down, and I was talking to the captains. In those days they had two player captains for each team; one was Chick Reiser, player-coach for Baltimore, who was a vicious ballplayer. The other one was Al Cervi, one of the toughest ballplayers I ever saw. I think he matched Chick Reiser in being nasty.

We were out in the center court, and they recognized the fact that I had never refereed a game. I was going to do the game by myself, that's how stupid I was, because the other fellow didn't show up. The other official comes tearing in and takes off his coat. He was already dressed and puts the coat down. His name was Max DiBachi, an old-timer. We shake hands, showing everyone that we do not know each other. He introduces himself. He says to me, "Is this your first game?" I said, "Yeah." He said, "Let them play," which means do not blow the whistle too much. We let them play. There were bloody noses, guys bruised, and guys on the floor. He got very angry in the second half. He said, "Okay, they want to play this way. Let's call it tight." We called a tight game. I do not have to tell you what happened. End of the game, he once again goes right to the scorer's table, puts on his coat, and leaves. I had to fight my way upstairs. That was my introduction to NBA basketball.

Over the years, things were good. That was like 1952. I came back at the end of the 1953 season. I did not start the season; it was around January or February. They must have lost officials or dropped them, and they brought me in. I was a regular from then until I left to go to the ABA. Each and every referee had another job. There was no way you could live on being a referee. The league was made up of that, too, coaches and players had other jobs. This is a carryover, the psychology of the old American Basketball League, where you supplemented your job playing ball on weekends or evenings. I was in the school system, and then I worked for the Office of Continuing Education, which permitted me to take off more time during the winter because I worked summers. Mendy Rudolph sold time for GNTV of Chicago. Arnie Heft was in real estate. Jim Duffy was a car salesman. Earl Strom worked for General Electric. It went on and on.

We worked around the main jobs, as the games were primarily on weekends, and also most all the teams were in the East. When I went in the league, there were only eight teams, so New York, Baltimore, Philadelphia, Boston, and Fort Wayne [Indiana] was the Wild West. Traveling was easy. We worked a game in Boston on Saturday night and in New York on Sunday night. Wherever you were, you could get home in three to four hours. They paid you by the game, and if you got hurt you did not get paid unless Mr. Podoloff thought you deserved it and gave it to you. I think everybody started at forty dollars a game, and every year that you came back you got an automatic five-dollar raise. Expenses were on the side. Of course, today referees would laugh at those expenses. For a while we had to hand in exactly our expenses so you would put down lunch, $1.25; dinner, $3.20; cab to airport, $1.30. Then they changed it later on where you got ten dollars a day for meals, do what you want with the money. A funny anecdote, after my third year in the league I was making fifty dollars [a game]. I knew I was going to get an automatic five-dollar raise, so I thought maybe I should be getting a little more. So I called and asked to see Mr. Podoloff. He was about 5'1", short, rotund, wore big red suspenders, spoke very well, and he sat behind a desk that magnified his smallness. That desk must have been about six feet by three feet, rectangular. When he sat down, his head just looked over the top of the desk. You constantly had to look to see if he was there. I got to know later on that although his outside veneer was brusque, he was rather soft inside. Anyways, he says, "Okay, what is on your mind?" No informality, you're doing a good job, nothing. I said, "I know I'm up for a five-dollar raise and with all my great financial expenses; I'd like a ten-dollar raise." Of course, in those days there was not a lot of money. With that, he pounds the desk, stands up, and said, "Are you trying to bankrupt the NBA?" Today it seems so funny. I said, "No." He said, "You'll have to get the same as everyone else." I walked out thinking I did not get it. However, in my check, I got the ten-dollar raise, so that was my first negotiation session.

There were two games a week. In those days, to save money I would assume, the teams played back-to-back games. In other words, Boston would play New York on a Saturday night, and they would go back for a Sunday night game in Boston. The referees were the two same referees most of the time, so they saved money on traveling for the teams and the referees. There was a common practice in those days; you had the same two referees. Generally, the policy was to try not to travel with the teams, but you were constantly thrown into the same traveling mode as the teams. By that I mean if there was a train leaving Penn Station at 11:20 p.m., that was it, you would get on that train. Then, if you ran to get a sandwich in the club car before they closed, the ballplayers would be there, and you would be there.

We would take the Empire to Rochester in the morning, and if you had a game in Rochester Friday night, on Saturday night you had a game in Syracuse. They'd make them very close. So if New York was going up there, they were on that train, so invariably you kept being thrown in with the same players of each team. I think you got to know them much better. I'm not saying it's good, but the mere fact that ballplayers played for longer stretches of time than I guess today, and today with twenty some odd teams in the league, you do not see the same teams more than once or twice a month. Yes, I socialized. We did not go out with them, but it was on the train. Referees used to tell me, we would stay at the same hotels, and at night after the game we would be down in the bar having a drink, and the coach and the ballplayers were there too. So today you cannot do that. When I was a supervisor, it was forbidden to stay at the same hotel, forbidden to socialize, so that has completely changed. In many ways I think it is good, but as you analyze it, the fact that nearly everyone had an avocation in basketball, there was not the same kind of pressures they have today, and also the kind of big money problems.

I followed the NBA from its inception. However, I went into it in 1953. When I left in 1968 to go to the ABA, I had worked fourteen years in the NBA. I saw the beginning of changes, the inception of the bigger, faster ballplayer, and the changeover in shooting, and of course today it is up to about 50 percent. At one time in the NBA 33–34 percent was considered pretty good. No doubt they did not keep as good records. Sonny Hertzberg was a teammate of mine. He could be correct. There is no doubt the shooters are better today. It has become an art. I could really say it is even becoming a science.

Baseball is an enigma. As you sit back and recognize the fact that you can compare a ballplayer that played in 1930 and in 1980, there is very little difference really. One big difference I see in baseball is the introduction when they opened up the color line. For some reason, the black kids are so much faster that it shows up in stolen bases, which they did not have in the old days. Catchers' records of throwing out runners are much lower than they were in the old days, but that is the one thing you have to remember. In bygone days in baseball, they were throwing out slow men, slower men. Today we've got running at an unbelievable speed. You watch a baseball game, and these teams have two or three guys that fly to second base. The comment made by a broadcaster the other night, the catcher had thrown out twenty-three of seventy-seven runners, and he is considered pretty good.

However, basketball is measured like track. That may sound crazy, but this is what I mean. In track, you can really see who is faster, 2.3, 2.1. You can see what happened in the mile. When I was a kid, they all spoke about Glenn Cunningham [who set the world record for the mile at 4:06.8 in 1934]. Kids had their sights on that. Today they run a mile and losers come in under four minutes. We went from 33 percent good shooting to 48 percent good shooting. That is unbelievable. Everything else has become rebounding, if they could measure it that way. Who we thought were good rebounders, Harry Gallatin, Nat [Sweetwater] Clifton, these fellows, they could not get three rebounds a game today. You can see what has really happened to the game if you measure it that way. It is a totally different game. The twenty-four-second rule was not in when I started. Guys like Al Cervi helped make it. He could freeze the ball by himself, ten minutes at a time. There were teams proficient at that. You can imagine how boring it was to see a team leading by eight points, maintain eight points, and with eight minutes to go they would start freezing the ball.

We had doubleheaders at Madison Square Garden, fifteen hundred people, so that is not good. The game was boring, although it was a very artistic game that was played. They tried many different things. One year we had a jump ball after every basket in the last five minutes. You had to line up with the same ballplayer that was your man. The last five minutes took forty minutes. Can you imagine getting everyone together, lining men up? What they were trying to do was after each jump ball give the losing team a penalty to get the ball again. At that time, they thought that would be a good idea. There was a little more excitement because the losing team got the ball back. But a jump ball after every basket, I do not have to tell you. That went by the boards. Then they tried fouling in the last two or three minutes and getting the ball back. It was good because it stopped the fouling. They had the deliberate foul rule, which gave them the ball back. They tried all these band-aid things that did not work out. Now they tried to see if there could be a clock. I will tell you one thing; I only refereed in college two or three years. The pros, being like a business, do not have the problems that colleges have. When they think they have to make an improvement, they meet in a room and they make it tomorrow morning. So they knew they had a problem and a way to make the ball change from team to team, and they met. They said a clock. They had a scrimmage at some point, and Danny Biasone and some of the other men, and they timed the amount of time it took teams to score. In those days, it was about sixteen seconds, which was the average. There was no scientific way of dealing with the twenty-four-second clock. They said to let us add eight seconds and make it twenty-four, and that is how twenty-four came in. It, in my estimation, saved professional basketball.

Games became more exciting, and not only that, the teams losing had a built-in psychological advantage. The team that is winning, especially the first few years, they still remembered freezing the ball. They tried freezing the ball for twenty seconds. In Boston they put that strategy to rest. If you wait twenty, nineteen, eighteen seconds to use up that time, you are taking a bad shot in the last four seconds. You must get your good shot and take it whenever it comes. Boston played that way for many years. They played like they were losing the game all the time. I think the clock is a built-in advantage for the losing team.

When I started refereeing in 1953, I kept myself in good shape because we ran five or six miles a night. The game changed. It became faster only by the fact that the ball was changing hands so much faster. With the advent of the very fast ballplayers, the changing, the total speed up and down the court, a referee had to be in pretty good shape. As you become more experienced, you learn tricks that saved some of your running. It does not mean you are necessarily out of shape. It means you are in better shape, really.

When I was supervisor, no referee saw a team more than six or seven times a season, so what happened was we got to know the teams. We knew what Oscar Robinson was going to do. I have always said great ballplayers, you do not know what they are going to do; only the average and good ballplayer you can really tell what they are going to do. I always felt, I never said this publicly; you have to be a good statesman to be a referee. I preferred the better teams because they ran, and there were less crazy fouls. You get the poorer teams, like one year Minneapolis was down, and Detroit, and you get two poor teams playing, we used to say it was like a bar-room brawl, everybody jumping on each other, tripping, not deliberately, but not getting out of each other's way. Good teams, they played hard, ran the court well, so it was much easier to referee a good game produced by good teams than two average teams that may play a good game, but they had a lot of problems.

With the advent of teams coming in like Minneapolis, they had a rough, tough team one year. They had guys like Dick Schnittker, who played for Minneapolis, a rough character, and that was his image. We did not allow him more roughness than he deserved.

My reaction, by our training, everybody would start off at the same level. He will have to demonstrate. That is important. As a fan, you can see that. The reason you are out there is to have this professionalism. Any guy that gives you a hard time, you may dislike him, and subconsciously if you dislike him it may show up in your calls.

It is common knowledge, one player, who since retired, we see each other, and we are friendly. I have gotten to know he is different, Rick Barry. We had constant problems, not that I thought I was creating, but it was his way of doing things to win. Red Auerbach as a coach was the same way. I felt that he was trying to browbeat every referee to get an edge, and I was not going to let him do it. Some of the other officials felt the same way. Did that spill over? I do not know. At the time, I thought not, and hopefully I was good enough professionally not to let it.

The problem in those days was security. No team had security. You got on and off the court yourself. Later on, about 1966–67, we had a lot of problems. The league put out a rule that you had to have somebody take the referees on or off the court in a security-type uniform. I remember in Saint Louis, the man in charge of taking us on and off must have been about eighty years old. An old ticket taker they had no job for so they put him in charge. You can imagine what type of security that was. We used to say to him, "Here, sit in the locker room." We used to leave the beer they brought us and say, "We will be back."

There were many, many incidents. I do not know if they are recorded. Syracuse was a constant battle getting on and off the court. Boston, one night, Earl Strom and I had a real thing with the fans coming off with a fistfight. In Los Angeles, when they first got there, the fans were pretty raucous. Mendy Rudolph in Cincinnati, getting off the floor, had to go through the stands. They had about twelve rows of loge seats right against the court, and the teams and referees had to go through these rows to get to the locker rooms. You go through twelve rows of angry fans, and we had incidents. This was common all over the league. It was a common practice that referees would go off the court, take off their belts and wrap them around their hands, and leave the belt buckle out in case some guy came at you. That was a common practice. I recall in Syracuse, they had a guy named "the Strangler." I was not there that night, but the Strangler roamed all over the place. Some of the courts had fans about a foot off the sidelines. Today they at least move them back some. Sid Borge had a fistfight in Syracuse. Anyway, the Strangler, I understand he attempted to strangle a referee, that is where he got his name. Boston and Syracuse were playing in Syracuse, and Boston was well hated in Syracuse. The Strangler was doing more and crazier things, now rather close to the Boston huddle, screaming at the Boston players, and as the story goes, Jim Loscutoff grabbed him and brought him into the huddle, and they took a couple shots at him. He came up bleeding from the eye. This is the story. I just played golf with Loscutoff. He has gotten bigger and gained about sixty pounds.

We had run-ins in Los Angeles, Boston, and several in Fort Wayne. The fans were tough. It is identification with the team, and they are there to protect them from you. That is one of the reasons referees became so well known in those days. Not only were we in the same city ten to twelve times, but there was raucous behavior of the fans. Many times we had arenas where they used to shake the back of the basket. One night going off the court in Philadelphia a guy came at us. Earl Strom punched him, and he broke his thumb. Referees are very poor fighters. We used to complain, but nothing ever happened. After you had a relationship with the ballplayers, which you do not have today, and it was a very tough game, very difficult, one of the ballplayers would say, "Hey, walk off with the team," which would give us protection. Never a problem with a player. I had a player deliberately go to jump me, but I got out of his way and threw him out of the game. The only time it ever happened was with a player named John Briskei, who played in the ABA and NBA. He was mad and tried to run through me. He was 6'6". He was a kooky kid. He got in trouble with the police.

In the old Madison Square Garden, they used to bet in the hall. Betting goes on today, but it is more sophisticated. In those days, there were five-dollar, ten-dollar bets, and guys screaming all over the place. There has always been a gambling aspect to sports. I think the problem is making sure the players and referees and coaches are not involved in any way. I do not think they will ever stop that. Alex Groza and Butch Beard, I do not think they had a scandal in the pros; they go back to the college days. However, Groza and Beard came in as a team into the NBA. Anyways, they had a pretty good team, but they had something they were investigated for in college, and it had repercussions. They had some other repercussions in the NBA while I was there. A fellow played for Columbia [University], played for Fort Wayne, he bet on some games. He was murdered, by the way. He was Jack Molinas. He was a great ballplayer, and then it came out he bet on ball games, and he was involved with gamblers. He was in the pros, and he played for Fort Wayne. He was the kind of guy that somebody did a study with, and he was really a product of his environment. He grew up in gambling. There was one, many years ago, in 1954 or 1955, a referee was under a cloud of suspicion, but nothing ever came of it. It was a little before my time, maybe not that good of a referee. There should be awareness because a referee can no doubt influence a ball game, and I think in subtle ways. If a referee was devious or was susceptible to taking money, he could influence a game. You do not have to do it by being outrageous. Subtle things like five guys going for a rebound, picking out the guy he wants to get out of the game, a walk, a trip. They ask the referees not to go to the same bars, not to be seen with gamblers, and not to go to the tracks.

I always felt that you make your reputation by showing the ballplayers that you are fair and good. If you make a mistake, you could not help it. You do not compound a mistake by saying, "I gave you one, now I will give you one." Then they know you are weak. The history of the NBA is that weak officials do not make it. Today they have more protection. They protect their referees more, but in our day if you did not establish your reputation with the ballplayers you could not last. You do not last by saying, "That was a bad call." After thirty-four years of refereeing, I am too intelligent to tell anybody every call was correct. I like to think 95 percent were good, but there were some bad calls. Everybody saw it differently. You do not make it up. I think making it up is a product of broadcasters. There is a bad call, somewhere down the line, maybe three periods later, there is a call that looks not as good to him the other way, and right away he says "That was a make-up call." In his mind it is, but the good officials out there are not doing that. It would be a very poor official who would do that.

[The best players] on strict ability, I would say Wilt Chamberlain, Bill Russell, Bob Pettit, Oscar Robertson, Jerry West, Elgin Baylor, and then of course Kareem Abdul-Jabbar. These men performed every night. We have loads of guys, on an eighty-two-game schedule, that played forty-five great games, thirty bad games, and twenty average games. I cannot remember these men playing out of a season more than four bad games. Now that is amazing. Guys like Bob Pettit, every night he performed the same way, a phenomenal basketball player. He could not pass the ball, could not dribble. He could shoot and rebound. He could not do two of the five things, and he was unbelievable, and every single night he did it. Bill Russell did it. Wilt Chamberlain did it. He may have been the strongest human being on the basketball court I ever saw. I also think the fact that he is a nice man saved a lot of guys from physical harm. The only time I ever saw him get mad is when he chased Bob Ferry up the stairs. I saw him throw a punch. He decked Clyde Lovelette. San Francisco was playing Boston, and Lovelette was the backup for Bill Russell toward the end of his career. They were playing in Boston, a playoff game, and Clyde had been pushing Wilt around. Wilt said to him to cut it out. Of course, he is in Boston, so he is throwing his elbow. He hits him again, and with that Chamberlain says, "That is the last time I am going to tell you." Clyde went as if he may throw a punch, and Chamberlain just hit him with a shot to the jaw, and if you ever saw 280 pounds falling, he fell down, and as he is starting to get up one of his teammates said, "Clyde, take the full count." That is the only time I ever saw Chamberlain get mad.

When Nat "Sweetwater" Clifton came in, there were only a few black ballplayers. The league was predominantly white kids, a good smattering of kids who had been raised in the South. I am not trying to be a sociologist. There were antiblack feelings, even anti-North feelings. They were playing Boston, and the referee told me they had a kid named Harris, a southerner I think, and things went down. He made some comment to Clifton. At one point after a comment he looked like he was going to do battle. With that Clifton hit him, and the story is he spit out three or four teeth. With that the Boston bench starts to come after Clifton, and he says, "Let's go, come on." The whole Boston bench stopped. Nobody came to help Harris. Clifton was known for that. Nobody messed with him. Walter Dukes and Clifton played together.

Saint Louis was horrible for the black ballplayer. They accepted the black ballplayers on the Saint Louis team, very interesting. Saint Louis had really an all-white team, Bob Pettit, Cliff Hagen, and Clyde Lovelette. Detroit had Dukes and Clifton. Red Auerbach used five black ballplayers. Playing in Detroit something happened, and Clifton and Dukes went for a loose ball, and Dukes ended up in the stands, in like the first row. You would expect him to come right out. Suddenly, Dukes was fighting with a guy and all I really heard was "Don't you ever say that again," something of that nature, and with that Clifton goes to help him, and Clifton yells, Clifton's sense of humor, "You take the first row, I got the second row."

All the games sort of blend in, although I can really see every game. It was the seventh game [of the championship], Boston and Philadelphia in Philadelphia. Philadelphia had won the first three, and Boston had won one. They then tied the series, and they were coming back to Philadelphia for the seventh game. I worked that day with Mendy Rudolph, and I do not have to tell you the place was wild. The Philadelphia and Boston series was always a wild series. That was the game that Bill Russell played a great game. Everyone played a great game, but they won the game in the last few seconds, and it was just wild. Getting off the court was wild. In their wisdom, Philadelphia sold about ten thousand standing-room seats behind the basket, and that was the way we had to get out. With two seconds left to play in that game, we decided not to go the usual route. We went with the Philadelphia team around the back way. That was an outstanding game, because it was important, the big game of the year, and a lot of great ballplayers. Philadelphia had a great team. Boston, they won eleven championships.

Another game that stands out is the Los Angeles and Boston game in Los Angeles, either sixth or seventh game. I worked that with Earl Strom. I remember that game vividly because that was a big game, the place was jammed. Very interesting, the bigger the game, the referees psychologically became uplifted. Extra hours of sleep in the afternoon, get to the arena an hour early, things of that nature. So I think there is a carryover.

I was always impressed with a coach like Red Auerbach, his mode of behavior. I read his book. It seems to me he constantly tries to portray the image of how bright and intelligent he is as a coach, and to me I relate that to if somebody in my normal life kept doing that, I would be very unimpressed. I am more impressed with people who do not say things, and I find it out. He deliberately took a technical, and he relates that to winning the ball game. He says that was [the] reason he ranted and intimidated the referee, and he got the calls at the end of the game. His arm is not long enough to slap himself on the back. He says he has always done this, and I know in 90 percent of those cases it is not true. I know the referee's thinking and behavior. I am not certain I buy all this. He may have gotten away with it with one or two referees. I am not saying no. His success I do not think is related to the referees at all. When he says something like that it demeans the team. He is saying, "My team was not good enough," Cousy and all those guys, and I had a referee to help us. This is what he is saying. I never liked that, and it demeaned the sport and the league. That type of coaching I never bought. Surprisingly, most of the coaches are not like that. There are some that think if he was brilliant in that way we would have copied him. However, I daresay if you are a psychologist that type of behavior towards officials does not buy anything. It may buy you with one or two guys. I think it may have hurt him. The fact that he had a lot of talent is what made him successful. I am not knocking Red. He did a job, whether you like him personally or not. He was successful. There were a slew of coaches that impress you. This fellow in Los Angeles, the Lakers coach, Pat Riley. He is quiet, efficient, and he works. In my day, we had quiet operators like John Kundla in Minneapolis for years. He had good teams in that era.

I personally think for years the NBA had poor coaches for the fact that they thought because a man was a good ballplayer he made a good coach. If the criteria for being a coach is being a good ballplayer, that would be okay. However, the measure of a good coach is so much more than having the ability to play basketball. In fact, I might say the reverse may be true. The very good ballplayer, by reason of his own effectiveness, cannot see how guys cannot do all the things that he did. With most of the superstars, cooperation is a lost word. They scored. They did not help anybody to score or to do anything else. They performed very well. Except for Larry Bird; he helped everyone. They did not understand cooperation, getting the maximum out of them, how to handle men.

When I came into the league that was acceptable—jumping around, screaming, and yelling. I made a decision not to do that. I was forceful when I had to make a loud call. A technique really. But that screaming, jumping, I felt it was strictly for show. A lot of ballplayers did too. A lot of ballplayers resented a Pat Kennedy or Sid Borge, who would call a foul screaming. As a ballplayer I would have resented it too. They did it, and they were unique in their own time. No one is really doing that anymore today. When I was a supervisor, we started toning that down. We wanted a game called; the official is part of the game, no bigger than any of the parts of the game. Just do the job. Each official has a personality, and they referee a certain way. When I came into the league, the principle of officiating at that time was to let them play without getting anyone killed. That is something that many officials in those days could not really fathom. In colleges, they want you to call the game, and a foul is a foul. In the pro game, if a man is driving to the basket and there is incidental contact, complete the play. It is tough for a referee until he gets the hang of that. Even today, you see plays come through where a poor referee stopped the play at the top of the key, and they start all over, but that is a big part of the game. At no time did we want it to get rough. Play itself was rough in those days.

I came back in 1976 to the NBA, but had been in the ABA, which was not as rough as the NBA. The game did not get any rougher. The reason it was rougher in the old days was there was no real speed, no jumping ability. Everything was done from the front position. It is like comparing two plodding heavyweights. They stand toe-to-toe, and all they can do is slug each other. Muhammad Ali, dancing away, jabbing, coming back. That is what basketball has become. It is like ballet. Years ago, it was stevedores. That is the best analogy I can give you. The game itself lends itself to this type of fitness.

At one time, the players were up for the TV games, no doubt about it. When we first got TV, it was a tremendous honor as an official to say you had a TV game, unheard-of. But now these kids are so sophisticated that every time they come in, the cameras are there. I think it's lost that. If a game is important, it is important. I think TV alone does not make the game. When we first started, they had a deal with ABC for fifteen games, maybe $3,000 a game. The good teams like New York and Boston did not want to play TV games because they had to be played Saturday afternoon. You get $3,000 and you would lose the revenue from a night game, so they used to sell the games to poor teams, say when Detroit was down. Poor teams used to be on five times a year, and the public was getting a horrible picture of basketball in the NBA. They did not see the good teams except maybe once or twice. That was a weakness in the league. They were in a tunnel and did not see that the end of the tunnel could be good for them. So the poorer teams were on most of the time.

We knew the owners because for the owners that was their livelihood. Danny Biasone used to sit on the bench. Eddie Gottlieb of Philadelphia, he was the owner-coach for a while. Ned Irish in New York was aloof. Fort Wayne had a guy named Zollner, lived and died with the team. Ed Turner of Saint Louis lived and died with the team. These owners identified with the team. I daresay today I do not know more than maybe two or three owners. I do not know who the other fellows are. I doubt if the present-day officials know or see them. You would meet them on the train. You would see them. If you were fifteen times in Syracuse, you saw Danny Biasone fifteen times. You knew him, and he knew you.

I had worked fourteen years in the NBA. At the end of fourteen years, we were making $140 a game. We were considered the top officials in the world, I guess, Mendy Rudolph, myself, Earl Strom, and John Baschu.

I broke in on the road. Rochester was playing, and Lester Harrison at that time was the owner, maybe coach. This was my first game in that era, 1953. They won on the road. In those days I do not know what the statistics were, but not too many teams won on the road. The first night after we won, there was a knock on the door. Lester Harrison, who did not know me, said, "What is your name? You are okay. You are going to be a good referee." Second night, he won again, unheard-of, same knock on the door, "Hey, Drucker, you are going to be some referee." About a week later I had a game in Rochester, Minneapolis playing Rochester, and this night he loses to Minneapolis in Rochester. There is a knock on the door and he says, "Drucker, forget what I told you the other two nights." That is Lester Harrison. A million stories about him, by the way. The team did not really think much of him as a coach. He had great ballplayers—Bobby Davies, Red Holzman, Fuzzy Levane, Bobby Wanzer, and Arnie Risen. When they had their huddle, part of their gag, they would go shoulder to shoulder, and they would not let him come into the huddle to speak to them. He coached. Eddie Gottlieb coached. Biasone sat on the bench. Ben Kerner sat in the front row. They were there all the time.

The best was Mendy Rudolph. He had the greatest impact from a refereeing standpoint. He was an artist. Also, Sid Borge at the beginning. Those two did the most to help the league, like Bob Cousy did in those years that nobody else will ever do.

17. Sonny Hertzberg was a player, scout, assistant coach, and television analyst for the New York Knicks. Courtesy of City College Archives Collection.

SONNY HERTZBERG

- Sonny Hertzberg had the distinction of playing in the first game for the Basketball Association of America (later the NBA) on November 1, 1946, when the New York Knicks played the Toronto Huskies in Canada. Hertzberg captained the first Knicks team. After a season with the Knicks, Hertzberg signed with the Washington Capitols where he played under a first-time coach, Red Auerbach. He then spent the next two seasons with the Boston Celtics before retiring. He stayed involved with the game long after his playing career, working as a scout and an assistant coach for the Knicks and then as a television analyst. He later enjoyed a successful career with Bear Stearns.

I went to City College of New York and played under Nat Holman. At City College I played on two metropolitan championship teams and never lost to any metropolitan team in the couple of years I played varsity ball, playing guard. I was 6' tall. My backcourt partner at the time was Red Holzman, who went into the army. In later years we played against each other. He was with the Rochester Royals. I was with the New York Knickerbockers, Washington Capitols, and the Boston Celtics in my career. In recent years, of course, he became the Knickerbockers coach. Professionally, I started while in the service in the American Basketball League, the New York entry, which was the New York Jewels. They later changed their name to the New York Gothams, and I led them in scoring I guess for five consecutive years until the BAA was organized in 1946. It was called the Basketball Association of America. The teams in the ABL were the Philadelphia SPHAS, Trenton, Wilmington, Saratoga I think, and Albany. I played weekends and evenings. Mostly weekends, sometimes there was a weekday night, depending on what city you were playing. I got fifty dollars a ball game, and we played either two or three times a week. Most of the men had jobs and probably they earned more in those years in basketball than they did in their five-day employment.

I was in the service at the time and fortunate enough to be stationed in New York, and I had permission [to play professionally]. I was married and was able to sleep at home, so after duties I had free time to do what I wanted to do. Most of the games were two or two and a half hours away, so you could get out, play the game, and come back the same evening. I didn't have to sleep over. The only time we slept over is if we played a Saturday night game in Philadelphia or Sunday afternoon game in Wilmington, and then we'd be back on Sunday night. I was fortunate enough in the service that I was off each weekend.

They didn't have the twenty-four-second clock of course, and it was a better defensive game than they play today. The men who were playing the game were all experienced college ballplayers and were not in top condition because they were working and didn't have time to practice, so there was a great deal of holding, shoving, body contact, and if you took a shot, you'd get fingers in your eyes accidentally. Also, the rules in the American Basketball League were a little bit tougher than the current rules.

There were rules at that time that you couldn't keep your back to the basket more than three seconds, so it eliminates some of the pivot playing, maneuvering. For that game, incidentally, you had to be strong physically because these fellows who were earning $150 a week playing three times would not give that sort of job up. They were going to earn more than in a regular job, so if you were a new kid in the league, you had to take your lumps, show them you could put up with everything, and if you couldn't, word spread around the league. This new kid isn't so tough. You can bang him around, so there were plenty of fistfights and you had to take care of yourself. It was good play because in order to score you had to really know basketball, every phase of the game, whereas today you're a specialist in either jump shooting or fadeaway shot or a good defensive ballplayer, terrific dribbler. In those days you had to be proficient in boxing out your man and setting up plays. You couldn't be weak on defense or else they'd take advantage of you because you could milk that ball or hold onto that ball for a minute and a half if you wanted. Here where it's twenty-four seconds, get it up and shoot, whereas they could take advantage of anybody who was a weak sister, work on him long enough until he made a bad step, crossed his feet or something of that nature, and I found that that was real tough basketball, when you finished a game you knew you had played. I think I still hold a record of a forty-minute ball game in Paterson, New Jersey. I think I scored thirty-eight points. They didn't keep statistics like they do today; if I averaged twelve to thirteen points a ball game that was a lot of points. I don't even know if I led the league in scoring. There wasn't that type of statistic. I know I led my team. For instance, there wasn't a publicity office to afford putting out that type of publication. The length of the season depended on the arenas. Sometimes they would cut it short. But I would think we averaged approximately forty to sixty ball games a season, including playoffs. As I said, it was a physical game, a slower game, yes, because you always had someone holding you or a fist in your chest, and every, shouldn't say dirty trick, but cleaver maneuver was pulled on the court.

There were a few big men, 6'7", 6'8", jumping center, a variety of sizes. But height, whether being 7' or 6' 8" was not that important because everybody knew how to box out a man. I could hold a man 6'6" out from getting a rebound. City College had a pattern offense called moving pivots; everybody was actually a pivot man. You didn't have to be 6'3", you could be 5'8" as long as you came out of the corner to set up a bounce pass coming into you or a chest pass, you were a pivot man, and it all revolved.

Depending on the arena, we'd get anywhere from two thousand to five thousand spectators in the American Basketball League. With the creation of the NBA, I guess there was an owner-arena franchise, Madison Square Garden, that owned a franchise with the Knickerbockers. Walter Brown owned the Boston Garden, and the owners owned the arenas so they weren't going out on a limb financially, they just could place the nights that were available for them. If there was no ice show or boxing match, they could fit in pro basketball. In the American Basketball League, they would rent the arenas and they were promoters, but the NBA started as an owner-arena organization, and as far as I was concerned, the first one who approached me was Washington. Red Auerbach, who was coaching Washington, just got the job in 1946, and he asked me to come down there to play for them. I had played my college ball, my high school ball, and my pro ball in New York prior to the NBA, and my wife was pregnant, and I was also involved in business after I got out of the service. I was an optician, working with my father-in-law, who was an optician, and I figured if I stayed in New York rather than traveled out of town, I could still devote time to the business, which I did. I signed with the Knickerbockers, earned less money than I would have with Washington, but I figured business came first and basketball was always a sideline. I enjoyed playing, if they didn't pay me I'd still play. I signed with the Knickerbockers the first year. I think it was $4,500 my first contract, but in discussion with Ned Irish of salary, who was president of the Garden [Madison Square Garden] at the time, in charge of basketball, he didn't know how the thing would develop and he thought I would be able to maintain my job in the optical business while playing. It just so happened that the schedule was too rough, and he promised me a bonus at the end of the year, which he fulfilled. I think $1,500, and my entire salary was $6,000. I could have got more in Washington, but I was at home, which was important to me. I was high scorer of the Knickerbockers the first year. The team went to the playoffs, we lost to Philadelphia in the semifinal round, and they won the championship in the 1946–47 season.

It was called the BAA at the time. It took several years before it changed to the NBA. The first year my coach was Neil Cohalan, who was coach of Manhattan College for some twenty-odd years I believe, and he only coached the Knickerbockers the first year. The second year, Joe Lapchick from St. Johns became the coach of the Knickerbockers, and I guess I didn't fit into his style or there was something awry there. It wasn't a trade of bodies, just money, and a waiver price of $1,000. I don't know. I went to Washington and played for Red Auerbach for two years, and we went into the finals of the playoffs against Minneapolis while I was there. I was in the top five in foul shooting in the league in two or three consecutive years.

Washington had the best record in the league the first year, although we didn't win the championship. We had the best streak going in the third year; I think 1948–49, which was recently broken by the Boston Celtics. I think we had eighteen or nineteen [wins] in a row. We had a really good ballclub, including Bob Ferrick of Santa Clara [California], who held the league percentage. I think he had the best shooting percentage in the league for a couple of years. Freddie Scolari, who also came from San Francisco and was a great scorer. Bones McKinney from Wake Forest later coached for Wake Forest. That was a big team. John Mahnken was about 6'8" or 6'9". It was a fast-moving ballclub. Auerbach as a coach was the same as he is a general manager. He recognized talent better than anybody I ever played for. I played for quite a few coaches, some of the best. Red never wasted time in being the cheerleader, never said let's go, let's fight. It was always corrective criticism: Sonny, your guy goes to the right, play him a little bit to the right. Ferrick, your guy is shooting slow, go up an extra six inches.

It was one play after the other. He saw all ten men on the court, and I think he could review the entire game when it was over, how the scoring went, where the mistakes were. If you were out there, you didn't dare take it easy because you knew Red would recognize you loafing or that you did something wrong. And I think he has that extra something that most coaches do not have. Nat Holman, my college coach, was, in my opinion, the greatest teacher. He could develop a ballplayer to do things. He would teach the game, but he would lose sight many times. He was so intent on teaching, of the balance of the court, the rebound, the scoring. Red was cognizant of everything that went on at all times, and I feel that is his claim to fame.

Joe Fulks was the first good jump shooter around. There were one-handed shooters. It started with Hank Luisetti before I started my college days. Yes, one-handed shots were used, but jump shooting was not. It was something that everybody started developing, because if you could hang a half a second longer than your opponent, you could get in closer to the basket on his way down and you could release the ball and get off an easy shot, whereas if you're both together on a set shot of a one-handed shot, it's very difficult to have an edge, so the fellow who could jump higher or hang higher and add time had a distinctive edge. I didn't even attempt it because I was fortunate enough. I was shifty enough and had enough experience that I didn't have to do that. This was mainly for the big men closer to the boards. My scoring was done in a drive or set shots from far out. Maybe I made two jump shots in my entire career, but that was maybe against Ralph Slater or somebody a head shorter, but I never attempted to develop that shot.

After two years in Washington, I was traded. They fired Red and made Bob Ferrick coach. Red went out to Tri-City and coached Davenport, Iowa; Moline; and another team. I never found out what the reason was, but he appointed Bob Ferrick as coach. Bob and I were roommates, and the thorn in Ferrick's side was that they were knocked off the first year of having the best record in the league by Chicago, who had the tallest men in the league, Charlie Halbert, West Texas State, 6'11" or 7' tall, and he dominated the boards when Washington played Chicago during the season and knocked them out of the playoffs. At that time Boston had Charlie Halbert, and during the off-season after the second year at Washington, and I was quite popular there, he traded Charlie Halbert from Boston to Washington for me. Unfortunately he made two trades, and the reason he made the trades was if he won any championship it would have been Auerbach's team. This way if he made some changes it would be Ferrick's team. He got rid of Jack Nichols, who was also on the Washington team. Washington I think wound up in last place that year, and that was the end of the Washington franchise. Washington was an hour-and-a-half plane ride from New York and Boston was the same, so it really had no effect on me. If I was going further west or something, I probably would have packed it in, but I was able to get home on off days, contribute to the optical business, and fortunately it was a family business so I came in two days a week or one day, and it was fine. Physically it meant no change as far as I was concerned. Boston was not a very good ballclub in those days. I joined Boston in the 1949–50 season after they had a very poor year the year before, and I was high scorer of that team. The coach was Doggie Julian from Holy Cross. He was not a well man and after a year he couldn't take the travel, and he retired after that season. Walter Brown, the owner, was quite a gentleman, interested in international sports, hockey, wonderful man, and he asked me about a coach, and I recommended Auerbach. I said I had played for him in Washington for two years, told him what I thought, and fortunately he got him. I don't know if I was the big influence in getting him, but I recommended and suggested Red for the job.

That year with Julian we had a pretty good team, and we improved considerably. The next year we had several ballplayers from Holy Cross who only lasted a year or so in the league. He [Julian] had his local ballplayers, who played college ball for him. The following year we had Ed McCauley join us. He was my roommate. Then there was a breakup in the league where there were three ballplayers we had to pick out of a hat. One was Max Zaslofsky, Andy Phillip, and Bob Cousy. There was a breakup, teams folded or something, and we got third choice, and we wound up with Cousy.

He was a substitute in the backcourt when we started that year. Eddie Leede played with me in the backcourt, and then Cousy got the job. He wasn't that good at the beginning. Cousy was a phenomenal passer, a great team ballplayer, but was not that good a shooter. And I think he realized that to be a 100 percent ballplayer and not a 95 percent ballplayer he had to develop his shooting. He also was a little too fancy for the pros. College ball you have one or two good defensive men against you, but in pro ball all five men are experienced. Instead of giving a man a direct pass in pro ball as we did, Cousy would get up and do a pirouette of some sort and get the ball. By the time he had the ball, the man either had someone on him or wouldn't be an easy shot, and we had to tell him to cut out the whip cream and just make it bread and butter.

He learned very quickly. He was a smart ballplayer, and he knew the game, and it was just a matter of developing with better ballplayers than he had played with in college.

He was All-American in college, and he had unusual hands. Cousy was about 6'2". The ordinary man, the wrist breaks here. I think Cousy's wrist broke up here, so he had like a dangling hand, and he had wonderful control of the ball and great peripheral vision. He could spot a free man and get a pass. Once he cut off the whip cream, and he developed into a tremendous ballplayer by the end of the first year, we had a pretty good ballclub. After ten games or so he started.

Kleggie Hermsen who played with me in Washington was on that Boston club. Bones McKinney who was with Washington was on that ballclub. Red never forgot his old ballplayers. We could pick up an experienced ballplayer, even in their last year, he could get something out of them because Red, I don't think ever looked at a box score to see who was scoring, who got most assists. He wanted five men to fit together, and if he could get something out of a ballplayer that could help the cohesion of a ballclub, he used them and gave them an extra year. We wound up in second place in the 1950–51 season, and that was a real good ballclub.

In fact someone once passed a remark about Chuck Cooper, "He's the whitest guy I know." He was a delightful guy, and married to a nurse. Coop was a scorer, but a real team ballplayer who would give you forty-eight minutes of hard play. I heard he passed away. Talking about that, unfortunately, my first Knickerbocker team, which was in 1946, Stan Stutz passed away, Tommy Burns, Leo Gottlieb, Neil Cohalan, there must have been five or six of the original eleven that are gone, which is unusual for fellows who should be in pretty good physical shape.

[The] 1950–51 [season] was my last year. My wife was now pregnant with the second child and it was not important to me. The salaries were not that much. I think I was earning $13,000 or $14,500 at the time. I was in the top 5 percent in scoring, considered one of the top echelons. Yes, there was a problem with retiring. Walter Brown had written me several letters when I told him I wasn't coming back, and he says, you Jewish ballplayers, you and Auerbach, get together, you're stubborn, and so on. I said, no, it isn't worthwhile for me to come back, and Red spoke to him and so on, and I stuck to my guns. There's another story that involved Bill Sharman coming to Boston because of my retiring. But they said I'd be at training camp, and I said I wouldn't, and they thought I was holding out for money, but I had no desire to play anymore. I had enough years, I guess five in the American Basketball League, and five here was enough. The family and I just had our fill. I was twenty-nine years old, had one of my best years with Boston. I think I scored a little over ten-point average, and the twenty-four-second clock wasn't in force at the time, so maybe you could double that because you didn't take too many shots in those days. But I decided I'd had enough, and they were stuck. They said they didn't draft backcourt men. I spoke to Auerbach about Sharman, who had started with Washington and had a very poor year, and Bill said he would probably stick to baseball, that his career was there. I said, "Why don't you offer him a contract?" He said, "No, he doesn't want to come here; he's property of Fort Wayne anyway." We had a ballplayer named Bob Kinney who originally came from Fort Wayne, and he said he was hanging his shoes up too, so Red worked some sort of a deal. He gave Fort Wayne the rights to Kinney, and Boston got the rights to Sharman, and I think Sharman called me and asked me about Boston. They offered to pay his transportation or some little extra. He wasn't getting much money. I think he was getting $6,500 in Washington. He said no, but they influenced him, and he said, "All right, I'll try it one more year." The one more year playing with Cousy, he developed into a sensational player.

So in reality I was quite instrumental in getting Auerbach involved. I hope I was, and in getting Sharman involved. That was the building of their dynasty, really, because after that Red got Bill Russell and Tommy Heinsohn and the rest of them, which lasted for many, many years.

I started to do television work at the time, and [Ned] Irish asked me to be an assistant coach [with the Knickerbockers]. I had to get permission, to get a release from Boston. They wouldn't give me my release because I was still a decent ballplayer, and they were afraid I would play. This lasted for years and years that they wouldn't give me my release, because I had stopped playing at the time, but they had given me permission to do TV work, be an assistant coach, or scout. I guess it was scout with Knickerbockers, and I did that for several years. In scouting, I was fortunate enough for the two or three years I worked for the Knickerbockers. I picked up Richie Guerin, who became All-League, and he wasn't a first choice. I also picked up Gene Shue, who also became All-League. Both became coaches, and they were not heralded ballplayers by any means, like the All-Americans who had the publicity. I think it was Holman's teaching and Auerbach's eye, and I recognized the talent and was very fortunate that nobody grabbed them before I did, and they both proved to be excellent ballplayers.

Then I did some television work. I worked with Bob Wolff, who I met in Washington when he was doing the Senators baseball games. He got an invite to come up to work for Madison Square Garden, WPIX I think, to do basketball, and he wasn't that familiar with basketball. He did some play-by-play in Washington but never did it on a big-time scale. Since I was retired and knew Bob, he asked if I would help, so I did some of the color for him and analyzed. I think I was probably the first professional ballplayer to be an announcer, and now they have it in every sport. At the beginning, I used to whisper to Bob. I wasn't on the air. He was paying me personally. Then I did some work where I did the interview at halftime, did the analysis. I enjoyed that. That had to stop because I became a partner of a New York Stock Exchange firm, and the stock exchange frowned upon it. They said I should be doing stock exchange work full-time, so I stopped that. And that was the end really of my being mixed up in basketball. The first year was very difficult.

I would go to the game, and I would be maneuvering and I'd perspire, my hands would get wet 'cause I would be inwardly making moves, watching somebody make mistakes, and so on, should have shot, should have one this and that. But that only lasted for a year. I used to give time to my local temple three nights a week for youth programs, and an occasional speaking program. I stayed with it for a good number of years, but then as my family grew my obligations changed. I had a good time, and as I said before I would have played anywhere. I didn't have to get paid. I enjoyed it.

The change from the ABL to the NBA was a big change. The ballplayers in the ABL, as I said, had jobs. They were strong and all experienced. When you came to the NBA you went to a training camp for a month or three weeks; you had to be in tip-top shape, physically. The ballplayers in the ABL could not stay with the ballplayers in the NBA; it was a much faster game. It was a cleaner game, a more youthful game. The ballplayers in the old American League, I would say the majority, never went to college. They were just tough, good pros, but when it came to the forming of the NBA, the ballplayers all had good college coaching, say 95–98 percent. Most of the ballplayers had college experience. There were very few, like Connie Simmons, I remember, who did not attend college, was a very good ballplayer in Baltimore, and there may have been one or two others, but there was quite a change physically with the athlete. The ABA to the NBA was a name change, and they dropped some teams. The play was the same. They included some of the National Basketball League teams. There was the National Basketball League at the time, which consisted of Rochester, Syracuse, Oshkosh, Sheboygan, quite a few teams, and they incorporated them into the NBA. Max Zaslofsky started with Chicago, and I played against him fifty or sixty times. He was a great ballplayer. He was offensive minded, had a good touch, was a good competitor, deceiving in his size. About 6'3", I think. There wasn't a phase of the game that he wasn't proficient in. He was court-wise. A fellow who only had one year of college experience, he was outstanding.

The guards. Max was one of the better ones. Johnny Logan started in the league. I can't remember which team he was with, he was an All-American. John was a great ballplayer. Bobby Davies was a great backcourt ballplayer. Ralph Beard became an excellent backcourt ballplayer. Shooting percentages were much lower. I don't think they kept them accurately. I don't think they had a system, where one man today will keep shots, and one man keeps rebounds. Angelo Musi of Philadelphia was a good back player. Howie Dallmar was a great ballplayer from Stanford. He must have been 6'7", but he would play like Magic Johnson of Los Angeles does today. He would bring the ball up and shoot and score, a good team ballplayer. George Mikan played for Minneapolis, and when I was with Washington we went into the finals and played a seven-game series. George was a great pivot man. I don't know whether he would do as well in today's game, because the 7' man today is much faster than George was in yesteryear. George's scoring was done on the pivot. He didn't face the basket. His back was to the basket, and he was throwing enough to ride somebody on his back and turn and make the score. He was a very good rebounder. He'd plant himself close to the keyhole, the ball would come in to him, and he would maneuver. They had an enormous team, Jim Pollard who was about 6'7" or 6'8". Vern Mikkelsen, who joined them a little later on, was as tall as George and a little more agile, so they had three good rebounders, and they dominated the league for quite some time. Freddie Scolari, from Washington, I played against the first year and then when I was traded to Boston. I played against him. He was a tough man to control.

I don't remember scores or statistics very well. I do remember the games where I had fights. They stand out. One particular game, we were playing the Knickerbockers in the playoffs. I was with Washington, and I had a phenomenal night. I think I made every field goal I attempted and every foul I attempted. I didn't miss a shot. And it wasn't that many points, maybe eighteen, twenty, or twenty-two, something like that. It was a particular night we knocked the Knickerbockers out of the playoffs, and Lapchick came over to me and said, "You're probably the biggest mistake I've ever made in basketball," and I appreciated it. That really stands out—not only for the scoring, but after leaving a team that I was high scorer, and you feel a little bit bitter because it was my best year, I lived in New York, it was a New York team, I would have loved to spend my entire career there.

But the other games that stand out, they are not where I made the foul shot when time was run out or a winning basket with no time left, that's a blur. But the fistfights and that particular game stand out. We were playing Minneapolis in Washington, and I think this was the fourth or fifth game in the playoffs, and I was having a very hard hand, and Mikan wasn't doing too well. Kleggie Hermsen was playing center or John Mahnken at the time, knocked Mikan down, and Mikan fractured his wrist. He had to play the rest of the playoffs in a cast, and it was dangerous to be throwing that around. Mikan had a friend who played with him, Whitey Skoog, who probably wouldn't have been a pro ballplayer if it wasn't for Mikan, his close friend. And we had played Minneapolis two or three years now, and Whitey Skoog was on that team. He never guarded me, he wasn't capable. He came in this game of the playoffs to guard me, and he was so pent up, upset that Mikan was hurt, that the first shot I threw at him he slapped me in the face, no foul. "Whitey, what's that for?" He said, "Mikan broke his wrist." Something like that. The second time he did the same thing, and I said, "The next time you touch me I'm going to deck you." And he did, and I decked him, and we were both fined something like $200, $300. In those days that was big money, and he was quite upset because he didn't do anything! But I've had my fights. Those days are gone.

Travel. The league had a rule, you could fly, and if your plane was cancelled you had to be able to get there by train. Many of the trips were by train. Some of the tough trips, of course, were flying to Chicago and going to Minneapolis. We'd fly there, and then have to take a train out of Chicago to Minneapolis. We had trips to Toronto, Saint Louis, Indianapolis, and many of them were by train. We would read, some would play Hearts, not much gambling, they couldn't afford much. It was storytelling time.

Most of the time we slept. We were tired, because you couldn't go cross-country in three or four hours. We didn't have jets. Those were propeller planes. Chicago was four and a half to five hours, and those were very difficult trips. We had one trip to Toronto where we played a game, we had to go to a small town in Toronto to catch a train where we had three cars pick us up and drive us to an outlying station, and the last car was the starting five because we were the last to get dressed after showers. Our car broke down. We were stuck in the mountains of Canada and had to hire cars to get out. It was an all-night affair, and we got there the next night in time for a ball game in Providence [Rhode Island]. Sandwiches, peanuts, whatever we could buy. We killed ourselves getting there. We had some bad experiences traveling, a lot of funny situations, they seem so silly because you're overtired.

Once incident, I think in Indianapolis, I was with Washington at the time, and Bones McKinney would not fly. He said, "If he'd [God] meant me to fly he'd have given me wings." That was the first time I heard that expression. We'd leave there for the game from Washington a half a day after Bones because we were [not] going by train, and on this particular evening . . . He would always get there in time. There was a meal we used to eat together, and Bones didn't make the meal. We're on the court practicing and Bones walked in with a patch over his eye and a cane. The train he was on had an accident, and the cabby he paid extra to rush him to the arena had an accident. Harrowing experience. Yes, the ballplayers were close.

On the road, we were always together, eating, movies. At home in Boston, Ed McCauley and I shared a room at a hotel and took a suite. Yes, we were quite close. We knew each other's families, and our wives would sit together at ball games. Close association. I still speak to McCauley every once in a while, and some of the old-time ballplayers, coaches, and referees. I spent the weekend with Red Auerbach and his wife, my wife, two years ago at his place in Washington. We're quite close.

The only injury I had in all the years I played was a broken nose, and I was out maybe two or three games at the time. That was an experience. We were playing at the armory, Lexington Avenue. We didn't play all games at Madison Square Garden. We must have been twenty points ahead, third quarter, winter night. I lived in Manhattan Beach with my wife at that the time, in-laws really, just married maybe two years or so, we were looking for a place. I go for a ball, and a fellow tried to kick the ball and kicked me in the nose. My wife was pregnant, sitting in the first row. And they all ran over to her instead of me. There was no doctor at the game. I had to go back to Madison Square Garden to Dr. Nardiello, the fight doctor. Here I am, no shower, my wife has a big stomach, grabbed a cab to Madison Square Garden, he says, "It's nothing, Sonny, I see these all the time," and snapped it, says, "Go over to St. Clare's Hospital, get an x-ray." It was negative.

It was a snowy, miserable night, and we had to go back to Manhattan Beach. We got on a BMT [Brooklyn-Manhattan Transit] subway. You have to see this picture. A fellow with two black eyes, broken nose, all perspired, shirt and tie open, and this woman with the big stomach, were sitting on the train. I was carrying a Knickerbocker [bag], so everybody probably assumed. But I won't forget that night. We got back to Manhattan Beach. We were a mess.

My strength was court savvy. I could set up plays. Well, Red called me his second coach on the floor. Cousy said the same thing. I could tell somebody that his man was weak here or there, capitalize on what was going on. I was a very good shooter, where my defensive men would play very close to me, and it was easy for me to get around. I wasn't fast, I was quick, and my getting around my man would cause someone an easy pass. McCauley loved me. He would say, "Drive some more instead of shooting," so his guy would come up to take me, I'd give him a bounce pass; he'd have a decent lay-up. The scoring didn't mean anything, the assist didn't mean anything, and it was the win that was most important.

The twenty-four-second clock started the year after I stopped. I think it was a great addition for the spectator. If you're brought up in a basketball environment, you can appreciate good ball handling, dribbling, passing, but 90 percent of the people go there to be entertained, and this is marvelous entertainment.

I think it's a great thing for the game to have scores of 100, 150, and the percentage of shooting [now] is phenomenal. These guys are much better scorers. The old players didn't shoot as much, and the more you shoot, the more proficient you become. Average scores when I was playing were in the eighties and nineties. Oh sure, I would have scored much more. I'd go through some games, make six or seven baskets out of nine attempts, where these fellows take that many shots in a quarter; there would be a big difference. That twenty-four-second clock is great. These fellows want to shoot, they could shoot in three seconds, and they don't need a twenty-four-second clock. They're so fast, their strides, they are down court in two seconds, and the ball goes up within five or six seconds. All they need is somebody to stand in front of their defensive man, they take one step, and the ball goes up. I always enjoyed the game.

I find ex-athletes, especially basketball players . . . this is not to pat anybody on the back. I find they're sharp, alert, they're pleasant to be with, good dispositions, they know how to lose, how to enjoy winning, don't take advantage of people.

I find it with most basketball players, I don't know how it is with other sports, maybe because their background, going to school, most getting an education, Jewish ballplayers because it's an urban sport. I would think so. As I said, I started shooting through the rungs of a ladder. There was no dribbling. Then later on in elementary school, thirteen or fourteen started high school, the schools would be open again in the evening. The ceilings were not high, you had to be a good ball handler, the trajectory of your shot was kind of low, and the New York element were all good ball handlers, dribblers, and good passers. They started this league. You asked about Jewish ballplayers, so many of them came from the East, and they were predominantly from Jewish areas. But the second year [of the BAA] we got the influx of the midwesterner and far westerner who had a physical advantage over the easterner. Bigger, faster, rangier than the Jewish ballplayer. The eight or ten that started in the league just fell by the wayside. There's no reason they shouldn't have because of the ability. No, they didn't play defense the way the eastern players did. They were physically stronger, and they relied on their strength and speed and would give more space defensively, but when they came upon an eastern ballplayer who became a better shooter, their game changed too. Once they developed better defense, the eastern ballplayer faded out of the picture. Joe Fulks was so fast, he was more interested in getting that rebound, and he didn't think a man could score. He'd let them shoot.

18. Jerry Fleishman was a member of the 1947 BAA champion
Philadelphia Warriors team. Courtesy of Bill Himmelman.

JERRY FLEISHMAN

- Growing up in New York, Jerry Fleishman learned the game of basketball with his friends in the neighborhood. Fleishman would improvise, sometimes using newspapers or rags for balls and boxes or ladders for baskets. It was a crude form of the game, but one that spurred a lifelong interest and led him to accept a scholarship to New York University. He led the Violets to the 1943 NCAA tournament. Turning professional, he joined the Philadelphia SPHAS during the war years; his play was interrupted by his war service. Notwithstanding, he helped the SPHAS capture the 1945 American Basketball League championship. With the new Basketball Association of America, Fleishman stayed in Philadelphia and helped lead the Warriors to the 1947 title.

I was born in Brooklyn on Valentine's Day, February 14, 1922. When we were growing up, we were poor kids. We did not have basketballs. We rolled up newspapers and tied them together with a cord. There were fire escapes on the building, and the lower rung had a hole there, and we threw it through the lower rung. If it went through, it was either a basket or a touchdown. That was our football and basketball.

My parents were from Europe, and they did not think basketball was something to look forward to. They said, "Jerry, don't get hurt." It was safer than football, though.

We moved from our poor neighborhood to a nicer section of town. I went to Erasmus High School. The coach was Al Badain.

One day I walked into the gym and there were twenty basketballs, and everybody was shooting. It was free shooting. So I started to shoot, and the coach says, "Let's start a game." We start the game, and someone passes me the ball, and I run with it like it is a newspaper under my arm. The coach stops and says, "You need to dribble." I said, "What is a dribble?"

My folks moved to Florida, but I stayed in Brooklyn with my sister. Coach Badain taught me everything I know about basketball and how to act socially. He was my mentor. He was a wonderful man.

At Erasmus we played against James Madison High School in Madison Square Garden. They were coached by Jammy Moskowitz. They had won thirty-six games in a row over two years. There were five high school games on a Saturday afternoon. We were the underdogs. We played well, and towards the end of the game, and they put in a basket to win. Afterward we came into the locker room, and coach was laughing and thanked us for playing so hard. He said, "The next time we play them we will win." And the next time we played them, we beat them. I had seventeen points.

I was the first ballplayer to make All-City first team in New York City in all the newspapers two times in a row. At the time, the city had eight newspapers.

I went to college at New York University. NYU in those years was like playing for the New York Yankees. I got a full scholarship, which was rare in those days. Usually, you got one year, and if you played well then you got another. I told them I would not come without a full scholarship. As a freshman, I broke all the records. On the varsity, I broke all the records. In one game at Madison Square Garden, I made ten field goals (nine in a row), which broke the record at Madison Square Garden.

I enlisted in the army in 1943 and was stationed in Fort Jackson, South Carolina. There were teams in the army then. I was also captain of the volleyball team.

Eddie Gottlieb lured me to the SPHAS after seeing me play against Penn State University. He saw my ability. He would fly me in on the weekends to play ball. In those days you were paid for each individual game.

We would play in Philadelphia on a Friday night, and there would be a game and a dance. We would stay over, and on Saturday afternoon we would play at Wilmington, Delaware, and on Saturday evening we would play against the Trenton Tigers. I got $100 a game, and that would be $300 cash for the weekend. However, if there were not that many spectators you would have to take a cut or you would not be asked back the next time.

All the players would meet every Saturday night on Track 16 at Pennsylvania Station. You would not need to remind anyone. We would get on the train and play cards until we got to Philadelphia. One time we were on a train and going to Hartford, Connecticut, and we could not get off. So finally we got off, and we took a cab from Hartford to Philadelphia. Well, Eddie wasn't too happy, but all the people waited around for the dancing at 11:00 p.m.

Eddie was a wonderful man. He stuck to his word. He would keep talking until he ran out of breath. One time we were playing in Detroit, and we lost. We are in the bathroom of the airport, and Matt Goukas says he wanted to win in the worst way. Eddie says that he wanted to win more. So Eddie locks the door, and they argue over who wanted to win more. The people in the airport had to call security because Eddie would not let anyone in the bathroom.

Dutch Garfinkel was a terrific passer. He loved to play with me. I would run without the ball, be free, and he would get me the ball. He used to call me the rabbit.

The Broadwood Hotel where the SPHAS played was a family hotel. The ballroom could hold three thousand people. It was a fine hotel for residents who lived there. It was on Broadwood Street. It did not have a big lobby. The ceilings were high for a dancing room. The baskets were removable, and we would put them away after games. There would be a dance at halftime and after games. At halftime, we asked them not to put wax on the floors. We did not want to skid on it. Three thousand people came to the games, and it was always the same 99 percent who came. Saturday night [it] was the place to meet people. The stage was good for shows. Many groupies went to the dances.

It was at Erasmus High School where I first heard of the SPHAS.

Irv Torgoff and Dutch Garfinkel would work out against us in the alumni scrimmage. They were our heroes. They were only five years older than we were.

The SPHAS were the best team in the world. We were better than the Harlem Globetrotters. There was a feeling between each one of us. Lots of the SPHAS players stood together. We played the toughest teams in the towns we went into, and we usually won. We were the same type of fellows, and we played well together. The New York players made the SPHAS the best team in the world. Our uniforms were blue and gold.

We went into towns like Oshkosh or Sheboygan in Wisconsin, and we would have the Jewish star on our jerseys, and it took courage to do that. Most people were for us because of our ability to play. Each team always had one football player who would bully us. The Jewish star on the jerseys got us into trouble. We got into fights, but we got out of them. We were proud to represent the Jews, who were supposedly the weak ones. But we could handle ourselves. We became lifelong friends with the basketball players who played with us and against us.

The war ended, and I got out of the army in 1946. Eddie called me and signed me up for a new league, the Basketball Association of America. Everyone then was a free agent. Most of my buddies signed with the New York Knicks. Abe Saperstein owned part of the Warriors. We played in the [Philadelphia] Arena or the Palestra, which was home to the University of Pennsylvania. Joe Fulks was on our team. He was an unbelievable player. We won the first BAA championship by defeating the Chicago Stags. I signed for $7,500 and got a $2,100 bonus for winning the championship. In the off-season I worked for Cedars Country Club, which was like the Catskills. Every Friday night we had basketball games, and I would get ten ballplayers to come for the weekend with their wives, and we would play some games.

My contract for the following year was $5,000. I called Eddie and told him, "I played my heart out for you, and we won the championship, and I made $7,500." He says, "But now I own you." See, in those days there were no representatives or agents like today.

We would spend a month in Hershey, Pennsylvania, or Atlantic City, New Jersey, and there would be thirty college kids trying out and trying to take your spot. I played five years and then retired. After I retired, I got a call from Joe Lapchick, the coach of the New York Knicks, who asked me to play for his team. They had lost the first two games in the playoffs against the Minneapolis Lakers. I got the okay from Eddie and Maurice Podoloff, the first commissioner of the NBA. So I played for them for two playoff games, and we lost. But I played well. They gave me a contract for 1953–54, but I went to work with my father-in-law. I had played for nineteen years, since I was fourteen years old.

In the BAA we took either propeller planes or buses to games. From Chicago, we usually took a bus to Tri-Cities, Iowa. Once we were going from Washington DC to Chicago, and there was smoke in the plane so we needed to turn around and start again. When I was with the SPHAS, we took a train from Penn Station, New York, to Broad Street in Philadelphia. We would take a cab to the arena. Then we usually rented cars to travel to Wilmington or Trenton.

When the NBA started, there were groupies in Syracuse who always knew the teams. They knew all the fellows on the teams, the hotel rooms, and they would sit in the lobby. At the games, they would sit under the basket screaming. It was difficult to shoot a foul shot.

One time we played an exhibition match at the Uline Arena in Washington DC to help raise money for the widow of Sonny Boy West, who was killed. Our team had six SPHAS and six members of the Harlem Globetrotters. In those days Uline Arena had two balconies, and the blacks had to sit upstairs. After the game we got a hotel, but they would only let the six white players stay there. We were with Nat [Sweetwater] Clifton, Marques Haynes, and Zach Clayton. So we all left and drove back to New York City that night.

After I retired from the NBA, I would play games on the weekend with Scranton of the American Basketball League. It was like a minor league, and if someone in the NBA got hurt, they would pick up a fellow for a few weeks. We had jobs and played on the weekend. It was dangerous in those days. If it was snowy in the Pocono Mountains, then you had to follow the white line carefully. Driving the bumper onto the guardrail would save us. It is not like Route 80 today.

Basketball was growing up then. The ballplayers today are much better than we were. It is a different game. We moved more without the ball.

After our playing days were over, we became part of the Retired Players Association, and everyone was like a brother. We would meet once a year either in the Bahamas or Puerto Rico, and they would have golf and tennis tournaments. I won the tennis tournament two years in a row. One year it was Dave Bing and I versus Bill Russell and Patrick Ewing. In the second year it was Jason Collins and I versus Patrick Ewing and Dave Bing. I got two beautiful watches for winning.

19. One of the NBA's first great scorers, Max Zaslofsky retired in 1956 as the third leading scorer in league history. Courtesy of Bill Himmelman.

MAX ZASLOFSKY

- A native of Brooklyn, Max Zaslofsky played one season of college basketball at St. John's before entering the newly formed Basketball Association of America. Playing for the Chicago Stags, New York Knicks, Baltimore Bullets, Milwaukee Hawks, and Fort Wayne Zollner Pistons, Zaslofsky enjoyed a successful career that saw him retire in 1956 as the NBA's third-highest scorer. An All-League player, Zaslofsky led his team to the NBA finals five times, losing out on the ultimate prize each time. He was named one of the top twenty-five players in the NBA's first twenty-five years. Most famously, when the Chicago Stags folded in 1950, his name was thrown into the dispersal draft with Bob Cousy and Andy Phillip. Zaslofsky was selected by the Knicks.

I was brought up in Brooklyn, Brownsville. It was an area in those years having very, very difficult times. It certainly was in the very early thirties, in the Depression days, and I can remember very, very vividly the people in the neighborhood. It was a melting pot, if you will, of many, many different cultures, many ethnic groups that were there. But we lived as one family very, very happily. Of course in those days we had the bad element, so to speak, if you will. Murder Incorporated [the enforcement arm of organized crime groups] was around at that particular time. These are things that I certainly would like to forget, but as a youngster it never really bothered me too much because I wasn't aware of it, and all I was aware of was playing basketball.

I would say that it [the neighborhood] was predominantly Jewish. I would have to say at least 90 percent Jewish and some other ethnic groups compiled the people in the particular locale that I grew up in.

I think the first time I picked a basketball up I was about age six, and at that time this was the only interest that I had. My interest at that particular time was just to be a player and probably to be one of the best if I could. I played basketball from six or seven years of age right into my late teens and certainly into my professional career. I did play in the NBA for some ten years, and that was my love, and I did this eighteen hours a day.

It was predominantly schoolyard basketball. We did have some intramural basketball where we played various teams and leagues, temples, churches, things of that nature, where we had various clubs that participated in tournaments and so forth. But primarily, most all of my time was spent in the schoolyards.

I was born December 7, 1925. My father's name was Morris, and my mother's name was Ida. Both were from Russia. I believe it was either Minsk or Kiev. My father did a number of things. I think in Russia, he was a painter by trade. I think when he came into the New York City area in the early 1900s he continued that profession, but I would say that in the last fifteen, twenty years of his life he was involved in buying and trading merchandise. My mother was a housewife. I have two brothers besides myself. I'm the youngest of three, and in those days, like any good Jewish mother, her main concern was to raise her boys in a very orderly fashion and to make sure that they didn't go astray and keep bad company, and we never did. We never really gave her any headaches, and it was very typical. We never really had much money. In those days nobody did, but there was an awful lot of love in the family and whatever was there was sufficient for all of us. My oldest brother's name is Irving. My older brother is Abe.

We're talking about people coming from the Old Country, and they didn't know anything about sports really. She [my mother] never discouraged me. She never encouraged me. She knew this was a labor of love that I had, and at least one thing she always knew, that if she ever needed me she'd find me in the schoolyard.

So this is what made her very, very happy. Certainly down through the years when I migrated through my college career and certainly when I entered the pros, she became interested in it, as my father did, and very, very excited about it with some of the things that I established as a professional basketball player. Needless to say, she was very, very proud of the fact that I did play. In those days, they had the various scores submitted on some of your sports shows, and whether it was a basketball score or football score or hockey score, she'd be listening in to see if she got some word on how her son Maxie did. She was very, very proud of the fact that I did attain stature in the professional ranks, and we had a beautiful life together.

My brother Abe played basketball, though never on a professional level. He attended high school and played in high school. He was a very, very prominent player in high school, but I guess he felt that rather than go into or attempt to go into professional or even college ball, he'd rather go out into the business world. One professional athlete was enough, and inwardly he probably felt that he might not have had the ability to go into the professional ranks. My brother Abe is about 6'. My other brother, Irving, is about 5'11". I am 6'2".

I never did [know my grandparents]. They were in Russia, and I never got to know them. I don't know exactly [what year my parents emigrated]. It might have been around 1914, 1915.

I never really had a religious training. Both my parents, I would think you can probably call them Orthodox. I never really was. Not that I am proud of it, but I always had many, many things to do, and I observed the most holy days, Yom Kippur and Rosh Hashanah and things of that nature, and abided by it. Those days, on the High Holy Days, I certainly would attend services and everything like that. I think the reason why I never really got as deep as I would have liked to is the amount of traveling that I did while I was playing. I never really had the time to conform to the things that possibly, if I were just in the business field, I would do some of the things I really wanted to do.

My mother kept a kosher home. She had separate plates, separate dishes for the various foods and everything else like that. As I got to be in my early twenties, and I was playing basketball, it was very, very difficult for her, to the extent that while you are playing it is a very, very difficult time as far as applying yourself to the kosher tradition and everything like that because there were not so many of these places on the road. When you go into places like Oshkosh, Indiana, and Anderson and Moline, Illinois, there are not too many Jewish people around there. I have to say that basically I drifted from that track. My mother used separate dishes. They were always very kosher in the house and always had separate dishes for your meats and your dairies.

I know that my mother and father always went to synagogue. We had a synagogue about a block away from where we lived, and they would always observe, not only wait for the most holy days or anything like that. I can remember as a youngster my folks were in there for Shabbos, both Saturday and Friday night services. They always did this, and they always observed the Jewish tradition and the Jewish laws very, very strictly. I would say most of them [my parents' friends] were Jews, and it was a clique of people that more or less migrated about the same time from Russia. They all were on an equal basis more or less, and they all had the same things to share with one another.

I lived at 317 Riverdale Street in Brownsville. I went back with my son Jeff about fifteen years ago. Jeff today is twenty-three. We took a look at it and to see it today everything was bombed out. Ironically enough, the house that I was born in still stands, and I noticed people still living in it. But everything else is rubble, down to the barest necessities, and the culture has changed. I know that it is predominantly Spanish there and black today. In talking to my son Jeff, I just said that you have to close your eyes and go back some twenty-five years ago. This was predominantly a Jewish neighborhood and a very, very happy one, not too much money around, but everyone loved one another.

I went to cheder. I did not go very, very long. I probably attended about three years. I think I started when I was about ten, and I went up there until I was thirteen for bar mitzvah. Then again, as I say, unfortunately, I drifted somewhat from it because as a youngster I used to play an awful lot of ball and we traveled, and I am talking even as a youngster at age fourteen and fifteen. I would travel to various cities and play, because what you have to appreciate is that what you see today at 6'2", at age thirteen I was 6'2". I was progressing in the basketball games, and then there were various tournaments throughout the country that I participated in.

It was really an all-star team. It was comprised of many, many different fellows from various parts of the country, and we would tour many, many of the cities and play these various tournaments and represent a particular locale. So as much as I would have loved to really stress the Jewish heritage as a youngster, I was pulled somewhat from it, but certainly my ties to the Jewish religion and heritage are very, very strong today.

I would say that ever since I was certainly rational enough to believe that I could be what I wanted to be in life my one desire was to be a professional basketball player. I went to Jefferson High School in East New York. From there I attended St. John's University. [At Jefferson] I played baseball and basketball, but my first love was basketball. We won three championships there and, prior to going to Jefferson, at junior high school we won two Brooklyn city championships. I went a year to St. John's. I spent almost two years in the service, and when I left the service I went to St. John's for one year and then professional basketball was born in 1946. I felt that going to St. John's at that particular time, I was married, and I felt that I certainly could not support a wife going to school. It would be very, very difficult. When the opportunity arose where I might become a professional basketball player, well, I jumped on it, and I went out to Chicago.

Joe Lapchick was our coach [at St. John's]. He was a very, very stern type individual. Background-wise, you have to appreciate he played with the old Celtics, and it was a very, very rough game in those days. I'm talking about the early 1900s, 1920s. He always wanted to instill the same kind of basketball in the fellows going to school as when he had played, which was very, very difficult. I think he was a very fair man as far as that goes and certainly his record would indicate he was a successful coach. He tried to instill competitiveness, I think, more than anything else; rather than to be a very meek player, to be a very strong, strong-willed, competitive player, and if you see a loose ball on the floor, do not wait for somebody to pick it up, dive for the ball, make the play, and get it over to one of your teammates.

As far as I know [I was the only Jew on that team]. No, Harry Boykoff. I played one season with Harry Boykoff, who was our center and 6'9". Harry came out of service, and I played one season with him. Harry was the only other Jewish player.

It [Chicago Stags] was certainly exciting for me because I never realized or ever dreamt that professional ball would be a real, paying job. Prior to professional ball being born, they had what they called the Eastern League, and they still have the Eastern League, where fellows for the weekend maybe can go out and play for thirty or forty dollars a game. To me, this was the utmost as far as professional basketball. Needless to say, when the NBA was formulated, this was a dream that I always had that I would be a professional basketball player.

I was the youngest member, I think, playing professional basketball. When I entered I was just about twenty years of age when I went out to Chicago. To have four really glorious or outstanding years was just something that was a dream come true. It was exciting, and all the accolades that were bestowed upon you and all the monies that you earned from something like that was really something that you had always hoped for as a youngster, and the dream had become a reality.

We had some very fine players there, and I might add that throughout my career I've never witnessed any problem as far as being Jewish. I know that the players received me very, very well. I received them well. I think there was an awful lot of respect among all of us. I certainly know the fans wherever we traveled, wherever we performed, whether they knew I was Jewish or not, it never entered the picture, other than treating me very, very fairly and just applauding for everything that I did out there.

I never did [hear any antisemitic remarks from other players]. Of course, the old adage being that you never hear it, but you do not know what the thinking is, and that is something I could not control. There might have been some of that thinking there, I do not know, but I could not care less if there were. I knew that I had made a certain niche in professional basketball, and I was going to continue to go that route regardless of what other people did think of me. In all the ten years that I played, I had nothing but very, very warm welcomes from the various stadiums that we played in. I never witnessed anything like that at all. In those years, you never had too many Jewish players, and the thing that makes me a little more proud was the fact that I was Jewish. I was more or less maybe blazing a trail for future Jewish players that might be coming into the game, where they could come by and maybe ask certain questions, some of the things that you might be up against, what are the problems being a Jewish player and so forth and so on. So I was proud of the fact that I was a Jew playing the game of basketball and probably maybe one of three that were in the game at that particular time.

I never really thought about it [religion] too much. My main concern was that there were people paying two and three dollars a game to watch you perform. I had to go out—it would be the same if I were an entertainer on the stage or in the theater—and I had to give my best performance. I never really thought about it in any way like that because the fact that I was Jewish was always something that certainly I was very, very proud of and still am today. My job out there was just to go out and give the best performance I could for the people that were watching.

We did that [joking around about religion] kiddingly many, many times in the locker room, but everything was in good faith. I must say that with all the teams that I played on I do not think there was any malice or any type of thing that was unsatisfactory as far as I was concerned. Again, you really do not know. You do not know the envy. You do not know the thinking of some of the other players that you are playing with, but I can only say that with all the players that I played with I've always been received royally.

I did witness some of it [antisemitism]. I witnessed it in the service. When I was in the navy, for the two years that I was in there, I witnessed it quite a bit. Basically it was from some of the southern fellows that were out there, and they would pass some of the sly remarks and some of the ethnic jokes, and as a result we had many, many scuffles. There came a point in time when people would mention to me, "You know, why go through something like this? Your name is Zaslofsky. I mean, it is not a common Jewish name. It could be Russian or it could be something else. Take the easy way out, you can deny these things and save yourself so many black eyes." Certainly, I would never go that route. I was very, very proud of what I was and what I am, and we continued to have battles. I did witness some of this when I was growing up in the Brownsville area, when we did play in various church groups. I did hear some of those remarks from some of the visiting players, but those were few and far.

I had many, many scuffles, many, many fights, and everything else like that. As a youngster, I would always, as long as I can remember, I would always either wear a Star of David or something like that. I would have it today, but my chain busted, and I do not have it on. I would put it on in full view, not to advertise or anything like this, but certainly be very, very proud.

I was in the service from 1945, I think, until about 1947. It was almost two years, maybe a couple of months shy of two years. I never went overseas. I took my boot training up at Sampson Naval Training, which is in upstate New York. From there I was assigned to a heavy cruiser out in Newport, Rhode Island. We just had some shakedown cruises, and I always stood within the United States. I never went overseas.

I am what I am and [the feeling of being Jewish] was as strong ten years ago as it is today as far as that goes. I do not think it is any stronger. I may be a little more cognizant of the fact today. I think I have a little more time than I had when I was playing ball so I can get myself involved. If there is a temple that is looking for some coaching for some of the kids or things of that nature, whenever I can find time I go down there and I instruct, which I could not have done when I was playing ball. I may be thinking a little bit about it more today than I did years ago only because I have more time on my hands.

They say that [Israel] is our mother country. I have never visited Israel. I may go out there next summer. They are putting on a tour there, a basketball tour. To me it is home. When I see a Jewish face, regardless of whether it is in Israel or around the corner, I am very, very comfortable because they are my people. You will hear remarks that Israel is strictly interested in the Israeli people; they do not like the American Jew or something like that. I cannot react to that because I have never been in a position to really talk with the Israeli people. I would say that the greatest thing in the world certainly was the formation of the state in 1948. It gave our people a place that they can call home and be with their own, but of course the turmoil that's gone on through this and the fighting that they are doing to establish what they feel is right, I have the highest esteem for the Israeli people. I do not know how I can certainly be supportive to them, other than maybe to put on some clinics one day, to go out there and perform and teach and instruct maybe some of the youngsters out there in the way we play American basketball. It is something that they are trying to work out with the Maccabiah Games, where they will be visiting certain countries, but hopefully if we can work something out, I will be affiliated somewhere along in the coaching staff or something like this to instruct and try to develop some of the younger talent there.

When I played, the game was a five-man game, and that is the way basketball should be played, five fellows playing with one another, working with one another for the ultimate that is victory. Today, I do not think the young men have all that great a desire. I think they're making tremendous salaries, but I just do not think they have the desire to play. They are not hungry enough, because their attitude is, "Well, fine, I am making an awful lot of money; I do not have to get myself hurt out there." Years ago, we never thought about that, the money was secondary; the game was first because we loved the game. Today you will have a coach call a practice from twelve to three. The fellows will come out at twelve o'clock and at three o'clock sharp the floor is empty. When we played, if it were twelve to three, we would hang around until about six because we loved doing what we did. The game has changed. Today it has become more of an individual game than a team game. You have tremendous talent in the game today, but in order to watch it, and I watch it because I love the game, an awful lot is taken out of it, and this is the response I get from many basketball fans. They do not enjoy it anymore because everything is isolated for one man. He goes and four watch. The game of basketball, it is really a thing of beauty to play and to think and try to outguess your opponent and do other things with it, but it takes five men that have to be involved with the things. With this game today, it is really run, run, shoot, shoot, shoot, and they do shoot and shoot very, very well, but I just do not think it is the same game.

This question [of being born too early] has been posed to me many, many times, and I have a very, very simple answer for it. It is just something I could not control. If I would have had to pick a time, certainly I would say now, where the salaries are phenomenal. Had I been playing today I might have been playing for $400,000, $500,000 a season. My top salary when I retired was about $45,000, but you are talking about $45,000 in the years of 1954 to 1955, which was an awful lot of money in those days. But certainly if I were playing today, it would be ten times that much.

Well, I was very, very happy coming back to New York because it meant home again, certainly spending an awful lot of time with my family, living in the area once again, visiting some of the old neighborhoods that I grew up in, and talking with some of the people that I knew for many, many years. I was very happy and delighted to come here, and I played here for three years, and I had a very, very nice career here. The funny thing about professional sports, like anything else, you can only play for so long. While you are playing, your productive years anyways, you have to see that you can get as much money as you can get out of the game. The only problem with the Knicks was the fact that one year, my last year, I held out because I wanted more money and I felt I deserved it and they did not want to pay it, so I asked to be traded. They did trade me, which was probably the greatest thing that could have happened. Although I was leaving New York again, going out to the Fort Wayne Pistons at that time, which is now the Detroit Pistons, the amount of money I made there was probably three times the amount that I made when I was in New York.

I enjoyed Fort Wayne. I was there from 1953 to 1956. I would say the population as far as Jewish people were concerned was probably maybe 5 or 6 percent total. I think the total population at that time was about 200,000, 250,000 people. What I enjoyed about Fort Wayne was that the people were very friendly. It was a small town, so to speak, so you could walk down Main Street and everybody would recognize you, and everybody would sit and talk about last night's game. No matter where you went, you were well received, very, very warmly, and I enjoyed the people. They were very, very nice people, and I spent three very nice years there before I retired.

I played for about a month in Baltimore, but this was a package for me, going to Baltimore and then to Fort Wayne when I left New York. The time I spent was mostly the four years in Chicago, three years in New York, and the other three years in Fort Wayne.

I played in the Garden [Madison Square Garden] many times prior to my being a professional, because when I was at Jefferson High School for the city championships we always played in the Garden, and needless to say, you have made it if you played the Palace Theatre on Broadway. This was the ultimate. It was exciting, certainly thrilling for me to step on the Garden floor as a youngster of maybe fifteen, sixteen while in high school playing in the big house, the Garden. This was where it was at. One of the biggest thrills that I had certainly was when I was with the Knickerbockers in 1952. They had a night for me in Madison Square Garden. This was the first one that they did for any professional athlete in New York City, and this was really the ultimate. My mother and father were in attendance in a box seat, and my wife was called out at half court. I think Jimmy Powers, at that time with the old *Daily News*, emceed the affair, and I received a tremendous amount of gifts at that time. It was just something that you can never forget.

I did not remember the points. It is a funny thing, people say that most every athlete that is given a night or a day, whatever the sport may be, usually is jinxed, and that is why I scored nine points. I do not really feel that way. It is just that that particular night I just did not do the things that I normally could do for every other night that I went out. I remember fouling out with about four or five minutes to go in the game, and I was very, very disappointed with it because in all my career I do not think I fouled out more than three or four games in ten years and that had to be one of the games that I fouled out before a full house, and the family and all the friends and everyone else who was there. I was delighted that we did win. I remember that it was a very close game and an overtime game, but unfortunately I had to watch it from the bench.

I have had many, many sessions with the sportswriters of that day, and all of them are my friends. They have been very kind to me through the years, and they have always given me tremendous publicity. What I tried to impress upon the people was that many of them have mentioned that if you won you were never very happy and if your teammates scored you were never very happy, and I said that was a fallacy. If I won, I was extremely happy, and when my teammates scored I was very, very happy. The one thing that I did not show was emotion, and that is why they termed me a loner. Now, again, when we would go into the locker room at the end of the game, I was very comfortable sitting off into the corner where my locker was. Not that I wanted to be away from the players, but this was the way I was. I was a very introverted type of person in those days.

It might have been the upbringing, the time that I spent as a youth in Brownsville. I do not know, but I was very, very happy to do what I had to do without fanfare. I guess the same association has been told to me by many people and by the man himself, Joe DiMaggio, who is a friend. He never showed emotion on the field. He was that type of player. If he hit the home run, he would have a stone face, and I was really maybe the same way naturewise. I never got excited, nor was I jubilant when I scored a basket or we won or something like that. Inwardly, I was very, very happy and jumping within myself. I never expressed that enthusiasm; so as a result, many of the New York writers termed me a loner-type personality.

I was never thin-skinned. When I had to voice my opinion, when they called a call on me that I felt was not a right call, I would yell and rant and be hit with technical fouls by the referee. It is just that I guess this was my nature, and this was the way I was built. I certainly was not going to change for any New York sportswriter or anybody else for that matter. If I was happy doing one thing, then I would do it. I did not want to do it to make you happy. That was the point. So I kind of think that there was a misconception on many people's part that possibly Max is only interested in Max, and if he had a good night, fine, he was happy. If he did not have a good night, he could not care less whether the team won or not, and really that is not the truth. That bothered me more than anything else because I did feel very, very happy when we won, and it was always nice to get the points that I did get. That was not the criteria. When I was labeled as "the loner" and "interested in himself," that bugged me. I did speak to some of the writers, and I just told them exactly what I am telling you, that this is the way I am constructed and nobody is going to change me.

The press was always very, very good to me. I can remember fellows, and some of the fellows are still around today, some are gone, some have retired, but fellows like Milt Gross in those days who wrote for the *New York Post* was a giant. Dick Young today is still here. Lenny Koppett was with the *New York Times*. There are a number of people—Maury Allen, Lenny Lewin. These were fellows that covered the scene when I was with the Knickerbockers, and they were always very generous to me, I mean as far as write-ups and interviews. I was always ready to talk to them when they wanted some story and everything else like that. I would say it is probably no different than it is today. Every year brings a new crop of people, but I guess they had their style, as some of the young men have theirs today.

The loss always bothered me deeply, and it was something that, especially if it was a tough loss and if it was a championship game type thing, I would carry for a long time with me, because I wanted it so badly. I wanted to win so badly. I would store this up. The difference then as opposed to today is that if a kid loses, okay, fine, there is always tomorrow. I always said there was tomorrow, there is another ball game, forget it, it is done with, but I carried many of the important losses. When I say important losses, I am talking about the playoff games, where it meant that possibly if I had another opportunity to take a shot, we might have won or things of that nature. The fact that we lost by one point or we lost at the buzzer, you know, was something that really stayed with me for a long time, maybe a month or two after a game. Then, like anything else, in time, you have to forget and go on.

Max Zaslofsky • 243

I could not leave it at some bar or something like that because I never drank, and to this day I do not do any drinking. On occasion, if we socialize or something I will have a glass of wine, but I took it home with me unfortunately, and in some areas unjustly gave it to the family, which was really none of their concern. Certainly they always wanted to see me happy and everything going right for me. If we lost a crucial game, I would replay the game over and over and over again and become angry with it and let out some of the frustrations to the family, who were very innocent people.

I think I have a diamond in my wife. We are married thirty-four years, and she knows me probably better than I know myself. She has put up with an awful lot because during the course of a season, I could become very, very moody. I had the temperament that most athletes have, and it is not easy living with an athlete for the woman because she has to put up with an awful lot. She has to soothe, appease you, and do everything to erase whatever's bothering an individual. I have been very, very fortunate. I feel, again, I have a gem in a woman. We go back many, many years, because I met my wife when she was thirteen. It was a childhood romance up until the time we got married. She knows all my quirks and everything else that goes with it, and she simmered me down.

We had them [groupies on the road]. I do not think that has changed very much. You had them in every town that you visited, every hotel, certainly at the games. I think the same thing applies then as it does today.

Just to recollect quickly, I went into the insurance business for a while. I did that for a few years, and then I managed and I was a partner in two bowling establishments, I guess in the late 1950s, '57, '58, '59 or something like that. I invested some money in that, and it proved to be very, very successful. Then I got out of there, and I did an awful lot of promotional work. I represented many athletes from all major sports as their manager-advisor-agent, and down through the years I guess I did quite a few things, an awful lot of public relations work for many companies, so I have been busy all through.

Being a new league [ABA with the New York Nets] that was being formed, it took the same steps as the old league that was formed when I first started in 1946 and 1947. It was frustrating for me, and I was general manager and coach for two years. I think the first year was 1967–68 and then 1968–69. The club at that time was sold to Arthur Brown, of the ABC Freight Forwarding Company, who I worked for about eighteen years on and off. While I was performing, I would work in the off-season, and when I finished playing ball, I went there full time. I hired athletes throughout the country from every major sport to work in the off-season. When the ABA came into existence, he bought the New Jersey Nets, and we played out in Teaneck Armory the first year, which was a very, very interesting year and statistic-wise we did not do very badly. The second year was a disaster. We then moved to Commack Arena, which was a barn as far as I was concerned. The conditions were horrible. There was an ice rink there, and it was just freezing. People were coming with overcoats and mittens, and you could not really watch a game, and attendance was maybe three or four thousand people. So Arthur Brown lost an awful lot of money, and at the end of the second year he sold the club. It was frustrating for me because of the fact that you did not have any talented ballplayers around. You were really getting the high-class schoolyard player or maybe a mediocre college player at the time before some of the NBA names came into it. The thing that I found most frustrating was the fact that I knew what I wanted them to do, but I could not do it for them because they just did not have the talent. It became very frustrating, and I became very angry and I said, "Max, I think you are asking too much of these fellows. They just do not have the ability to do the things that you want them to do." So realizing that, I went through the second year, which was pretty agonizing for me, and we had a very, very bad season. I think we ended up winning twenty-five games and losing something like thirty-five or forty games. [The team was actually 17–61.] Arthur Brown decided that he wanted to sell the club because he lost probably about $750,000 then, and he said, "I am used to making money. I am not used to losing money." He was a very successful businessman, so he sold it. He sold it to Roy Bowle, who took it over and nurtured it out in the Island Gardens before the [Nassau] Coliseum was built. That was the extent of my contact with the ABA.

As far as I was concerned, this is something that is always in your system, and this was a new league, and I wanted to be a part of the new league. I felt I wanted to get in because it is a labor of love, and I do not care if you are out of the game twenty or thirty years, there is always that feeling that you would like to participate in some fashion in the sport that you played your entire life. I gave it considerable thought, and then I said I would like to get back into this game, just to be involved and find out what it looks like. I did this, and I had a discussion with my wife and naturally I think [she said] the easiest thing for any woman to say, "Honey, whatever makes you happy, do." So I did it, and I got back in. I certainly did not enjoy the traveling because I had an awful lot of that as a player, but I felt that it was a new league and perhaps this thing here maybe can be elevated on the stature of the ABA in some years to come. I wanted to be a part of that new thing. I was pioneering now another league which was at the same stage, similar to where the NBA was.

[Longevity] I would think really quickly is the type of life that I led. I am a very clean-living guy. I do not drink. I never went to clubs and everything else like that. I was a homebody guy. When the game was over, I would come home to my family, and I think just because I was a clean-living individual, I think this would prolong any athlete's life rather than going after the game into some gin mill or what have you and just dissipating yourself with drink. I think this would cut your lifespan very, very short. I played ten years, and I could have played another five years because I retired just about age thirty, which is very young. I had ten years in at that time. The reason I retired is because my kids were growing up, and I wanted them to say that they had a place that they can call home and to stop pulling them around from one school to another when they traveled with me on the road. I felt that perhaps getting into the business world would be the best thing at that particular juncture, and making it at age thirty rather than still making some fairly good money for another five years. You know, you are old for the game and maybe then the opportunities would not be as great as they were then, and this is why I made the decision of leaving at that early age.

I can recall that when playing with the Knicks or with Chicago or even with Fort Wayne, if I were fouled or going to the free-throw line, it was very, very rare where they would say, "Zaslofsky for two shots." They would say, "Max goes to the line." I always felt that this was nice, and it would build your ego and it is a wonderful thing, but I paid my dues. I have established certain situations where if you would say "Max," it would be recognizable to the fans. So it was nice. It was nice, and they referred to me as Max many, many times. Even in scoring situations when I made a basket, "Max scores," things of that nature, which was a very, very personal type of thing and certainly the people could identify, the people that watched me play through the years. It was encouraging enough for Lenny Schechter at the time if he was going to make comparisons to say Willie Mays or something like that; I am thrilled to be in that company.

I was Dad and they [my children] knew that I was a performer. Of course, they were young. They watched me a year or so before I retired, especially then with the two girls. Jeff is the only boy I have, and certainly he was not around then. There was no special treatment. I think they might have said to their friends that "My daddy plays for a team," things of that nature, but I was Dad at home. There were no airs and nothing, just very plain folk and everything else like that and I tried to do the right thing by them.

I never really had heroes. I really cannot identify with anybody. The only one that really sticks out in my mind somewhat is that as a youngster I remember going to Ebbets Field when the Brooklyn Dodgers were there, and the one man that I really became infatuated with was Dolph Camilli. For whatever reason, he was a hero to me. I do not know why, but of all the fellows on the team in those days, I would watch him and for one reason or another I loved the guy. I never met the man. I never said a word to him. As far as heroes, I never really had heroes in sports because there was really nobody that took me aside and developed me. Everything that I did, I did on my own. I made the progress by myself, so I really could not identify with anybody. When I entered high school I was a finished player. The coach had very little to do. Give me the ball, let me do what I can do, and hopefully we would win.

Certainly at St. John's the same thing prevailed, but I was only there for a year and then right on to the pro leagues. I never really had anybody take me aside and say do it this way, do it that way, or this is the correct way, this is the incorrect way.

I will tell you the man that I really enjoyed playing under the most was a gentleman named Harold "Ole" Olsen, who came from Wisconsin. He was the coach for my first four years with Chicago. He was a gentleman. He was a man that treated the fellows like men. He was a great basketball mind. I do not think he really got the acclaim that some of the fellows had in those days, but he came from Wisconsin with a very, very good record. He was a great athlete in his own right prior to coming to basketball. He was an excellent football player. I respected him the most, and I enjoyed playing for him, I think, the most of all the other coaches.

I would not think that was the reason I had my best years. I just think that things fall into a certain groove. You are with a club and basically what happens, everything is centered on you. You can go to another club, and they have certain situations, and they want you to play a certain way so now you have to adapt and adjust to their style of playing. In Chicago I more or less did everything that I wanted to do. There were two people that they celebrated in Chicago as far as athletics went, and it was very complimentary to me. They said one was Sid Luckman, who was playing then with the Bears, and of course I got identified with him, being the other Jewish player. The other was Max Zaslofsky, who was playing with the Chicago Stags. They were the kings. I know that in Chicago anything I wanted I had. The people were loyal to me, and I just had a fantastic career there. When I came to the Knicks, I had to make an adjustment because the style was very different. The Knicks never really wanted any one person to excel. They would rather have team balance so that if you go down statisticwise, you will see I had a fourteen-point average. With Chicago, I could have had a thirty-point average because it was geared to me. The same thing happened with the Pistons.

My career average was 14.8, 14.9, something like that. I played two years with the twenty-four-second clock. So the situation was that had I played with the twenty-four-second clock for six or seven or eight years that I played prior to that. There is no question that it [my scoring average] would have been a lot higher because if we had a two- or three-point lead with five minutes to play in a game, we would stall the game until we had thirty seconds to play, so that cut down, certainly, on the shooting and the attempted shots that you would take. Normally I would average anywhere between eighteen to twenty shots a game. If I was playing with the twenty-four-second rule, it would have to be close to thirty shots, because I was primarily an offensive player. So that, again, times and different situations come about. I know that certainly had I played with the twenty-four-second clock it would have been a lot higher.

I would say that [the two-handed set shot] was my chief asset, anywhere from maybe thirty, thirty-five feet out. Today that would be worth three points with the new rule that they have. Primarily, I would say most of my scoring came with the two-handed set. At 6'2", I played a backcourt position, and as a guard most of your shots either come from the outside or in a driving fashion if you are going to the basket. I would say that if we were going from one to ten, I would say possibly seven would be for my outside shooting and maybe three for my driving ability. I always felt that I was a very good ball handler, but they never wanted me to really become a playmaker. I always prided myself on being a very good passer, and a guy that can hit the man, but whatever club I played with, they said, "We want your shooting ability. We have guys that can make the pass." So I was really somewhat turned back on that because I knew I could do that particular portion of it.

Joe Lapchick was the coach of the New York Knicks. The three years I spent there he was the coach. When I was at St. John's, he had me for the one year. Then, of course, when I went out to Chicago, the big hullabaloo when I established the career that I had in Chicago was how does a young fellow from Brooklyn go to Chicago and not end up with the New York Knicks? The New York Knicks could have had me very easily. All they had to do was say, "Fine, we want to sign you to a contract," but they never did. I crucified the Knicks every time I played against them. I would average maybe twenty-eight points a game against the Knicks. Lapchick would say, "We have to get Max Zaslofsky. We have to bring him into the Garden. We just cannot leave him out in Chicago." I think that everybody was jubilant, in fact, when Chicago folded and Ned Irish picked my name out of a hat, that I was finally coming back to New York. Lapchick, I know, made the statement that when I was playing, pound for pound I was probably the best basketball player he ever saw, which was a compliment to me.

Chicago folded after four years, and they had to disperse some of the players from the Stags. At that time I think Chicago had drafted Bob Cousy out of Holy Cross, and everyone wanted Max Zaslofsky. There were only two fellows that they felt had merit, that was Andy Phillip and I, but every club in the league wanted Max Zaslofsky. From what I understand, the story goes that they sat up all night in the commissioner's office, some of the team owners there, and they could not resolve anything, so finally the commissioner said, "Well, let us put three names into the hat. We will put Max Zaslofsky, Andy Phillip, and Bob Cousy, and you pick out. Whoever picks the names, those are the clubs that these fellows will be assigned to." So Irish picked first, and he picked my name, and he was ecstatic, from what I understand, and he says, "Great, we finally got him back home, right?" Then the Philadelphia team, Eddie Gottlieb, picked Andy Phillip. Walter Brown, who was then the owner of the Celtics, was left with Bob Cousy, and he said he did not want Bob Cousy. He said he will take any player in the league. He did not want Bob Cousy because he did not think he could make the league. Too much of a Fancy Dan and so forth, and he will never fit in with us. Well, needless to say, everything is history. He [Cousy] went on to be one of the greatest players that we had in the game of basketball. That was it. That was the way the thing turned out, so I ended up in New York, Phillip ended up in Philadelphia, and Cousy ended up in Boston.

There were so many greats. I cannot pinpoint the greatest. Of course, George Mikan in his era was a fantastic center. Today it might have been a little different story. He was not as mobile as the guys are today. He was a big, bruising-type guy. He would muscle himself under the basket three to five feet and do most of the scoring. He was the big, dominant force in those days. Jim Pollard was a great player with the Lakers. Joe Fulks, I thought he was an outstanding player. Bobby Davies with the Rochester club, little Bobby Wanzer, they were great. Dick McGuire played with me with the Knicks, and I thought he was a great player. Then down through the years certainly Dolph Schayes and Bob Pettit, Elgin Baylor and John Havlicek, and Rick Barry and Julius Erving today. There are so many great players. I can never really pick, and people have asked me the question, can you pick your all-time ten great, and I cannot because there were so many great ones, and everyone filled a certain niche. It would be unfair to some of the other people to slight certain people. I look at some of the stuff today, and I saw something just the other day on ratings of various players. It is kind of ridiculous to me to have certain people above other people, and you say, "Well, how is that possible because all around this fellow certainly was a far greater player than the one that you gave a higher rating to." I think it becomes a personal type of thing in evaluating a player. I do not know. I know that I have been associated with many great players. I had the privilege of playing against some of the greatest players that ever lived, playing with them and against them, and I let it go at that.

I speak to a lot of the fellows here in the city because many of the fellows are around, fellows like Dick McGuire, who is the head scout of the Knicks. Carl Braun is a stockbroker. I get to speak to him on occasion. Ernie Vandeweghe I have not seen in years. He is out on the West Coast. Sweetwater Clifton, I understand, is in Chicago. Ray Lump is here at the New York Athletic Club. We bump into one another, and we speak to one another. We do not lose contact.

Well, I enjoy it [today's game] to a degree. I do go to the game really because of the atmosphere. I love the game certainly. I am not really truthfully happy with the way the game is played today because I played it at a different stage, and I think it should be played a certain way. I cannot change the times. This is what it is. I enjoy being there and reminiscing with some of the people, some of the sportswriters, some of the newspaper people, and I just love going into the locker room and smelling the old smelly uniforms. I mean, this is I guess like the circus people with the big tent and smelling the sawdust. It is something that will always be with you. It can never leave you. It has always been a part of me, so I enjoy going in on that basis. It is something that you always have to feel, something you can always relate to, and people ask me this or that and it is very difficult for me to really respond to the question only because you have never been there so you do not know what I am talking about. If I talk with another athlete today or former athlete, to me we belong to the same club. We know exactly what we are talking about. But to talk to the very, very good fan, it is difficult to convince him of what I am trying to say because he has never been a part of something like this. Basketball has left me with great memories, wonderful things. They are in the books. You can cuddle up one winter night and reminisce, and it makes you feel good, builds your ego once again, and it has been a gratifying experience for me.

I miss it. I miss it to an extent. I would be lying if I said I did not, because it is something that is in your system. I know as a player I loved to step out on the floor. I was stepping out on center stage. I mean, this is what I was geared to do. I loved the applause and everything else like that. That was the rewarding thing for me, and contributing and doing what I could do best was the rewarding factor. I loved that kind of thing. But again, being realistic, I always knew that one day this had to stop because you cannot play forever. I try to make the adjustment now and everything else like that. I do not crave the attention. There are many people that come into our collectors' store, and we talk basketball and reminisce, and I feel good talking that way. I do not feel that if I walk down the street and somebody does not recognize me, I am hurt or I am offended. I had my day, and it is the new young man that is coming up. I do not crave the attention, but I know when I go to a ball game it starts all over again, because people now start to huddle around, and we start talking. Some of the youngsters, if you say "Max Zaslofsky" their answer is "Who?" and their fathers say, "Well, when he played, take a look at the books and see the things that he established." Again, now we are talking about the ego type of thing and that makes you feel good, but when I leave the stadium it is forgotten. It is a glorifying experience but not a lasting experience. You were there when you were there, and when it is all over the curtain comes down. The next show goes on, and that is the way I have always interpreted this.

It is something that you really cannot describe in words. You are out there, you are on an island by yourself, and all you hear is thunder, the applause, and it is for you, and that is something that is very difficult to relay to other people because they have never experienced that particular situation. When I was out there, and if we had fifty thousand fans, it was great. I felt like I really wanted to perform because they gave me that incentive. The spotlight was on you, and I craved that at that particular time when I was an athlete. The more people out there, the better I felt. The adrenaline flowed that much more and possibly I extended myself a little more.

I would think the crowd had a major effect upon my performance, because if we played before twenty-five thousand I think unconsciously I might have worked a little harder to get their approval as compared to playing before three thousand or four thousand. I would play hard, but I do not think the thinking was maybe as strong as for twenty-five thousand.

Unfortunately, we came very, very close [to winning a championship]. In all the years that I played maybe three or four times to the final game and probably until the final second. Three times with New York, we lost probably in the last second or two, and one with the Pistons we lost in the last second. The ball went up and the gun went off and the ball went in and we lost. That was the closest. The one thing, if you say, "Did you harbor anything?" or "Did you take it home with you?" These are the things that really stuck with me for a long time because I wanted to be on a championship team very badly, to know that I played with a championship team. This is where it was at. Not the money, but to know that you were world champs one time. We came close four times, and it just escaped us every one.

It did certainly hurt at the time. But like anything else, time is a great healer of everything and you forget it. If you are going to reminisce about it, then I can go back to games and point out how we lost because it was that important.

I can remember the three games. Two of them we had with the

Rochester Royals we lost in the last two seconds, one when I was with Fort Wayne, we played Syracuse and we lost in the last second. We lost to the Lakers when I was with New York.

The one we should have won, there is no question in my mind, was the one with the Lakers, and I hate to say it but I think the game was taken away from us. I think that was 1952. We went there for the final game out in Minneapolis, and the big controversy at that time was that Al McGuire scored a basket. He was fouled and scored the basket, and nobody saw the basket go in, the officials or anybody sitting around it, which was ridiculous. The ball clearly went through the basket for two points. As it turned out, the game went into overtime. Had that basket been allowed it never would have reached overtime, we would have won by two points. That is the one game I know that was taken away from us because the ball clearly went into the basket, but the two officials did not see it. We lost in overtime to the Lakers, I think by three or four points, who had George Mikan, Jim Pollard, Vern Mikkelsen, and Slater Martin. But had that basket been allowed, we would have been world champs. Those things hurt. The game was taken away from us, but that was the closest. The others, it was just one of those unfortunate things. In the last, waning seconds, the last second or two of the other three times, the ball went in for the other club, and you got beat. Tough defeat, but you cannot do anything. But this other one was really the toughest to swallow when we had the game, and they took it away.

I really do not think expansion has hurt the game. I know that there are many cities each and every year looking to come into the league, and it is very difficult for me to really comprehend because of the salaries that they are paying. I do not see how any of the owners really can make money or stay in business. The television rights are very heavy, but that is a portion of it because when you analyze it, I would say the payroll of most every club exceeds $3 million. You are not talking football or baseball, where you can put in sixty thousand or seventy thousand people at a game. You fill up an arena, and probably one of the largest arenas is Madison Square Garden, and they seat nineteen thousand people. I do not care if you fill up nineteen thousand people every game for forty-two games; you are not going to make it. The other arenas are not that big. I just sit and think, "How is it possible that these people make money and how can they stay in the game?" The other thing I look at is you are talking about very wealthy people; they are probably looking for tax situations and tax shelters. Then there is the big ego factor that they want to get involved, and they have the money to do it and they remain. This is where it is at for them.

A few years ago, I said I might like to get in, but certainly in the area of the administrative end, possibly a general manager. I would never, never really go into the coaching ranks. Never again will I ever anticipate something like that. I would think about the administrative office up until about three years ago. But today I am very happy. My partner and I are here at the sport collectors' store in New York City. We have a beautiful store, and I think we are on the right track. I think the people that come in here and buy our merchandise are very happy with it, and I think I have a very fine future ahead of me in this.

20. Dolph Schayes played his entire sixteen-year career with the Syracuse Nationals. Courtesy of Bill Himmelman.

DOLPH SCHAYES

- During the 1950s Dolph Schayes was one of the most con-
  sistent players in the National Basketball Association. In a
  sixteen-year career with the Syracuse Nationals and later
  their successor, the Philadelphia 76ers, he led his team to
  the playoffs fifteen times. He was a twelve-time N B A All-
  Star and a twelve-time All-N B A selection. He won the 1955
  N B A title with Syracuse and was named to the N B A's fifti-
  eth team in 1996. He retired as the league's all-time leading
  scorer. A stickler for improving his game, Schayes practiced
  his free throws using a fourteen-inch hoop that was placed
  into a regulation eighteen-inch basket. Prior to his time in
  the N B A, Schayes starred at New York University, where he
  led the team to the N C A A Finals.

My father was 6'4". He was a boxer. Well, he was not a boxer.
When he came to this country he was very, very strong,
and he worked for Consolidated Laundries in a midtown
location. He would deliver to barber shops, and I think one day
he told me that there was a manager called John the Barber who
looked at him and said, "Boy, you are a real strong guy. I would
like to make a boxer out of you." My father told him his feet were
frostbitten during the First World War. John the Barber suggested
that he get an operation on his feet so he could become more
agile, because you had to be pretty agile in the ring. My father was
very strong and got into a lot of barroom brawls and came out
victorious. At least, he told me. He got this operation. However,

the operation was quite painful, and a cast was put on his feet. It became so painful that, with a cast on, it restricted his movement so much that he broke the cast by smashing his foot against something hard and this left his feet in bad shape. So because of that he never was able to pursue a boxing career. Maybe that was good because this was in the early twenties and Jack Dempsey was at his height, and had my father fought Jack Dempsey maybe I never would have been born.

He was born in Romania, or at least he was from Durohoi, which was in the northeastern section of Romania, close to the Russian border. My mother was born in Iasi or Yashi. They were born twenty miles from each other, in a very Jewish section of Romania. I did not know my grandparents at all. My grandmother on my mother's side I had met a few times. I never met either of my grandfathers, whom I think died at young ages.

We lived, as I can remember, at 2275 Davidson Avenue, which was on the corner of 183rd Street and Davidson, one block up from the Jerome Avenue El. I remember the Jerome Avenue El because as a youngster I was kind of put to sleep by the trains coming back and forth at that time. It was a crowded existence. We had a one-bedroom apartment, apartment 3G, and my brother and I would share a couch, which was bought from Ludwig Bauman. By the time we paid for it, they had to get a new couch. We lived in the living room and my mother and father, with my younger brother, Herman, lived in the bedroom. He was quite young at that time. So it was a crowded existence. I was in the middle. I have an older brother, Fred, and a younger brother, Herman. There were a couple of other boys that were stillborn and one boy lived and died of pneumonia at about six months. So there were quite a few Schayeses around.

My parents were not religious at all. Of course, I do not know what their background was in Romania. I have a hunch that on my mother's side there was quite a lot of religion because I recall my uncles were quite religious in Brooklyn and Queens. However, growing up in the Bronx, there were not any organized shuls or synagogues, and I think that had a great deal to do with the non-religious upbringing. Of course, everybody in the area of the Bronx where I came from seemed to be Jewish. We had an Irish person, Brigit, who lived above us, who we were very friendly with, but as far as I was concerned that was the only non-Jewish person I could remember.

I cannot recall if we did [celebrate holidays]. I am not really sure. I was not formally bar mitzvahed, as I remember, and neither were my brothers. So we did not have much of a formal religious background, although the Jewishness was ever-present. My mother always kept kosher, in that I could remember well. The steaks were always kind of stringy, kosher steaks, and she made a lot of Romanian-type dishes like *kasha veranekas*. Well, there were a lot of dishes that I could recall that were very Jewish. Rolled beef in cabbage. Other things like that. My mother seemed to have kept a very kosher home. I think the Michael part of the family, my mother's side of the family, was the more religious coming from Romania. My father's family was not nobility, but they were landowners in Romania. My mother and father's families did not get along that well in that my father's family looked down upon my mother. There was not a problem, but you could feel sparks that they looked down upon her because she was lower class and they thought that my father could have done better. I always had that feeling that that was what was occurring during the many visits. My mother's family would visit quite a lot, but my father's family would not. My father's family, a lot of them was in Manhattan and Brooklyn, and my mother's family was mostly from Brooklyn, although we had an uncle and aunt in the Bronx.

We grew up in this area of Davidson Avenue, and I went to school and made lots of friends. Clubs were formed amongst the guys in the neighborhood. At that time the World's Fair was on, and our club was called the Trilons because the symbol of the fair was a Trilon and Perisphere [two structures, a spire and a sphere, at the New York World's Fair] and we were skinny, or else we would have been called the Perispheres. Then we had jackets, and we were a bunch of guys, and my whole world revolved around this group of friends. After school we would sit on the corner and play ball. I think the existence was school and playing ball was what we liked to do. I do recall playing stickball, playing softball, playing touch-tackle and baseball. We went to Van Cortland Park, and we would have organized games in leagues there, in football and maybe touch-tackle and in baseball.

I was a good athlete. I seemed to catch on to things quite easily. I was a pitcher in baseball. I thought baseball was my better sport because I was long, rangy, and could play both first base and pitch and because if you are long and rangy you could put a little whip on the ball. When I was twelve or thirteen or maybe even a little younger I pitched against an excellent player, and he hit a line drive right back at me and it hit me right in the mouth. I think from then on I was gun shy to be a pitcher. Basketball I gravitated to because that is what you basically did in those days. The schoolyards were full of baskets. Saturdays and after school you would play ball, and since I was taller I played a lot with the older players because they would pick you. I was taller, so I was able to get more experience. I can recall climbing over the schoolyard fences when they were locked, and I was a playground rat, you might say, in those days. We played a great deal of outdoor basketball as I remember.

I was more of a "mama's boy." I went shopping with her. I was very close to my mother. My father was not around as much as my mother was. I guess he got into a lot of scrapes. As I said, he drank a little bit. He would get into lots of fights in the local bar on Jerome Avenue. He was a taxicab driver. Then he worked for Consolidated Laundries through his entire life and there were always financial problems as I can recall. I would say we were middle class, lower middle class. I think the rent at that time was forty-five dollars a month, and whether they were even getting the rent I do not know. We never had a car as I recall. I can recall my father did play the numbers once in a while. I guess everybody did in those days. The numbers were a real lower-middle-class way of maybe getting out, making a few extra bucks. I think the odds were five hundred to one if you won. For instance, I can recall one specific time I used to be the runner for my father. He would give me a quarter, let's say, to bring to this barbershop, and you would give it to the barbershop and then the runners for the people who handled the booking action would pick it up. This was based on horse races, I guess. So your number had to be in by one in the afternoon because the horse races got off a little later than that. I can recall specifically at this one particular time I was always a nut for going to school and being on time and for some reason I would eat lunch at home. I would walk to school, and I was a little late so I did not put the money in at 12:00 or 12:30 because I was late for school. So I just went to school, figuring after school I would bring the money in. I brought the money in after school and the barbershop said, "Well, it is too late." Then I just glanced that it was twenty-five cents for the number 058. I will never forget the number, and I figure I was maybe ten or eleven. I figured I would save my father's quarter because the chances of winning, of course, were about a thousand to one, triple-zero to ninety-nine. The pink edition of the *Daily News* came out that night at about eight o'clock. My father picked up the edition and 058 came out, the number came out, and then I told my father I did not put the money in. That was the first time ever my father laid a hand on me. He was really angry, because I think it meant $125, which was a great deal of money in the midthirties. That is a story that sticks out for obvious reasons. Later in life he did hit a few numbers. Obviously, he probably never came out ahead, but this was the pastime for almost everyone in those days.

I can recall that there was always friction. There was friction. I think money was not always available. Whether he gambled I do not really know. He was a great, great person to me. He loved baseball, loved baseball and loved this country. I can recall going to Yankee Stadium on holidays and Sundays for doubleheaders at ten o'clock in the morning. The game started at 1:30, the doubleheaders. We would sit in the bleachers from eleven o'clock on, as soon as they opened up. In those days you would take your shirts off. This was summertime, hot, and it was like a great block party with all these guys. Those were wonderful times because my father was just free and happy like all the guys in the bleachers. I think you paid fifty cents to get in, and you would see the Red Sox and the Tigers, Jimmie Fox and Hank Greenberg. For some strange reason I never rooted for the Yankees. Yankee Stadium was on 161st Street, and we would take the Jerome Avenue El from 183rd to 161st Street and watch the games. I can remember that home plate did not seem so far away, but late in the afternoon with the haze and when your eyes got tired it looked like a million miles away. We would sit through these doubleheaders, and it was just a wonderful time.

The worst team in baseball at that time was the Saint Louis Browns. I was the greatest Saint Louis Browns fan you ever saw. I knew every player. I rooted for the underdog of underdogs. I could tell you the players—Harlond Clift and Oral Hildebrand and Jack O'Connor—they would lose a hundred games a year. I would go with my mother, and she rooted for the Browns too because she was my mother and I rooted for them. We would go to the stadium, and I can remember a specific time sitting in the upper deck with her, going through a doubleheader, and they had at that time DiMaggio, Hendricks, and Keller, and Red Rolf. The games were eleven to two, nine to three, and the tears would be coming down. Everyone knew I was a Saint Louis Browns fan. Maybe it was their uniforms, maybe just to attract attention, to be different. The Yankees would wear the pinstripes, very conservative, kind of sharp. The Browns would come in, and their colors were brown and orange, and they would have orange stripes and they were just a different-looking team. Everybody in the neighborhood knew I was a Browns fan. I would be kidded mercilessly. Maybe they would have a good player every once in a while like a Bobo Newsom. He was so good that he had to pitch doubleheaders, and he would lose twenty games, but maybe he would win fifteen or sixteen. Maybe they had a good hitter like George McQuinn. The way the Browns stayed in business is once they had a great player then they would sell him for $100,000 to make the payroll.

My mother knew the game. She knew the game, and she knew I loved the Browns, and we would go and watch once in a while. I do not think they ever won. Maybe they won one game. They would never win in the stadium [Yankee Stadium]. How could you win at the stadium against Murderer's Row? But it was interesting. The Yankees were dominant. Everybody was a Yankees fan. Maybe you would find a Giants fan because they were in the Polo Grounds. No Brooklyn Dodger fans at all. I did go to the Polo

Grounds a few times but always to the stadium. In fact, many times my father would take me to the park across from Yankee Stadium. McComb Dam Park had great semipro baseball games. Sometimes on Sunday if the stadium was filled we would end up watching games because it was for nothing or twenty-five cents.

Finally, the Saint Louis Browns had an excellent team. Towards the midforties they started picking up some players like Vern Stephens. They had Johnny Beradino. They had some pitchers, Denny Galehouse, Ellis Kinder, Jack Kramer, and for some strange reason the Browns all came together. Luke Sewell was their manager and in 1944 the Saint Louis Browns won the pennant, and they beat the Yankees, I think the last couple of games. The Yankees had a decent team. They had Snuffy Stirnweiss and guys like that. This was during the war. Joe DiMaggio was away. Here was my time to crow. And would you believe it, 90 percent of the guys who kidded me were in the service, and I could not get at them.

I waited all my young life for that. I think Bill Veeck had come into the picture, and of course he tried out a lot of crazy things. People talk about the Saint Louis Browns—some people who really know and they were very few, I mean, they were just a footnote to American League history today—they would be known for the fact that they had a one-armed player named Pete Gray who I saw many, many times. He would catch the ball, put his glove under his stump, and then throw the ball in, and he hit over .300 banging out these singles with one arm. Then a couple of years after that, the Browns were known for the midget. Bill Veeck had a midget called Eddie Goodell, figuring, well, this is a free country. If a seven-footer can play basketball, then why can't a 2'6" guy play baseball? Of course he walked every time until they passed a rule saying he could not play.

[Hank Greenberg] did mean a lot because when I went to the stadium and the Tigers were there, I would secretly root for Greenberg when he came in. I do not think I ever saw him hit a home run in Yankee Stadium because left field was so far, so deep. Yankee Stadium was built for good left-handed hitters, a King Kong Keller and Tommy Hendricks in those years. If you were a righty it was Death Valley. Center field was like 490 feet away. The left-field line, right down the line, was 320 feet and then it was very, very sharp so that maybe 10, 15 feet toward center field it would go out to about 375 feet. If Joe DiMaggio had played in any other park he would have hit fifty, sixty home runs. Greenberg rarely ever hit a home run in the stadium. Greenberg was from James Monroe High School in the East Bronx. We always thought of the East Bronx as not the nicer part of the Bronx, those of us from the West Bronx. He was from James Monroe, and we would root for him.

I went to Public School 91 and then Creston Junior High School. Life revolved around the schoolyard on weekends, and we played a lot of community center ball at night in the junior high school gym, which is a very low-ceilinged gym. I played my first organized ball at Creston Junior High School in the seventh or eighth grade. The coach was Silverstein, but he brought Lou Rossini in because Lou was a high school player at the time and loved coaching. I think he was a senior high school player, I think at Teddy Roosevelt High School in the Bronx, and he just helped out. I can remember Lou teaching us a lot of our basketball.

I think the No. 4 [uniform] might have come from Lou Gehrig. I think Lou Gehrig wore No. 4, and I just liked the number four, but in high school I did not wear No. 4. In fact, I have a picture of my junior high school team, and I will look and see what number I wore. I do not think it was No. 4. Numbers did not mean anything at that time.

I was much taller [than the other players]. I can recall having difficulty getting into the movies at age nine, ten, and eleven because if you were a kid you could go in for like a quarter but if you were an adult you had to pay more. I can even recall just waiting around. I think if you were accompanied by an adult, you were able to get in cheaper. One time at the RKO Fordham— maybe the bigger movies—I can recall a kid coming up to me and saying, "Mister, would you take me in?" thinking I was an adult, fourteen or fifteen years old. I was always much taller. I can recall a lot of my friends were much shorter.

Not a freak, but I can recall sometimes just standing in the gutter and they were on the sidewalk so I could be almost their size. Just little things like that but nothing freakish. There were always problems getting clothes, but we did not have very much money and nobody had clothes for big people in those days. What did you wear as a kid? You did not wear that much. I do not recall having much new clothing.

When I got out of Creston Junior High School it was an early age because in those years you had rapid advanced classes. I guess New York City was trying something experimental by placing so-called smarter kids in advanced classes so the seventh grade was done in six months. So in one year, I completed two years of study. At that time there were two schools, again experimental-type schools that New York City was working with; one was the Bronx High School of Science and one was Townsend Harris. Townsend Harris was supposedly smarter kids. I took a test for Bronx Science. I do not think I passed it. I took a test for Townsend Harris and I passed it and I went to Townsend Harris, which was down on Twenty-Third Street where City College was for six months. But Townsend Harris ceased to be after I was there for six months, and then I went to DeWitt Clinton High School.

When I first tried out for DeWitt Clinton, I was cut from the team and just played a lot of intramurals. I cannot recall the exact dates. It is possible that after six months at Townsend Harris it was the middle of the season and I was not put on the team, but then the next year I was on the team. Or maybe then I was cut and then after doing well at intramurals they said, "We could use this kid."

We had a great team in those days. DeWitt Clinton was very large, an all-boys school in Mosholu Parkway in the Bronx, kind of a legendary school. It was more like a college campus–type school. We had a big campus and we had lots of kids to draw from. Although no blacks, mostly all Jewish kids, mostly Jewish kids, and we were very good. The star was a guy named Joel Kaufman. He was our star player, and then we had a good mix of role players. We played very good teams. I was the center. I did pretty well.

We won the Bronx championship. I do not think they had a city championship for junior high school people. In high school, the first year that I was in high school, we went to the semifinals and got beat by Benjamin Franklin. I think Benjamin Franklin beat us in the PSAL in Madison Square Garden. Then the second year that we were in the championship, I only played six months. I graduated in midseason, and the team did win the city championship that year. I only played for six months. For some reason, I graduated midterm.

I entered New York University at sixteen. My seventeenth birthday was in May, and I was at NYU in February. We played a game at Valley Forge Military Hospital on January 31, 1945. I think I matriculated to New York University on February 5th or 6th. We had this game, and I remember we played against some excellent college players, a couple from Notre Dame, and we got beat by eight or ten points. I had a lot of experience. In those years growing up, not only did I play organized basketball in junior high school and in high school, but there was also a club team called the Amerks. That was our name. Amerks was short for Americans. I guess we just took it from the fact that there was a hockey team. I think they were in the National Hockey League, called the Amerks, the New York Americans. They called them the Amerks. That was our name, and we were very much in demand because we were an excellent team. Most of the guys from DeWitt Clinton were on this particular team. We played almost every night, weekends, after the season, in tournaments, all over the Bronx. We were gypsy basketball players and for some reason it did not seem to interfere with school or anything like that. We played a lot, a lot of basketball.

I played a lot. We usually played three-on-three, or five-on-five. It was not just shooting around because it was hard to get a basket by yourself. How are you going to get a basket by yourself with hundreds of kids around? It was just like impossible. There were always lots and lots of guys waiting to play, and if you brought your own ball and took the basket, they probably would have killed you.

My second game was against Notre Dame in Madison Square Garden. I had played in Madison Square Garden before, in high school. We played against Benjamin Franklin and got beat. I think we played a game before that against Curtis and beat them in the first round. Curtis was from Staten Island. I knew Madison Square Garden, but of course it was an exciting place, especially with eighteen thousand people, Notre Dame, it was THE big game. In those days there were doubleheaders, but this particular game was just one game, because you did not need the second game to draw people. Notre Dame–NYU was such a natural.

My father was extremely proud to have his son in college playing ball. My name was in the newspapers, and of course basketball was big time. When we talk about newspapers, in those days in New York City there were probably fifteen newspapers, or maybe ten. My mother did keep a scrapbook, and I think within a week's clippings the scrapbook was filled, because she took it out of every paper. There was the *World Telegram*, there was the *Journal American*, there was *PM*, there were the *Times*, and there was the *Brooklyn Eagle*, the *Bronx Daily News*, the *Herald Tribune*, and the *World Telegram–Journal American*. There were lots of newspapers. I got my best write-ups, I will never forget this, from the *Daily Worker*. For some reason, there was a sportswriter who loved me and he would write about this new kid from NYU. Maybe he thought there was a Communist way back in my family.

The coach at NYU was Howard Cann. Howard Cann was NYU's only coach. He had played there in the early twenties. He was an All-American player, and he became the coach I think in the late twenties and had been their only coach whenever they were big time. He was an X's and O's coach. He was a coach who let the guys play. We were completely a New York City team. We had guys from Queens like Ray Lump and Joe DiBonus, and we had Brooklyn players. We had Sid Tannenbaum and Danny Foreman. We had Frank Mangiapanni from Queens. We had Marty Goldstein from Manhattan and Howie Sareth from Manhattan. He was the center at the time that I displaced [him]. I can recall we must have had twenty players on the team, only maybe ten or eleven played, but there were always a lot of guys in scholarship. What was interesting, and here is an interesting point why I went to NYU. Growing up in the Bronx, NYU was only at 181st Street and we were at 183rd Street, very close by, and we would often watch NYU play. I can recall getting thrown out by the guards trying to watch them play. When DeWitt Clinton had this great team in the midforties, we were asked to scrimmage against the NYU team. We did scrimmage the NYU team and no score was kept, but somebody kept an unofficial score and we were ahead. We were actually on par with this team, this high school team, and we kept playing and playing and playing and finally when NYU was ahead of us they stopped the scrimmage. I can recall, these upstart high school kids, it was a rough, very physical scrimmage. I think Howard Cann noticed me at that time, and I got scholarship offers from many schools.

We were offered a scholarship to Purdue but this was during the war years and the travel was tough. It was not knowing what was out there, but we almost took it. Also, we liked Nat Holman. Nat Holman, of course, was the legendary coach [at CCNY], considered the greatest coach in the history of the game. Of course Claire Bee was there, but for some reason Nat Holman was the person uppermost in all our minds.

Nat is still alive, close to ninety-five, a wonderful person. Nat had a camp, a camp called Camp Scatico, a children's camp, and during the summers we wanted to go to camp, play ball. We wanted to go to Nat Holman's camp, and he said, "You can go to our camp as waiters." Because we could not afford to go, we wanted to work there, make a few bucks and play ball. I will never forget, and it was me and Joel Kaufman, the heart of the basketball team. Nat obviously felt, "Those kids will be there, I will be with them, they will get to like me, we will go to City College." City College at that time was a power, second only to NYU. We go to Nat Holman's, and this is not a putdown of Nat Holman. We go to Nat Holman's apartment to get briefed on what we are supposed to do at camp. It was quite obvious, I do not know if Nat briefed us or his brother or his head counselor or somebody in charge, but whatever they told us struck the wrong note. We were going to be secondary citizens, second-class citizens. We were going to live in tents, you could not swim while the campers did this, and you could not do this, and you had to go to bed, and you could not socialize. We looked at each other. We did not say anything, but we left, and then somebody had a parent call up or we got one of the stronger willed guys to call up and say, "We are not going." Well, Nat Holman was so angry. The word came down that if we do not go to his camp we are blackballed from any college in New York. He was so angry. Of course, it was late and maybe he could not get waiters at that late date. This was like mid-June and camp opened in two weeks. But who knows, history could have taken a different course, because Nat was the man. So we decided N Y U, went to N Y U on a scholarship, and I went to the uptown campus. At that time, N Y U had two campuses, downtown and uptown. I went to uptown, merely because it was walking distance, and it had a lot of math courses, so I took an engineering course and went to uptown N Y U.

I did take [aeronautical engineering] but [also] a lot of math. I was very good at math in school, so I decided, well, if I am good at math, I might as well take math. I was a good B student. I do not think I studied extremely hard, but I was a good student. I flunked one course in high school. I flunked a course in English merely because it was the period before basketball practice, and I was always running out early. The teacher, I will never forget her name, a Mrs. Damon. I do not know why you remember things like that, but she flunked me. That was the only course I ever flunked.

All the players in New York were schoolyard players, and schoolyard players play schoolyard basketball, which is no plays, you just play basketball. You flash post and you shoot from the outside. I was always the tallest. I learned the game from every position. In fact, I disliked going inside, maybe because it was physical in there, maybe because I felt I was just taking advantage of my height, so I learned the outside game and the inside, the whole game, the complete game. All the players at New York University, the Queens guys, the Manhattan guys, we played the same game. So what Cann did was, he was a stickler for conditioning, you had to be in shape, so we ran and we ran. We'd do figure eights ad infinitum, an hour at a time until we were ready to drop. We were one of the first running teams, and I think that is why we were such a popular team. We would run teams off the court. When we set a half-court game, I can remember being the tallest man. I'd go in and Sid Tannenbaum would get in front of me and then Donny Foreman would get in front of him, and so on. Basically, we were just a good, smart team, and Howard Cann recognized this. We never played a zone defense. We never scouted an opponent. He picked the best five to eight players, and we played.

Sid Tannenbaum was the leader of the team, and he and Donny Foreman had a rivalry going. Both Brooklyn boys, both with their friends saying, "Don't let Foreman [or Tannenbaum] take the thunder, you take the thunder, you're the better player." Sid was a very quiet kind of guy. Sid was maybe a year older. None of these fellows were veterans. A few guys came back from the war and got on the team. Sid was young. He had gotten out of Thomas Jefferson High School. Donny Foreman got out of Boys High School. I was DeWitt Clinton. Then there was Frank Mangiapanni. He was from Queens.

As a center at New York University, I really was not a post player, a post-up player. I was a high post player. We played a lot of high post; pass the ball in and the guys would cut around, that kind of thing. I just shot the outside shot because I was not really an offensive threat. I would score. I would do a little of everything, but I was not really much of a threat. I was not the offensive player. Tannenbaum and Foreman were the two offensive stars of the team. I was more of a role player. I'd grab a rebound and stick it back in. They'd double-team them. I would get the ball and shoot it. I developed a knee injury in my second year, and I was kind of limited. I recall it was on v-j Day, and I had gone to the Polo Grounds to watch a baseball game. This was August of 1945. I think it was after my first year at NYU, first six months. I sat in a very tight seat because they never made seats for big people, and they still don't, and it was cramped, and I got a sharp pain in my left knee. I think it was a slight cartilage tear and that limited my play in my second year at NYU. I can remember going to the chiropractor in Washington Heights, and he helped me a great deal. It wasn't a major tear, but it caused me to lose a little quickness, a little mobility. For some reason it healed itself after that second year, and then I was able to develop pretty well in my senior year. I was a never considered a great player, but my senior year I somehow developed.

I probably wasn't aggressive. I never got into fights. I just played a pure kind of game. I wasn't physical or aggressive. In my senior year I did play some excellent games. I rebounded better. I seemed to have my timing. I was maturing and maybe was getting to be a better jumper. You've got to recall that I was still quite young at that time. I won an award that year, the Haggerty Award, as one of the better players in New York City. I think I was also third-team All-American. The team got into the NIT, and we were beaten in the finals by Saint Louis. I remember Ed McCauley completely outplaying me in that particular game. The NIT was the bigger tournament. You could play, actually, in both tournaments, but both tournaments at that time were on at the same time simultaneously. Then there was an Olympic trial in 1948. That was the first year of the Olympics after the war. We got into this Olympic tournament with Kentucky. Kentucky had the wonder team at that time. They won the NCAAs. Adolph Rupp was the coach. There was Baylor, the Phillips Oilers [Bartlesville, Oklahoma], and New York University. Those were the four teams. It wasn't Philips Oilers. It was four college teams. I forgot the other. I know Baylor was one of them, Kentucky, us, and another club. We played Baylor, and Kentucky played somebody else, because they felt they wanted a Kentucky-NYU matchup in the finals.

That is how they would pick half of the Olympic team. In those years, the Olympic team was picked; there were twelve players. Ten of the players—five from the championship of the college division and five from the AAU division, which was the Philips Oilers. They won there. So the Philips Oilers had five players and maybe one other player was going to come from that division. We were going to play Kentucky, except Baylor beat us. We were looking ahead to Kentucky. Kentucky won the tournament, and five of their players went and five from the Philips Oilers. It was between Ray Lump and me for the other college player. They had a lot of big men on that team, Alex Groza. So they had two centers, and they felt they needed a scoring guard so they picked Ray Lump, and I was an alternate. If Lump did not go, I was going to go. I was making jokes that I was looking forward for Lump to break his leg. I was an alternate on the Olympic team, but I never went because nobody got hurt.

I was very disappointed because that was, of course, something to look forward to. I do not think that [being Jewish] had any bearing on it at all. Not at all. I was never asked that question.

It was never broached in college or pro. [On whether he encountered antisemitism:] Not at all. I can recall we played Notre Dame once and Donny Foreman got into a fight with a player from Notre Dame, and they said it was because this player on Notre Dame said something racially to Donny Foreman, but Foreman, he would fight with anybody in those days.

I never did [experience anything because I was Jewish]. There was a game we played in Buffalo, I think it was my first year, and we played Canisius College. A brawl broke out very early in the game between me and a player named Tom Muller, who is since deceased. He pushed me, and I guess I pushed him back, and then he threw a punch. He did not hit me. I fell down anyhow, maybe from the wind, and then a brawl broke out. I recall later on, the crowd was . . . you know. I was maybe in a different world. I had blinders on. I just focused on basketball. I did not hear anything else. I was just focusing. I could recall that this Frank Mangiapanni got up and challenged a section of the crowd; why, I do not know, but I know that did happen. As I can recall, I never heard anything derogatory. Even in the pros, you never heard a thing. I think I tuned everything out but the game. I think I tuned everything out, and if something like that happened, I can never recall it happening.

At that time [after college], there were two leagues going. The Knickerbockers were the anchor of the BAA, the Basketball Association of America. After the war, it was started by arena owners who wanted some sport to fill up their buildings, use up the dates, and college basketball was big-time. The stars of college basketball were becoming well known. Professional basketball had a bad name. In those years, in the late thirties and early forties, there was professional basketball, but it was considered a rough-and-tumble sport played by ruffians. It was not the clean sport college basketball was. It did not have a good name, but it was thought that perhaps this arena association could capitalize on the game and the new stars coming out. After all, they were all young. They had ten, fifteen years ahead of them. The Knicks and Ned Irish started it. Then there was this other fledgling league, the National Basketball League, which was going on in the Midwest. The BAA was considered the stronger league because they had raided the

National Basketball League to get their better teams: Rochester Royals, Minneapolis Lakers, and Fort Wayne Pistons. There were four teams. There were no eastern teams left in the National Basketball League except the Syracuse Nationals, and the rest were out in the Midwest. Teams like Anderson, Indiana; Waterloo, Iowa; Sheboygan, Oshkosh [Wisconsin]; Calumet, Indiana; Hammond, Indiana. There was a team from Detroit, and this was the league.

I think the BAA had the superior attitude, and they were dollar conscious. They wanted to make it go, and they felt that they had to have a limit on salaries. They had a limit on rookies because they felt that rookies could bankrupt the league if somebody wanted to sign a big player for a lot of money. Ned Irish was the one who put the limit through for rookies, which was $5,000. The rookie limit was $5,000. There was a limit on the amount for the entire team. A fellow named John Golder, who represented Madison Square Garden, called me and said, "Well, we are offering you $5,000." Then I got an offer from the other league [NBL] for $7,500. I had never been in Syracuse in my entire life. To me it was like the North Pole, because I can remember going through to Buffalo and looking out the window of the sleeper, and it was ice and snow-white. For some reason Syracuse pursued me more diligently than New York did. Their owner, Danny Biasone, and general manager, Leo Ferris, came down, met me and my father and gave us a bonus of $500, all in $100 bills. It was a huge wad of dough. I said, "All right, I will play for Syracuse." I think the Knicks offered $5,500 and said, "Well, I will tell you what. We will get you a job with the Port of New York Authority or something like that, where you will work, but we got you a job so you will make a few extra bucks." So I signed with Syracuse. Then I got all kinds of calls from the Knicks. "Why did you do that? They are going to fold. It is a terrible league." That is how I signed with Syracuse.

I do not think they [my parents] thought much of it. I think they felt I would play basketball for a year or two. Who knew from professional basketball? It seemed kind of great to get paid for doing something you really love to do for nothing. I probably would have played for nothing. Of course, I had other offers from industrial leagues. I think the Phillips Oilers gave me a good offer, saying, "We're going to teach you a career. You will play ball. You will have the best of both worlds." AAU ball at that time was very big time, very big. I think the Bradley Company of Milwaukee offered a very nice deal. I think I even got a job offer from Boeing Corporation because I had this degree, but it was way out there. I just was going to start out playing basketball and see what happened after that. Of course, that lasted a career of twenty-five years, sixteen as a player, four as a coach, and four doing other things in the NBA.

I disagree with that [Ned Irish saying, "New York's failure to win a championship can be traced directly to our not getting Schayes"]. You never know what would have happened. It could be that the greatest thing that ever happened to my career was coming up to Syracuse in that they needed me right away. I was thrown right into the middle, as a player immediately playing forty minutes a game or thirty-five. I know that I played most of the game, and it was on-the-job experience.

The Knicks were a very good team. They had eight or nine good players. I might not have had that on-the-job experience. Lapchick was the coach, and they had fine players. There was Bud Palmer. They had Carl Braun. They had a very good team, and I might not have really developed because I developed by . . . you cannot learn the game, or any game, sitting on the bench; when you play and you play and you play, you learn skills. Then we had an aggressive coach, Al Cervi. I think by watching him, by being part of his system, it was like Gashouse Gang [a nickname given to the 1934 Saint Louis Cardinals for their rough tactics], it was like Dead End Kids [a group of young actors who played street toughs in the 1935 Broadway play *Dead End* and in subsequent movies]. We would fight at the drop of a hat. We would be fighting and scratching and scrambling and kicking. That was the type of ball we played, and maybe it rubbed off. I think going to Syracuse made me a player. Having played in New York, I might not have developed. This is pure speculation. I am sure that the Knicks for that $2,000 difference in the very first game could have had $5,000 more just from my family and extended family. Just from the gang in the Bronx.

I loved playing the game. I really loved the game of basketball.

I wanted to play, and coming to New York was always a big thrill. After the leagues merged we played many times in New York. I think at one time the Knicks did want to trade for me, but the deal was never consummated. I also understand when Syracuse was in desperate trouble Ned Irish offered to buy the franchise. I think that is what supposedly happened, but I am not sure. I was very happy in Syracuse, and I loved the town. I loved the coach. I loved the owner, a wonderful, wonderful man. He was a type of owner that was like a fatherly figure to everybody. He was the kind of guy who was a hands-on owner. He owned a bowling alley, made a living, but if the team sunk, he sunk. In fact, he had to recapitalize the team a couple of times in order to bring in partners so that he would not go under. In those days, professional basketball was on the brink of extinction because even though the game was popular, the rules stunk. The rules were awful. The coaches took advantage of the rules. First of all, you did not have the twenty-four-second clock, so when teams like the Rochester Royals or the New York Knicks got a ten-point lead, their ball handlers were so great, they would hold the ball forever. You know, like four corners, they would keep moving the ball. The only way you would get it, you had to foul. So you fouled. They would shoot the foul shot. Then you would get the ball and bring it down, and they would foul you. So all you were doing was trading fouls, keeping the ten-point lead unless you had terrible foul shooters who kept missing. The game developed into a horrendous foul-shooting contest toward the end of the game. Then they had rules for jump balls. If there was a jump ball near the end of the game, you could substitute. If I was jumping against Dick McGuire, the Knicks would call a timeout and substitute somebody for Dick McGuire. The last five minutes took a year. The game was in desperate trouble, and none of the owners were making any money. The referees were getting paid forty dollars a game, and the owners were intimidating every referee in sight because they had to win at home. If you won at home, maybe you would get a hundred more fans or a thousand more fans. You had the spectacle of owners sitting at midcourt, and the referees would go by screaming and yelling. One owner of Saint Louis even had his mother and lawyer sitting with him, and they would be shouting things in Jewish at these referees. The owner of Syracuse was sitting on the bench, so then the referees said they cannot do that. They passed a rule; no owner could sit on the bench. The owner said, "Well, I will get around that rule. I will appoint myself assistant coach." A coach can sit on the bench. So the game was in desperate trouble.

You could sit down with the owner, and I can recall one year when I was second in the league in scoring. I always played for not very much money, and my wife said, "I will divorce you unless you get more money." To me, playing the game was the most important thing, and I would hold out for a week at a time, and then they would go to practice, and I said, "Well, give me $5,000 more and I will play." There was no such thing as agents, and there was no other league to go to, no Europe to go to. Where are you going to go? You love the game. You got paid $10,000, $12,000, which was a lot money in those days.

I made $21,000 in my last couple of years. I think one year the owner would sit down. He was the kind of guy that you knew he was telling you the truth. I was second in the league in scoring. I made I think $13,000, so I said, "I would like a raise." He said, "We lost money. Would you take $1,000 less so we could . . . ?" But he said, "If we come out okay, I will give you $1,000 back." So I took $1,000 less, because he was that kind of guy. You just believed him. You wanted him to survive. I had a great year, and he gave me the $1,000 back.

I have been married forty years, so I was twenty-three when I got married. I met her in Syracuse. She was from Plattsburgh, New York. Her father worked for [U.S.] Customs, and she came down to Syracuse to work and study voice and music. I met her at a basketball game. What else? The rest is history.

I was Rookie of the Year in the NBL, the National Basketball League. We lost in the finals. I think we played the Anderson Duffy Packers. They were a small team in Anderson, Indiana, owned by Ike Duffy. He got together a great, great team even though it was a small town. The basketball was fantastic. I think we lost the sixth game to them in the finals. Then the next year was the merger of the two leagues, and it is interesting how that merger came about.

The BAA, which was supposedly the stronger of the two leagues, was floundering because they lost some teams. I think Chicago quit and Indianapolis quit. There was big turnover, but at that time the great Kentucky team had graduated, and both leagues wanted that team to come into their league. Ike Duffy, the fellow who owned Anderson, who was a meatpacker, very, very wealthy, went to these guys from Kentucky and said, "You can come into our league. We will give you the town of Indianapolis. I will pay the rent on the building. You come in as a franchise. You are a franchise." He signed them to a deal. When the BAA heard this, they said, "We need these kids. We've got to merge." That forced the merger, the fact that this guy got this Kentucky team en masse as one group. Of course, when the Kentucky team played as a group, when they got into Madison Square Garden, they played Syracuse first. We beat them by thirty points. We never lost at home. We were a great team. They went into Madison Square Garden, eighteen thousand people, which is how important they were to the league. They were a wonderful, wonderful team. After that a lot of stuff came out where a couple of their players were involved in scandals. They forced the merger, and the NBA became an unwieldy seventeen-team league. The year after that a lot of the smaller towns dropped out. One of the great stories, I guess Ned Irish, tells the story of the Sheboygan team. The National Basketball League teams played only once against the BAA teams. We only played the Knicks once. They played us once at our court. We played the Washington Capitols twice. The Sheboygan team traveled by station wagon, a huge station wagon seating twelve, one of those stretch station wagons. The story is about Madison Square Garden and the Sheboygan Red Skins. It is bad enough the marquee says, "Sheboygan versus New York." Eight o'clock game, the game starts at 8:30. Sheboygan drives up in front of Madison Square Garden and gets out. Ned Irish, who related this story, said, "Is this big league or not?" Then, supposedly, they kicked all those little teams out. "Waterloo versus New York." It did not fly for both leagues.

The 1949–50 team was 51–13. We were in the finals against the Minneapolis Lakers, and we lost in six games. The following year,

1951, I won the rebounding title with an average of 16.4 rebounds per game. That was the first year they started keeping statistics of rebounds. They are so many statistics now. You watch an NBA game, and they will have statistics after each quarter. People are statistics crazy. I was a good rebounder. I just had a knack to go get the ball. I was not a great leaper. In those years I was able to position myself, but the player I usually played against was not an offensive threat. In those years there was usually an offensive guard, a scorer and a play maker, and a defensive guard. Same with the forwards, an offensive forward and defensive forward. I was always against the defensive forward, and he would rarely ever get the ball to score, so I was able to cheat. If I had the inside position, I would not even box him out, I would just go get the ball, and because of that I was able to develop a sense to go get the ball. So I was able to rebound well, even though I was not a good fundamental defensive player, merely because I was not challenged. If the guy is not going to score, why box him out, why overplay him, why do all these things? Be a pragmatist. Just go get the ball. He is not going to get it. I have got the inside.

I was always a fairly strong player. In those years, you played with injuries. If it was a small injury, you played with it. It was like a badge of courage kind of thing. A sprained ankle, twelve stitches over your eyebrow, a broken nose, a dislocated finger, you got a charley horse; so you bandaged it up a little bit and you played. If you call that desire, desire to get paid, maybe that was what was behind it. Someone else would take my place [if I didn't play while injured]. You love the game. You want to play, and I was lucky in that I did not get a severe injury like a broken bone. Although I did have a broken bone; I had a broken wrist, and I played with that wrist. Luckily, the rule at that time allowed me to play with a cast on. The cast was a lightweight cast covered with a rubberized fabric which allowed the wrist to be protected but allowed the fingers to be free, and it looked like a loaf of bread. There were many stories where I took advantage of players. I would knock them over with the loaf of bread, all of that kind of stuff, maybe inadvertently, accidentally. I do not think I ever did that on purpose. It was a very slow-healing break. I think that loaf of bread was on for many weeks after the thing was healed. Today they are not allowed to do that. Luckily, in those days you were.

I developed the left hand. I always was able to go left, but at that time, that really developed my left hand. I was able to think and react as a left-handed person would, and that one accident, that break, was a break because I was able to now be completely ambidextrous. It is not only that you can shoot left-handed, but you think as a left-hander, and you go to your left. So my game, very simply, I was not a complex player. I was a very simple player. I had what I considered bread and butter, an outside shot, which I developed and worked on incessantly with extra practice, and a drive to the basket. That is all I had. Because I was ambidextrous, they did not know which side I was going on, and they had to guess. So a little fake right, I would go left. I would out-quick them right. I would out-quick them left because they did not know what I was doing. Because they did not know, they cannot react as fast. Then I worked incessantly on my foul shot because going to the basket you get to the line a great deal. Simply stated, that is all I did, and because of that broken wrist, that really made my game. In 1954 I broke my left hand, and I would rest the ball on my fingertips and develop fingertip control. Basketball is a game of touch and feel, and your feel and touch are in your fingertips, not your palms. The more fingertips you get on, the more of a touch, the more of a soft shot you can develop.

In 1955 we won the championship. In the seventh game, George King was fouled. Why they fouled him, I do not know. Maybe he was a poor foul shooter, but they did foul him. I think it was a tied game. They fouled him, and we got one point ahead. Then Andy Phillip got the ball out of bounds. He was double-teamed, and then the ball was stolen from his blind side. I think Paul Seymour played him, who was a very sure ball handler, and in order to get away from Paul Seymour, he pivoted and George King double-teamed, stole the ball, and then we won the game. I remember they fouled King, and I could never figure out why they would do that. Maybe they felt that they did not want to play in overtime, figuring we would win, and maybe King would miss the shot. He was fouled, and then that put us in the lead. I remember in that game, I did not play very well. I had foul problems, and we were way down in the first half. Our bench brought us back in that particular game.

That was our only championship. That was a very, very good team. Although in 1958–59 we had a player from Fort Wayne named George Yardley, a great, great player, the Bird. He was one of the great jumpers at that time, a great jump shooter. I guess the owner of Fort Wayne did not like him, and he was traded to us in a great steal. He was traded for a guy, Eddie Conlin, who was a good journeyman player, but Yardley was a star. That was a great break for me because I was the highest-paid player on Syracuse, making, I think, $15,000 at the time, and Yardley was being paid $25,000 by Fort Wayne. The owner of Fort Wayne said, "I will pay part of Yardley's salary but not all of it." Biasone would not pay $25,000, which was unheard-of in those days. I think he said, "I will pay him $18,000." Then he came to me and said, "Well, Dolph, I always told you, you will be the highest-paid player on Syracuse no matter what. Because we have Yardley, I am paying him $18,000; you are going to get $18,500." Something like that. Because Yardley came, I loved him. I got a $3,500 increase in salary because he came on the team. He and I meshed together beautifully. I averaged over twenty points per game. He averaged over twenty points per game. That was the greatest team we ever had. We almost defeated the Celtics in a great series. In the seventh game, we lost in the last minute or two after blowing a sixteen-point lead, and had we won that game, we would have been champs. I think they had Bill Russell in that year, that was his second year, and we should have beaten them. Yardley got thirty-four points. I got thirty-three points. It was one of the great games of all time.

I got fifty points in one game against the Celtics. I think one time they had a night for me where they honored me in Boston. I guess they had to draw some fans, so they figured as a scheme to draw fans, we will have a night, maybe we will get some more. I think I got forty points that game. I usually scored fifteen to twenty-five points a game. We played a team game. In 1957 I broke George Mikan's career record of 11,764 points. It was on a long set shot. Today it would have been a three-point shot. They gave me the ball. I think I still have the ball. It was a great feeling, but life goes on. The game goes on. I came close to twenty thousand points. That was one of the great disappointments of my career that I was not the first one to break twenty thousand.

Then I had a knee operation, and it looked like my career was over. Syracuse had just been sold to Philadelphia, and the new owner said, "We would like you to coach." They had a lot of young forwards, and I foolishly made a quick decision to coach and not play. The knee operation was a total success, and I had absolutely no problems after two or three years of problems. I knew I could have really been a devastating player for another year or two, and that was a terrible disappointment. It really affected my coaching. Then I did play a little there, but I could not coach and play. Some people could, but I could not. I could not divorce the two. I just could not do it. That was a terrible disappointment, and I suffered psychologically for a couple of years because of that decision because I was only thirty-five years old. You were breaking new ground because nobody ever played past thirty-three or thirty-four, so they said, "You are too old." I could still play. I knew it. In practice I was going by these guys like they were standing still. Be that as it may, I wanted to be the first player to have twenty thousand [points], but I made a quick decision, and I was not able to.

That first year in Philadelphia, we were in the playoffs. We played Cincinnati in the playoffs. I think in those years, almost every team made the playoffs. As I recall, there were nine teams in the league, and eight teams made the playoffs, but I am not exactly sure. We did make the playoffs. The Knicks did not make it. The Knicks had a poor team that year. We played Cincinnati and got knocked out in the first round to Oscar Robertson and that group.

In 1963–64, Syracuse moved to Philadelphia, and I became the player-coach. Syracuse was not drawing well. That was the time in the NBA when the game was not popular. It was like a lull period, and there was no television revenue coming in. There was no extra revenue at all, and the Syracuse situation was such that it looked like a break-even point. The people in Syracuse who ran the building were going to raise the rent, and the owner of the Syracuse Nationals saw that expenses were going to be much more the next year because of the NBA moving to the West Coast. The

NBA moved to the West Coast and expenses were way up. Also, players' salaries were going up because Wilt Chamberlain was in the league. Bill Russell was in the league. It was quite obvious playing in the small building that we had in Syracuse, about sixty-four hundred people [capacity], averaging four thousand [spectators per game], with low ticket prices. The owner had a viable bid from Philadelphia because Philadelphia was empty of basketball since the Warriors had moved to San Francisco a year or two before. He decided to just do the best he could, and he sold the team for somewhere around $500,000.

It came as a shock. There was no real indication that we were going to move, and I did not think about it too much except it might be a nice place to move. I did not think about quitting playing, but I had a knee operation, and the owner said, "It doesn't look like you'll play that much more, why don't you coach?" and I made the decision to coach.

I think we were 35–45 or 36–44 [actually 34–46]. There were only about eight or ten teams in the entire league at that point, and I do not want to go through the teams, but I know we did play Cincinnati in the playoffs and they beat us three out of four games. They had a great team that year with Oscar Robertson. We were kind of building again. We had a lot of young players.

The following year, I again coached Philadelphia, and in mid-season, a fantastic trade, probably one of the greatest in the history of pro basketball, was made. Wilt Chamberlain was traded to Philadelphia for Lee Shaffer, Paul Neumann, and Connie Dierking. They went to the San Francisco Warriors, and of course, that was a mega trade. I will never forget when Larry Merchant, then working for the *Philadelphia Daily News*, called me at three o'clock in the morning and said, "How does it feel to have one of the greatest ballplayers in the history of the game on your club?" Of course, I said it was great. What could I say? That started the turnaround of the 76ers. That year we ended up 40–40 and we took the Celtics to six or seven games in the playoffs and just lost on a controversial play in Boston. John Havlicek stole the ball. That is one of the more famous plays in professional basketball.

Johnny Most made a lot of bucks on it. Based on that, it looked like we were destined, with a couple of changes in our personnel, to become a very, very good basketball team, which we were the next year. We added Billy Cunningham, Hal Greer, Chet Walker, and Luke Jackson. Larry Costello was not with us until the next year. With that team, we won the Eastern Division. Instead of winning forty games, we won fifty-five games, an improvement of fifteen games, and we were not favored to win the championship. We won the Eastern Division, beating the Boston Celtics by one game on the last day of the season. We beat Baltimore, and at that point we took a rest. I think that hurt us because the Celtics went on to play the Cincinnati Royals and that series took, I think, ten days to two weeks. Meanwhile we were playing among ourselves, kind of relaxing. We lost our sharpness. We ended the season winning something like thirteen or fourteen consecutive games. We were on a roll, and then the lull came. Boston had made a very crucial move in their method of play. John Havlicek, one of the better players of all time, was their sixth man. In order to get more firepower into the lineup, Havlicek started. Red Auerbach started him, and basically that threw us off. The combination of the long layoff plus Havlicek starting, I think in the very first game we got beat and now we lost our entire home-court advantage.

We went and lost, I think, in five or six games because we could never regain the momentum. We could never just get going even though we did have a great team, probably the best team in the league at that particular time. Basketball is a game of confidence and rhythm and home-court advantage. We just lost our confidence and rhythm and home-court advantage. I was not playing. I was just coaching. I was named Coach of the Year, but then when we lost in the playoffs, I was let go as coach, although there were rumblings of that before. The owner, Irv Kosloff, was not too happy with the way I handled the team personnel-wise, so he decided to make a change after the season. I think it was the 1965–66 season. The following year it became the greatest winning team of all time. They added Bill Melchionne and Larry Costello came out of retirement, but they were not major additions. The team was just maturing.

There was another coach, Alex Hannum, who was a wonderful coach. I think they ended up winning sixty-six games. I played with him, and Alex was coach of the Syracuse Nationals for many years. Then when he left, I took over, and then he came back to Philly. Had Alex stayed with Philly, I probably would have played a couple more years and been a little wealthier. In the 1964–65 season, there were rumblings that the NBA was finally going to give a pension to all the players. There was new ownership in the league. They were not stonewalling us. Eddie Gottlieb, who was working in the NBA office, and he knew what was happening. He kept telling me, periodically, "The NBA is going to have a pension plan. Why don't you start playing again?" I said, "No, I do not think so." I retired in June 1964. [The year] 1963–64 was our first season in Philadelphia, and on February 1, 1965, seven months later, if you were on an NBA roster you were eligible for the pension, which would have meant I would have had seventeen years of eligibility at that time. As it was, my sixteen years went up in smoke because they would not allow it. In other words, that was the cutoff date no matter what. So that particular decision, not listening to Eddie Gottlieb, who was a very sage and very wise man. I still could have played, certainly. I was the coach. I could have put myself in any time I wanted to, and being the ninth, tenth, or eleventh player, I certainly could have played five or ten minutes a game. It would have been a little selfish. I would say conservatively it cost me $1 million. Later on, old-timers were brought into the pension but at a much lower rate of pay scale.

I think they had regard for us, but it was up to the owners. The owners had to make the decision whether to include older players. The owners at that time had to put in a major contribution in order to fund the pension. You just do not say, "We are going to start giving these guys money." They had to put in several million dollars overall, all the owners. They probably said, "Well, I do not know him. I was not around when he played. I am going to take care of my business today. Why should I take care of something that happened twenty to thirty years ago, I mean, that is not fair." Finally, the NBA was making so much money and David Stern, who was our champion, prevailed upon the owners to say, "Well, it is not going to cost you that much and you throw away so much money every year anyhow." So several years ago, I think the pension was put into effect. A watered-down pension, but a pension nevertheless. Frankly, I am very pleased about it. It was like found money for us, because there was really no reason, other than public relations, for the NBA to do that.

The NBA and basketball was my whole life and made me what I became, a person that was pretty well known. I did not think I was ready to just give it all up. There was an opening in the NBA front office to help out with referees. Not that I knew enough about refereeing to tell them what to do or how to referee a game, that should be done by a career referee, but I helped in scheduling and scouting for new referees. I did that for several years. It was fulfilling in one way in that I got to see referees in a different light. I got to know them as human beings rather than just guys on the floor who I felt were sometimes against me. They were just wonderful individuals, especially Mendy Rudolph, Norm Drucker, and Earl Strom. These three referees were the ones who really were the center of the staff. They were the heart and soul of the staff. They were the ones who knew the game of basketball and how to referee the game and when to blow the whistle, how to keep the pace of the game going, and they were the ones who really tutored the younger referees. In those days we only had two referees, so we would put in a lead man such as a Strom or Drucker or Rudolph with a kid, and they would do the teaching and give them the philosophy. I had a wonderful time just being around them because they were great people. Referees did have a tough life. In those days, refereeing was not like it is today. It was not their vocation, their main vocation. They actually had to supplement their income. For instance, Mendy Rudolph sold television time for WJM in Chicago. Norm Drucker was in the New York City school system, and Earl Strom worked for General Electric, public relations–wise, in Philadelphia. At times it was kind of hairy, especially during the wintertime, to get these guys scheduled into Detroit when they had to leave where they were at three in the afternoon. If there was a storm, we had to have guys in and around the Detroit area we could call. Many times, one guy worked a game. Several years later, the NBA realized a referee was just as important as the sixth man because a referee in basketball, not like in football, he is really part of the action. They made it a career job. Where you could not hold a second job during the season, you had to be absolutely ready to go and do nothing else. They made the salaries commensurate so that when they gave up their moonlighting jobs, they could feed a family.

After being in the NBA office, I still had the urge to coach, and since Buffalo was very close to my home in Syracuse, I decided maybe I will give it a shot, not realizing that an expansion team is a very difficult situation. No matter if you are Johnny Wooden or Bobby Knight or Dean Smith all rolled into one, you just do not get the personnel to work with. Even though I felt I wanted to prove that the firing in Philadelphia was a mistake, it was really difficult with an expansion team. Players never lose the game, according to them. They kept heaping the blame on the coach. "Why are they not winning?" and the players say, "Well, we got a rotten coach."

Our big star was a guy named Bob Kauffman, a 6'8" center who we got from Seattle in the dispersal draft. Then we got our first draft choice, a fellow named John Hummer from Princeton. We had several other retreads, and by the end of the season, we had twenty-two wins. It was a nightmare of a year because many times we were just blown out in the first half. We just did not have the personnel to either hold the ball or run with it. We had a couple of bright lights. We had a fellow by the name of Donnie May, who was a 6'4" small forward. He got twenty points a game. Bob Kaufman became an all-star because he worked hard. He was strong, but other than that, it was a nightmare of a year. Twenty wins for an expansion team is even a little better than the norm. If somebody were to pick up all the expansion teams in the history of the NBA, they would find a spread from eleven wins to twenty-five wins, which was Chicago in their first year. Most of them end up with fifteen or sixteen wins.

I was fired the first game of the next season. There were rumblings that the owner, a fellow named Paul Snyder, was not very happy with the way things went. On that particular day that we played, we played the Seattle Supersonics, and Paul Snyder was a big shot in the Democratic Party in and around western New York, and Hubert Humphrey was in town. Paul Snyder was the owner of the Buffalo Braves, and Humphrey and he were sitting center court to watch his team play. As luck or unluck would have it, Spencer Haywood played for the Seattle Supersonics. Lenny Wilkens was the coach, and this is the first game of the year on our court. We had a guy named Elmore Smith at 7' who was going to lead us out of the troubled waters. Spencer Haywood, I think he got forty-two points. They could do no wrong, and we could do no right. We lost by thirty, and from what I understood, Paul Snyder was embarrassed because this was his team and Humphrey was sitting right next to him. That evening or the next morning, I got a call, "Come into the office, pack your things, you are through." Now that Braves team which had new personnel, Randy Smith had just come into the league, who became a league All-Star, and Elmore Smith and several others, that team won twenty-one games that year. They won one less, and that coach was fired. Then the next year John McCarthy was fired and a coach from Philadelphia came in, Jack Ramsey, who was considered the dean, the smartest of all coaches, and he had Bob McAdoo and couple of other guys and he also won twenty-two games. I do not think it was the coaching as much as personnel. You cannot win unless you've got some pretty good players.

I was kind of sensitive. You are proud, and you have known success all your life, and now all you are getting is knocks and knocks and you have to be able to run with it and let it bounce off. I was a little sensitive, and it hurt. There is no doubt about it. I realized that I had spent so much time away from my family, my kids were growing up, and I really did not know them. I said, "Enough is enough. I love basketball. Basketball made me, but I gave enough to the game and so I am going to maybe get into a normal life." That ended my professional basketball career. From 1948 to 1971, we are talking about twenty-four consecutive seasons in the N B A. That was quite a lot.

The following year, 1972, I was elected to the Basketball Hall of Fame. When I graduated from college with a degree in engineering, and I had a party, one of my aunts asked my mother, "What is Dolph going to do now with his degree? What big company is he going to work for? "My mother answered, "Oh, Adolph is going to become a professional basketball player." She said, "What kind of job is that for a nice Jewish boy?" After twenty-four years, it really became a pretty good job. I was very proud, because at that time I was probably the youngest member of the Basketball Hall of Fame. The Hall of Fame was just starting out.

I was in the NBA for sixteen years, and for sixteen years the teams that I played on made the playoffs, which meant that, individual records aside, we were a winning team. I was part of a winning team every year, which means I was a pretty good team player besides owning individual records. That is what I am most proud of. Basketball is a team game, then, now, and forever. More than any other game.

The best players I personally played against would be Bob Pettit, Elgin Baylor, and Oscar Robertson. I did play against Wilt Chamberlain, Bill Russell, and Bob Cousy. I always felt that Oscar was the best, the most complete player, the player that, when he got on the court, could control the game and do whatever he wanted to. Yes, more than Magic Johnson but not more than Michael Jordan. Larry Bird cannot be far behind, and there is also Dr. J. There are so many guys out there, but if you had to pick one, I would have to go with Michael Jordan, and then I would go with Oscar a shade over Magic, which is difficult. You really have to have your head in the sand to say that we were in the 1950s just as good as they are in the 1990s. They are better athletes today. They run faster, jump higher, and shoot better. I think Wilt Chamberlain today could be making $5 million and dominate the league because he was so strong and he was inside. Bill Russell certainly could. Oscar could. There were very few of us in those years. I think I could.

I think a lot of players never got a chance to play. Remember, there were only eight teams, where today you have twenty-seven. In those days, a lot of players never got the chance to play because there were only eight teams, which was a shame because if you had more players, you would have found that there were a lot of great athletes out there. The sneakers we wore were the Chuck Taylor Converse. The soles were paper-thin. Now they have air pockets and a pump and you have two pairs of laces. It is like they are taping their ankles with their sneakers, and it is made very comfortable. That makes a big difference in the performance of a player night after night. We did not have good trainers. We had guys who knew how to tape, and when we went on the road, we would have to get another trainer who the home team would provide for us. We had nothing to do with weights or training or how to really take care of ourselves a little bit better and to build up our strength. Every team today has a strength coach, has a vitamin coach, and has an orthopedic man, a dentist. It is not that they are catered to, but there is such a big investment in them that you really need these people.

Basketball is a wonderful game. When the season was over we took a couple of weeks off. And we were out in the gyms playing again because it is just fun to play basketball and be part of the action. Especially if you knew you had some skills, and you are 6'8" and you can do certain things, and you are not hurting yourself.

My son Danny is a ten-year N B A player. Here I am, I am watching the games and I call him up and say, "Now, Danny, this is what you should do, this is what you should do." I do not realize that he has had ten years of professional, four years of college, three years of high school, and he went to all kinds of basketball camps. He has wonderful coaches, and I am telling him fundamental stuff that he had heard a million times, and that he knows. I guess once a coach, always a coach; once a father, always a father. He says, "Okay, Dad, I will do it," like I am really telling him something important, when in truth I know he knows it. He is really sharp, and he probably knows much more about basketball that I at this point because he lives it every day. I think he is a better defensive player than I. Of course, I was a scorer, so it is tough to compare. I was the guy that they went to all the time. Danny is more complementary. Danny has been a reserve mostly. Danny is a marvelous, marvelous team player. If there was an all-star team for team players, he would be the starting center. What I am most proud of in his record is that for the last nine seasons, his teams have made the playoffs. I think that is very significant. Many coaches and many people that are supposedly in the know, before each of those seasons, said, "The Denver Nuggets or the

Milwaukee Bucks, they won't make it, they don't have it." Each year, they surprise everybody because they do not understand that Danny adds so much to all of those teams. On every one of those teams, he was a big factor in bringing them all together because he is such a great team player. I think as Danny gets older, as each year goes by, he is going to get better. He might not be a Hall of Famer, but the bottom line will be that he was a winner. All his teams were winners.

INDEX

Page numbers in *italics* indicate illustrations.

fouls (*continued*)

Doc Sugarman calling, 69; Dolph Schayes on, 279–80; in game strategy, 25, 48, 193, 275; Max Zaslofsky making, 241; Moe Spahn scoring on, 79; referees calling, 201; technical, 50–51, 113; underhand versus overhand, 73, 137

Foxx, Jimmie, 36, 261

Frankel, Moe, 88, 144

Franklin K. Lane High School, 109–10, 131

Friedman, Marty, 2, 8

Fulks, Joe, 55, 176, 209, 220, 226, 251

Fuller, Alex, 2, 8

Fuller, Jackie, 2, 8

Furey, Fat Tom, 6

Furey, Jim, 5–6, 8

gambling and betting, 98, 196–97, 260–61

gangs, 37, 83, 98

Garfinkel, Jack "Dutch": background, family, youth of, 149–50; marriage of, 153; in military, 152; non-sports careers of, 153–54; pictured, *148*; playing, 150–53, 173, 182, 225, 226; refereeing, 154

Gashouse Gang, 274

Gates, Pop, 25, 119, 122

Gehrig, Lou, 16, 264

Gennity, Jim, 2, 8

Gil Fitch's band, 181

Goldberg, Lena, 93, 108

Golder, John, 273

Goldman, Moe: background, family, youth of, 131; pictured, *130*; playing, 72, 131–37, 142–43, 145, 158, 171, 173; teaching, 134

Goldstein, Jonah, 112, 117

Goodell, Eddie, 263

Gotthoffer, Joel "Shikey": background, family, youth of, 63–64, 72; coaching, 67; Jewish heritage of, 69–70; in military, 70; pictured, *62*; playing, 63–65, 67–69, 72–74, 129, 144, 145, 151, 171, 173; Rabin and, 128; scandals involving, 64–66; school years of, 64–67; SPHAS and, 145

Gottlieb, Eddie: Abe Saperstein and, 41–

44; automobile of, 38–39; coaching, 73, 81, 136, 143, 181–82, 202; Dave Zinkoff and, 144–45, 153; Dolph Schayes on, 250, 284; Harry Litwack and, 32, 41, 174; Jack "Dutch" Garfinkel and, 152, 153; Jerry Fleishman on, 224–27; Joel "Shikey" Gotthoffer and, 71–72; Louis "Red" Klotz on, 184; Max Goldman and, 133–34, 135; Ossie Schectman and, 158, 159; as Philadelphia Warriors owner, 53; Ralph Kaplowitz on, 171–72, 175; SPHAS and, 38–39, 44, 67–68, 128–29, 174, 180; as summer camp operator, 37

Goukas, Matt, 225

Granahan, Jack, 80

Grand Street Boys, 111, 117, 118

Grats High School, 45

Gray, Pete, 263

Greenberg, Hank, 64, 261, 263–64

Groza, Alex, 197

Guerin, Richie, 214

Haggerty, Horse, 17–18

Haggerty, Joe, 4

Haggerty Award, 271

Halbert, Charlie, 210

Hale, Bruce, 146

Hall of Fame. *See* Basketball Hall of Fame

Halpert, Charlie, 210

Hannum, Alex, 53, 283–84

Harlem Globetrotters: Abe Saperstein and, 41–42; Bernard "Red" Sarachek on, 118; Eddie Gottlieb and, 42; as independent team, xii; Jerry Fleishman on, 226, 227; Louis "Red" Klotz on, 43; Moe Goldman on, 135; Moe Spahn on, 82; NBA and, 43, 184–85; players in, 45; Sammy Kaplan on, 89; SPHAS and, 42, 153, 173, 183, 184. *See also* blacks

Harlem Renaissance. *See* New York Renaissance

Harrison, Les: background, family, youth of, 21–23; coaching, 23, 203; as franchise owner, 23–27; Jewish heritage of, 21, 22; managing, 23; on other players, 27–28; as owner, 89, 203; pictured, 20; playing, 23, 44, 53; Rochester Royals and, 55

Havlicek, John, 129, 251, 282, 283

Haywood, Spencer, 287

Hearn, Tiny, 132, 137

Henderson, Don, 48

Hendricks, Tommy, 262, 263

Henschel, Harry, 11

Herald Tribune, 267

Herkimer NY, and team, 118–21

Hermsen, Kleggie, 212, 217

Hertzberg, Sonny: background and youth of, 220; on basketball, 206, 215, 219–20; injuries of, 218; marriage and children of, 212, 218; in military, 206; as optician, 208; on other coaches, 209, 211, 212; on other players, 209–10, 211–12, 215–16; pictured, 204; playing, 171, 192, 205–11, 213; reminiscing, 216–19; retirement of, 212–14; televised games and, 213–14

Hildebrand, Oral, 262

Hillhouse, Art, 144, 173, 176

hockey, 26, 175, 266

Holman, Nat: background, family, youth of, 1–3, 6–7; baseball playing, 3; basketball playing, 1–5, 8–9, 11; Bernard "Red" Sarachek and, 103; coaching, 6, 7–8, 10–11, 78, 268; confronting Rabin, 128; Dolph Schayes on, 268–69; double championship win of, 10, 12; Harry "Jammy" Moskowitz on, 16; Harry Litwack on, 34; Jewish heritage of, 9; Joe Lapchick's friendship with, 4–5; Moe Goldman on, 132, 137; Norm Drucker on, 187–88; pictured, *xvi, 140*; scandals involving, 44–45; Sonny Hertzberg on, 209; as summer camp operator, 168

Holzman, Red, 23, 25, 55–56, 110, 153, 187, 203, 205

Humphrey, Hubert, 287

IAABO (International Association of Approved Basketball Officials), 154

Iba, Hank, 47, 49

ILGWU (International Ladies' Garment Workers' Union), 110

influenza epidemic, 94–95, 149

injuries, 129, 158–59, 218–19, 270, 278–79

International Association of Approved Basketball Officials (IAABO), 154

International Ladies' Garment Workers' Union (ILGWU), 110

Irish, Ned: BAA and, 153, 175, 202, 272, 277; Dolph Schayes on, 274, 275; Louis "Red" Klotz on, 185; at Madison Square Garden, 10, 43, 175, 208; pay issues and, 208, 273; picking Max Zaslofsky, 250; Sonny Hertzberg on, 213

Israel, 11–12, 42, 58–59, 121, 238–39

Iwo Jima, 168

James Madison High School, 18, 224

James Monroe High School, 64, 150, 264

Jefferson Barracks MO, 165

Jefferson High School, 235, 241

Jerome Avenue El, 258

Jersey City Atoms, 142, 147

Jersey City Reds, 34, 79, 128, 129, 183

Jewish Exponent, 183

Jews: basketball, connection with, xi–xii, 10, 90, 100, 105–6, 220; desiring to be American, xi, xiii

Johnson, Magic, 27, 288

John the Barber (manager), 256

Jordan, Michael, 27, 28, 55, 56, 288

Journal American, 267

Julian, Doggie, 153, 211

jump shots, 3, 55, 64, 132–33, 175, 185, 193, 209–10, 275, 280

Kaplan, Hy, 109–10

Kaplan, Mortimer, 12

Kaplan, Sammy: background, family, youth of, 85, 90; as business person, 91; early business experience of, 86–87; Jewish heritage of, 90; pictured, *84*; playing, 85–86, 87–90, 142–43; political career of, 90–91

Kaplowitz, Ralph: background, family, youth of, 163–64; flight-test incident and, 166–67; in insurance business, 176–77; Jewish heritage of, 167; Louis

Kaplowitz, Ralph (*continued*)
"Red" Klotz on, 181, 182, 183–84; marriage of, 167, 175; in military, 165–71; on other players, 172–74; pictured, *162*; playing, 163–65, 171–72, 174–76, 177
Kaselman, Cy: coaching, 173, 184; in military, 183; playing, 72, 128, 129, 134, 144, 151, 181, 182
Kate Smith Celtics, 80, 88, 142
Kauffman, Bob, 286
Kaufman, Joel, 265, 268
Kazin, Alfred, 90
Keller, King Kong, 262, 263
Kennedy, Pat, 201
Kentucky (college team), 271, 277
Kerner, Ben, 24, 53, 184, 203
King, Dolly, 119, 122–23
King, George, 279
Kingston Colonials, 79, 89, 128, 129
Kingston/Troy Celtics, 142
Kinney, Bob, 213
Kinsbrunner, Mac, 68, 134–35
Klotz, Babe, 181
Klotz, Louis "Red": background, family, youth of, 179–80; internationalizing basketball, 185; managing, 184–85; marriage and children of, 43; in military, 183; on NBA, 184; pictured, *178*; on players and coaches, 181–82; playing, 42, 144, 152, 179–81, 183–84
Knight, Bobby, 47, 49–50
Knights of Columbus, 41, 67
Kosloff, Irv, 53, 283

Lancaster, Burt, 89
Lapchick, Joe: coaching, 11, 151, 152, 208–9, 216, 227, 235, 249–50, 274; marriage of, 4–5; playing, 4, 8, 9, 17–18, 23, 67
Lautman, Inky, 72, 128, 129, 134, 143, 152, 172
Lear, Hal, 46, 51–52
Levane, Fuzzy, 18, 153, 203
Lewin, Lenny, 243
Lewis, Bobby, 165
Lewis, Guy, 61
Litwack, Harry: background, family, youth of, 31–33, 35–36, 38–39, 57; basketball camps career of, 39, 40; cigar-smoking habit of, 37–38, 51; coaching, 32, 45, 47–52, 53, 57–59, 144, 174; Jewish heritage of, 32, 33–34, 37, 44, 58–59; managing, 42; marriage of, 40, 53, 54, 56; pictured, *30*; playing, 31–32, 37, 38–39, 44–45, 72, 182; recruiting, 46–47; refereeing, 144; on retirement, 59–60; teaching, 32, 39, 45
Long Island University, 44, 127–28, 158
Loscutoff, Jim, 196
Lovelette, Clyde, 25, 198, 199
Luisetti, Hank, 9, 72–73, 128, 137, 185, 210
Lump, Ray, 251, 267, 271

Maccabiah Games, 42, 58–59, 61, 239
Mack, Connie, 36, 74
Madison Square Garden: attendance at, 193, 254; betting in, 196; college games at, xii, 6, 11, 54, 78, 127–28, 185, 224, 266; description of, 48; high school games at, 224, 241, 265, 266; holiday tournament win in, 46; importance of, 183; Jack "Dutch" Garfinkel playing at, 151; Max Zaslofsky honored in, 241; Ned Irish at, 10, 43, 208; NIT at, 49; owner-arena franchise in, 207; pro games at, 25, 277; televised games at, 214
Mahnken, John, 153, 209
Mahoney, Speedy, 119, 122
Mangiapanni, Frank, 267, 270, 272
Manhattan Casino, 8
Manischewitz, 109
Marx, Groucho, 105
May, Donnie, 286
McCauley, Ed, 211, 218, 219, 271
McComb Dam Park, 263
McDermott, Bobby, 81
McGuire, Dick, 251, 275
McKinney, Bones, 209, 212, 218
meat-tossing incident, 69
mergers, 26, 276–77
Metropolitan League, 16
Miami Heat, 60
Mikan, George, 24, 27, 216, 217, 250, 254, 280
Mikkelsen, Vern, 216, 254

offense, 49, 51, 110, 207
Olsen, Harold "Ole," 248
Olympic trial (1948), 271
operations, medical, 129, 257–58, 281, 282
Opper, Bernie, 144, 152, 173
Original Celtics, 3, 7–8, 16, 17–18, 23, 66, 82–83, 142
Outlaws, 180

Passon, Chickie, 16, 136
Paterson Crescents, 127, 183
pay for coaches, 39, 54
pay for players: in Hakoahs, 17; in Kate Smith Celtics, 80; in Knickerbockers, 240; limits on, for rookies, 273; Nat Holman and, 3; per game, 23, 41, 56, 67–68, 79, 128, 134, 135, 182, 225; per season, 39, 147, 175, 176, 202, 208, 226, 273, 276, 280; per week, 89, 171, 206; in recent years, 28, 239, 240, 254; salaries, 9, 17, 56, 80, 90, 208, 212, 213, 280; in SPHAS, 41, 128, 182; televised games and, 28, 68, 122, 202, 254; Wilt Chamberlain's effect on, 281; for winning, 176, 226
pay for referees, 189–90, 202, 286
pay for teachers, 39
Pearl Harbor attack, 165
Penn State League, 68, 78, 80, 82, 89, 134–35
pensions, 153–54, 284–85
Pettit, Bob, 53, 198, 199, 251, 288
Philadelphia Bulletin, 183
Philadelphia Daily News, 183, 282
Philadelphia Inquirer, 183
Philadelphia Ledger, 183
Philadelphia Record, 183
Philadelphia Warriors, 42, 53, 172, 173–74, 176, 183–84, 226
Philips Oilers, 271, 273–74
Phillies, 36
Phillip, Andy, 250, 279
Pittston team, 80–81
Platch, Mike, 69
PM (newspaper), 267
Pocono Mountain All-Star Basketball Camp, 40, 60

Podoloff, Maurice: Eddie Gottlieb and, 44, 184; Jerry Fleishman and, 227; as NBA commissioner, 44, 154, 184; Norm Drucker and, 189, 190–91; televised games and, 26
point-shaving, 44–45
Pollard, Jim, 27, 40, 216, 250–51, 254
Polo Grounds, 262–63
Posnack, Max, 67, 151
Princeton University, 65
Prospect Hall, 17, 137–38, 152
Providence College, 65–66
PSAL (Public School Athletic League), 64, 150, 163, 164, 265
punch ball, 87, 95, 96–97, 104

Rabin, Phil, 127–29; pictured, *126*
Radar, Howie, 18, 173
Radar, Lennie, 18, 173
Ramsey, Jack, 287
rebounds, 143, 192–93, 216, 278
recruiting, 46–47, 103, 214, 285
referees and refereeing: Bernard "Red" Sarachek and, 113; changes in, 82, 285–86; Doc Sugarman refereeing, 68–69; fouls and, 28; Harry "Jammy" Moskowitz and, 18; Harry Litwack and, 50–51; Jack "Dutch" Garfinkel refereeing, 154; Jerry Fleishman and, 145–46; Lenny Toff refereeing, 50; Norm Drucker and, 188–92, 193, 194–96, 197–98, 200, 201, 203; owners and referees, 275–76
Reiser, Chick, 88, 145, 189
Republican Party, 90
Retired Players Association, 228
Richmond, Ike, 45–46, 53
Robertson, Oscar, 27, 55, 198, 281, 282, 288
Robinson, Jackie, 12, 45
Rochester Royals, 25–26, 55, 153, 254, 273
Rodgers, Guy, 45–46, 50, 51
Roman, Ed, 10
rookies, 273, 276
Rosan, Red, 128, 144, 152, 182
Rosenberg, Petey, 72, 144, 152, 173, 176, 182, 183, 184